Hands-On Machine Le with scikit-learn and Scientific Python Toolkits

A practical guide to implementing supervised and unsupervised machine learning algorithms in Python

Tarek Amr

BIRMINGHAM - MUMBAI

Hands-On Machine Learning with scikit-learn and Scientific Python Toolkits

Copyright © 2020 Packt Publishing

Commissioning Editor: Mrinmayee Kawalkar
Acquisition Editor: Reshma Raman
Content Development Editor: Nazia Shaikh
Senior Editor: Ayaan Hoda
Technical Editor: Manikandan Kurup
Copy Editor: Safis Editing
Project Coordinator: Aishwarya Mohan
Proofreader: Safis Editing
Indexer: Pratik Shirodkar
Production Designer: Nilesh Mohite

First published: July 2020

Production reference: 1230720

Published by Packt Publishing Ltd.
Livery Place
35 Livery Street
Birmingham
B3 2PB, UK.

ISBN 978-1-83882-604-8

www.packt.com

Packt.com

Subscribe to our online digital library for full access to over 7,000 books and videos, as well as industry leading tools to help you plan your personal development and advance your career. For more information, please visit our website.

Why subscribe?

- Spend less time learning and more time coding with practical eBooks and Videos from over 4,000 industry professionals

- Improve your learning with Skill Plans built especially for you

- Get a free eBook or video every month

- Fully searchable for easy access to vital information

- Copy and paste, print, and bookmark content

Did you know that Packt offers eBook versions of every book published, with PDF and ePub files available? You can upgrade to the eBook version at www.packt.com and as a print book customer, you are entitled to a discount on the eBook copy. Get in touch with us at customercare@packtpub.com for more details.

At www.packt.com, you can also read a collection of free technical articles, sign up for a range of free newsletters, and receive exclusive discounts and offers on Packt books and eBooks.

Contributors

About the author

Tarek Amr has 8 years of experience in data science and machine learning. After finishing his postgraduate degree at the University of East Anglia, he worked in a number of start-ups and scale-up companies in Egypt and the Netherlands. This is his second data-related book. His previous book covered data visualization using D3.js. He enjoys giving talks and writing about different computer science and business concepts and explaining them to a wider audience. He can be reached on Twitter at `@gr33ndata`. He is happy to respond to all questions related to this book. Feel free to get in touch with him if any parts of the book need clarification or if you would like to discuss any of the concepts here in more detail.

I am grateful to a number of individuals who helped me build my technical knowledge and bridge the gap between the technical and the business sides of the equation. This list of individuals includes Khaled Fouad Elsayed, Amr Saad Ayad, Beatriz De La Iglesia, Dan Smith, Stephen Cox, Gilad Lotan, Karim Ratib, Peter Tegelaar, Adam Powell, Noel Kippers, and Mark Jager.

About the reviewers

Jamshaid Sohail is passionate about data science, machine learning, computer vision, and natural language processing and has over 2 years of experience in the industry. Currently, he is working as a data scientist at Systems Limited. He previously worked at a Silicon Valley-based start-up named FunnelBeam as a data scientist, working with the founders of the company from Stanford University. He has completed over 66 online courses on different platforms. He is an author of the course *Data Wrangling with Python 3.X* from Packt and has reviewed multiple books and courses. He is also developing a comprehensive course on data science at Educative and is in the process of writing books at multiple firms.

Prayson Wilfred Daniel bends Python, Bash, SQL, Cypher, JavaScript, Scala, Git, Docker, MLflow, and Airflow to make raw data tell their past, present, and future stories. Building business-driven innovative solutions with a strong focus on microservices architectures and taking into consideration DevOps is what he is passionate about. Prayson holds an MSc. in Information Technology and Persuasive Design from Aalborg University and seeks to help companies gain a competitive advantage from artificial intelligence, particularly machine learning.

Eugene Y. Chen is a machine learning engineer/researcher who wants to make the world a better place with smart software. When he is not building software, he enjoys thinking about and researching machine learning. He has published many peer-reviewed academic works, most recently at the KDD Workshop on Mining and Learning from Time Series on the topic of ensemble learning. He is a contributor to the scikit-learn project.

Packt is searching for authors like you

If you're interested in becoming an author for Packt, please visit `authors.packtpub.com` and apply today. We have worked with thousands of developers and tech professionals, just like you, to help them share their insight with the global tech community. You can make a general application, apply for a specific hot topic that we are recruiting an author for, or submit your own idea.

Table of Contents

Section 3: Unsupervised Learning and More

Preface

You have already seen *Harvard Business Review* describing data science as the *sexiest job of the 21st century*. You have been watching terms such as *machine learning* and *artificial intelligence* pop up around you in the news all the time. You aspire to join this league of machine learning data scientists soon. Or maybe, you are already in the field but want to take your career to the next level. You want to learn more about the underlying statistical and mathematical theory, and apply this new knowledge using the most commonly used tool among practitioners, scikit-learn.

This book is here for you. It begins with an explanation of machine learning concepts and fundamentals and strikes a balance between theoretical concepts and their applications. Each chapter covers a different set of algorithms and shows you how to use them to solve real-life problems. You'll also learn various key supervised and unsupervised machine learning algorithms using practical examples. Whether it is an instance-based learning algorithm, Bayesian estimation, a deep neural network, a tree-based ensemble, or a recommendation system, you'll gain a thorough understanding of its theory and learn when to apply it to real-life problems.

This book will not stop at scikit-learn, but will help you add even more tools to your toolbox. You will augment scikit-learn with other tools such as pandas, Matplotlib, imbalanced-learn, and scikit-surprise. By the end of this book, you will be able to orchestrate these tools together to take a data-driven approach to providing end-to-end machine learning solutions.

Who this book is for

This book is for machine learning data scientists who want to master the theoretical and practical sides of machine learning algorithms and understand how to use them to solve real-life problems. Working knowledge of Python and a basic understanding of underlying mathematical and statistical concepts is required. Nevertheless, this book will walk you through the new concepts to cater to both new and experienced data scientists.

What this book covers

Chapter 1, *Introduction to Machine Learning*, will introduce you to the different machine learning paradigms, using examples from industry. You will also learn how to use data to evaluate the models you build.

Chapter 2, *Making Decisions with Trees*, will explain how decision trees work and teach you how to use them for classification as well as regression. You will also learn how to derive business rules from the trees you build.

Chapter 3, *Making Decisions with Linear Equations*, will introduce you to linear regression. After understanding its modus operandi, we will learn about related models such as ridge, lasso, and logistic regression. This chapter will also pave the way toward understanding neural networks later on in this book.

Chapter 4, *Preparing Your Data*, will cover how to deal with missing data using the impute functionality. We will then use scikit-learn, as well as an external library called categorical-encoding, to prepare the categorical data for the algorithms that we are going to use later on in the book.

Chapter 5, *Image Processing with Nearest Neighbors*, will explain the k-Nearest Neighbors algorithms and their hyperparameters. We will also learn how to prepare images for the nearest neighbors classifier.

Chapter 6, *Classifying Text Using Naive Bayes*, will teach you how to convert textual data into numbers and use machine learning algorithms to classify it. We will also learn about techniques to deal with synonyms and high data dimensionality.

Chapter 7, *Neural Networks – Here Comes the Deep Learning*, will dive into how to use neural networks for classification and regression. We will also learn about data scaling since it is a requirement for quicker convergence.

Chapter 8, *Ensembles – When One Model Is Not Enough*, will cover how to reduce the bias or variance of algorithms by combining them into an ensemble. We will also learn about the different ensemble methods, from bagging to boosting, and when to use each of them.

Chapter 9, *The Y is as Important as the X*, will teach you how to build multilabel classifiers. We will also learn how to enforce dependencies between your model outputs and make a classifier's probabilities more reliable with calibration.

Chapter 10, *Imbalanced Learning – Not Even 1% Win the Lottery*, will introduce the use of an imbalanced learning helper library and explore different ways for over- and under-sampling. We will also learn how to use the sampling methods with the ensemble models.

Chapter 11, *Clustering – Making Sense of Unlabeled Data*, will cover clustering as an unsupervised learning algorithm for making sense of unlabeled data.

Chapter 12, *Anomaly Detection – Finding Outliers in Data*, will explore the different types of anomaly detection algorithms.

Chapter 13, *Recommender Systems – Get to Know Their Taste*, will teach you how to build a recommendation system and deploy it in production.

To get the most out of this book

You will need Python 3.x installed on your computer. It is a good practice to set up a virtual environment to install the required libraries into. It's up to you whether you wish to use Python's venv module, the virtual environment provided by Anaconda, or any other option you like. I'll be using pip to install the libraries needed in the book, but once more, it is up to you whether you prefer to use conda or any other alternatives.

In Chapter 1, *Introduction to Machine Learning*, I will explain the essential libraries you need to install to get started. I will show you how to install them using the same versions tested here, so we are both on the same page throughout the rest of this book. Whenever we need to install any additional libraries in the later chapters, I will also explain how to set them up.

I used Jupyter Notebooks to run the code in this book and display the accompanying graphs. I recommend that you also go to the Project Jupyter site and install Jupyter Notebook or Jupyter Lab. This setup is usually recommended when running experimental code. It helps you cut your code into pieces, iterate on each part separately, and display the resulting graphs alongside the code. When it comes to writing production code, then you may use your favorite **integrated development environment (IDE)** instead.

In addition to the software needed, you will sometimes need to download additional datasets. I will provide links to the required datasets when needed, and give step-by-step explanations on how to download and preprocess them.

I wrote the entire book and ran its code on a MacBook Pro with 16 GB RAM. I expect the code here to run on any other operating system, whether it is Microsoft Windows or any one of the different Linux distributions. It is more common for machine learning algorithms to hit a memory limitation before hitting a CPU bottleneck. Nevertheless, for most of the code and the datasets used here, I would expect computers with less memory than mine to still work fine.

If you are using the digital version of this book, we advise you to type the code yourself or access the code via the GitHub repository (link available in the next section). Doing so will help you avoid any potential errors related to the copying and pasting of code.

Download the example code files

You can download the example code files for this book from your account at `www.packt.com`. If you purchased this book elsewhere, you can visit `www.packtpub.com/support` and register to have the files emailed directly to you.

You can download the code files by following these steps:

1. Log in or register at `www.packt.com`.
2. Select the **Support** tab.
3. Click on **Code Downloads**.
4. Enter the name of the book in the **Search** box and follow the onscreen instructions.

Once the file is downloaded, please make sure that you unzip or extract the folder using the latest version of:

- WinRAR/7-Zip for Windows
- Zipeg/iZip/UnRarX for Mac
- 7-Zip/PeaZip for Linux

The code bundle for the book is also hosted on GitHub at `https://github.com/PacktPublishing/Hands-On-Machine-Learning-with-scikit-learn-and-Scientific-Python-Toolkits`. In case there's an update to the code, it will be updated on the existing GitHub repository.

We also have other code bundles from our rich catalog of books and videos available at `https://github.com/PacktPublishing/`. Check them out!

Download the color images

We also provide a PDF file that has color images of the screenshots/diagrams used in this book. You can download it here: `https://static.packt-cdn.com/downloads/9781838826048_ColorImages.pdf`.

Conventions used

There are a number of text conventions used throughout this book.

`CodeInText`: Indicates code words in the text, database table names, folder names, filenames, file extensions, pathnames, dummy URLs, user input, and Twitter handles. Here is an example: "We are going to use its `fit_transform` variable and a `transform` method."

A block of code is set as follows:

```
import numpy as np
import scipy as sp
import pandas as pd
import seaborn as sns
import matplotlib.pyplot as plt
```

Any command-line input or output is written as follows:

```
$ pip install jupyter
$ pip install matplotlib
```

Bold: Indicates a new term, an important word, or words that you see onscreen. For example, words in menus or dialog boxes appear in the text like this. Here is an example: "One-hot encoding is recommended for linear models and **K-Nearest Neighbor (KNN)** algorithms."

Warnings or important notes appear like this.

Tips and tricks appear like this.

Get in touch

Feedback from our readers is always welcome.

General feedback: If you have questions about any aspect of this book, mention the book title in the subject of your message and email us at `customercare@packtpub.com`.

Errata: Although we have taken every care to ensure the accuracy of our content, mistakes do happen. If you have found a mistake in this book, we would be grateful if you would report this to us. Please visit `www.packtpub.com/support/errata`, selecting your book, clicking on the Errata Submission Form link, and entering the details.

Piracy: If you come across any illegal copies of our works in any form on the Internet, we would be grateful if you would provide us with the location address or website name. Please contact us at `copyright@packt.com` with a link to the material.

If you are interested in becoming an author: If there is a topic that you have expertise in and you are interested in either writing or contributing to a book, please visit `authors.packtpub.com`.

Reviews

Please leave a review. Once you have read and used this book, why not leave a review on the site that you purchased it from? Potential readers can then see and use your unbiased opinion to make purchase decisions, we at Packt can understand what you think about our products, and our authors can see your feedback on their book. Thank you!

For more information about Packt, please visit `packt.com`.

Section 1: Supervised Learning 1

Supervised learning is by far the most used machine learning paradigm in business. It's the key to automating manual tasks. This section comprises the different algorithms available for supervised learning, and you will learn when to use each of them. We will also try to showcase different types of data, from tabular data to textual data and images.

This section comprises the following chapters:

- Chapter 1, *Introduction to Machine Learning*
- Chapter 2, *Making Decisions with Trees*
- Chapter 3, *Making Decisions with Linear Equations*
- Chapter 4, *Preparing Your Data*
- Chapter 5, *Image Processing with Nearest Neighbors*
- Chapter 6, *Classifying Text Using Naive Bayes*

Introduction to Machine Learning

1

Machine learning is everywhere. When you book a flight ticket, an algorithm decides the price you are going to pay for it. When you apply for a loan, machine learning may decide whether you are going to get it or not. When you scroll through your Facebook timeline, it picks which advertisements to show to you. Machine learning also plays a big role in your Google search results. It organizes your email's inbox and filters out spam, it goes through your resumé before recruiters when you apply for a job, and, more recently, it has also started to play the role of your personal assistant in the form of Siri and other virtual assistants.

In this book, we will learn about the theory and practice of machine learning. We will understand when and how to apply it. To get started, we will look at a high-level introduction to how machine learning works. You will then be able to differentiate between the different machine learning paradigms and know when to use each of them. Then, you'll be taken through the model development life cycle and the different steps practitioners take to solve problems. Finally, we will introduce you to scikit-learn, and learn why it is the *de facto* tool for many practitioners.

Here is a list of the topics that will be covered in this first chapter:

- Understanding machine learning
- The model development life cycle
- Introduction to scikit-learn
- Installing the packages you need

Understanding machine learning

You may be wondering how machines actually learn. To get the answer to this query, let's take the following example of a fictional company. **Space Shuttle Corporation** has a few space vehicles to rent. They get applications every day from clients who want to travel to Mars. They are not sure whether those clients will ever return the vehicles—maybe they'll decide to continue living on Mars and never come back again. Even worse, some of the clients may be lousy pilots and crash their vehicles on the way. So, the company decides to hire shuttle rent-approval officers whose job is to go through the applications and decide who is worthy of a shuttle ride. Their business, however, grows so big that they need to formulate the shuttle-approval process.

A traditional shuttle company would start by having business rules and hiring junior employees to execute those rules. For example, if you are an alien, then sorry, you cannot rent a shuttle from us. If you are a human and you have kids that are in school on Earth, then you are more than welcome to rent one of our shuttles. As you can see, those rules are too broad. What about aliens who love living on Earth and just want to go to Mars for a quick holiday? To come up with a better business policy, the company starts hiring analysts. Their job is to go through historical data and try to come up with detailed rules or business logic. These analysts can come up with very detailed rules. If you are an alien, one of your parents is from Neptune, your age is between 0.1 and 0.2 Neptunian years, and you have 3 to 4 kids and one of them is 80% or more human, then you are allowed to rent a shuttle. To be able to come up with suitable rules, the analysts also need a way to measure how good this business logic is. For example, what percentage of the shuttles return if certain rules are applied? They use historic data to evaluate these measures, and only then can we say that these rules are actually learned from data.

Machine learning works in almost the same way. You want to use historic data to come up with some business logic (an algorithm) in order to optimize some measure of how good the logic is (an objective or loss function). Throughout this book, we will learn about numerous machine learning algorithms; they differ from each other in how they represent business logic, what objective functions they use, and what optimization techniques they utilize to reach a model that maximizes (or sometimes minimizes) the objective function. Like the analysts in the previous example, you should pick an objective function that is as close as possible to your business objective. Any time you hear people saying data scientists should have a good understanding of their business, a significant part of that is their choice of a good objective function and ways to evaluate the models they build. In my example, I quickly picked the percentage of shuttles returned as my objective.

But if you think about it, is this really an accurate one-to-one mapping of the shuttle company's revenue? Is the revenue made by allowing a trip equal to the cost of losing a shuttle? Furthermore, rejecting a trip may also cost your company angry calls to the customer care center and negative word-of-mouth advertising. You have to understand all of this well enough before picking your objective function.

Finally, a key benefit to using machine learning is that it can iterate over a vast amount of business logic cases until it reaches the optimum objective function, unlike the case of the analysts in our space shuttle company who can only go so far with their rules. The machine learning approach is also automated in the sense that it keeps updating the business logic whenever new data arrives. These two aspects make it scalable, more accurate, and adaptable to change.

Types of machine learning algorithms

"Society is changing, one learning algorithm at a time."

– Pedro Domingos

In this book, we are going to cover the two main paradigms of machine learning—supervised learning and unsupervised learning. Each of these two paradigms has its own sub-branches that will be discussed in the next section. Although it is not covered in this book, reinforcement learning will also be introduced in the next section:

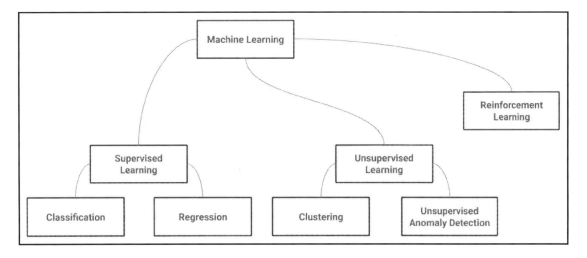

Let's use our fictional Space Shuttle Corporation company once more to explain the differences between the different machine learning paradigms.

Supervised learning

Remember those old good days at school when you were given examples to practice on, along with the correct answers to them at the end to validate whether you are doing a good job? Then, at exam time, you were left on your own. That's basically what supervised learning is. Say our fictional space vehicle company wants to predict whether travelers will return their space vehicles. Luckily, the company has worked with many travelers in the past, and they already know which of them returned their vehicles and who did not. Think of this data as a spreadsheet, where each column has some information about the travelers—their financial statements, the number of kids they have, whether they are humans or aliens, and maybe their age (in Neptunian years, of course). Machine learners call these columns **features**. There is one extra column for previous travelers that states whether they returned or not; we call this column the **label** or **target** column. In the learning phase, we build a model using the features and targets. The aim of the algorithm while learning is to minimize the differences between its predictions and the actual targets. The difference is what we call the error. Once a model is constructed so that its error is minimal, we then use it to make predictions for newer data points. For new travelers, we only know their features, but we use the model we've just built to predict their corresponding targets. In a nutshell, the presence of the target in our historic data is what makes this process supervised.

Classification versus regression

Supervised learning is further subdivided into classification and regression. For cases where we only have a few predefined labels to predict, we use a classifier—for example, *return* versus *no return* or *human* versus *Martian* versus *Venusian*. If what we want to predict is a wide-range number—say, how many years a traveler will take to come back—then it is a regression problem since these values can be anything from 1 or 2 years to 3 years, 5 months, and 7 days.

Supervised learning evaluation

Due to their differences, the metrics we use to evaluate these classifiers are usually different from ones we use with regression:

- **Classifier evaluation metrics**: Suppose we are using a classifier to determine whether a traveler is going to return. Then, of those travelers that the classifier predicted to return, we want to measure what percentage of them actually did return. We call this measure **precision**. Also, of all travelers who did return, we want to measure what percentage of them the classifier correctly predicted to return. We call this **recall**. Precision and recall can be calculated for each class—that is, we can also calculate precision and recall for the travelers who did not return.

  Accuracy is another commonly used, and sometimes abused, measure. For each case in our historic data, we know whether a traveler actually returned (**actuals**) and we can also generate **predictions** of whether they will return. The accuracy calculates what percentage of cases of the predictions and actuals match. As you can see, it is labeled **agnostic**, so it can sometimes be misleading when the classes are highly imbalanced. In our example business, say 99% of our travelers actually return. We can build a dummy classifier that predicts whether every single traveler returns; it will be accurate 99% of the time. This 99% accuracy value doesn't tell us much, especially if you know that in these cases, the recall value for non-returning travelers is 0%. As we are going to see later on in this book, each measure has its pros and cons, and a measure is only as good as how close it is to our business objectives. We are also going to learn about other metrics, such as F_1 **score**, **AUC**, and **log loss**.

- **Regressor evaluation metrics**: If we are using a regressor to tell how long a traveler will stay, then we need to determine how far the numbers that the regression evaluation is predicting are from reality. Let's say for three users, the regressor expected them to stay for 6, 9, and 20 years, respectively, while they actually stayed for 5, 10, and 26 years, respectively. One solution is to calculate the average of the differences between the prediction and the reality—the average of 6–5, 9–10, and 20–25, so the average of 1, -1, and -6 is -2. One problem with these calculations is that 1 and -1 cancel each other out. If you think about it, both 1 and -1 are mistakes that the model made, and the sign might not matter much here.

So, we will need to use **Mean Absolute Error** (MAE) instead. This calculates the average of the absolute values of the differences—so, the average of 1, 1, and 6 is 2.67. This makes more sense now, but what if we can tolerate a 1-year difference more than a 6-year difference? We can then use **Mean Squared Error** (MSE) to calculate the average of the differences squared—so, the average of 1, 1, and 36 is 12.67. Clearly, each measure has its pros and cons here as well. Additionally, we can also use different variations of these metrics, such as median absolute error or max error. Furthermore, sometimes your business objective can dictate other measures. Say we want to penalize the model if it predicts that a traveler will arrive 1 year later twice as often as when it predicts them to arrive 1 year earlier—what metric can you come up with then?

In practice, the lines between classification and regression problems can get blurred sometimes. For the case of how many years a traveler will take to return, you can still decide to bucket the range into 1–5 years, 5–10 years, and 10+ years. Then, you end up with a classification problem to solve instead. Conversely, classifiers return probabilities along with their predicted targets. For the case of whether a user will return, a predicted value of 60% and 95% means the same thing from a binary classifier's point of view, but the classifier is more confident that the traveler will return in the second case compared to the first case. Although this is still a classification problem, we can use the **Brier score** to evaluate our classifier here, which is actually **MSE** in disguise. More on the Brier score will be covered in `Chapter 9`, *The Y is as important as the X*. Most of the time, it is clear whether you are facing a classification or regression problem, but always keep your eyes open to the possibility of reformulating your problem if needed.

Unsupervised learning

Life doesn't always provide us with correct answers as was the case when we were in school. We have been told that space travelers like it when they are traveling with like-minded passengers. We already know a lot about our travelers, but of course, no traveler will say *by the way, I am a type A, B, or C traveler*. So, to group our clients, we use a form of unsupervised learning called **clustering**. Clustering algorithms try to come up with groups and put our travelers into them without us telling them what groups may exist. Unsupervised learning lacks targets, but this doesn't mean that we cannot evaluate our clustering algorithms. We want the members of a cluster to be similar to each other, but we also want them to be dissimilar from the members of adjacent clusters. The **silhouette coefficient** basically measures that. We will come across other measures for clustering, such as the **Davies-Bouldin index** and the **Calinski-Harabasz index**, later in this book

Reinforcement learning

Reinforcement learning is beyond the scope of this book and is not implemented in `scikit-learn`. Nevertheless, I will briefly talk about it here. In the supervised learning examples we have looked at, we treated each traveler separately. If we want to know which travelers are going to return their space vehicles the earliest, our aim then is to pick the best travelers for our business. But if you think about it, the behavior of one traveler affects the experience of the others as well. We only allow space vehicles to stay up to 20 years in space. However, we haven't explored the effect of allowing some travelers to stay longer or the effect of having a stricter rent period for other travelers. Reinforcement learning is the answer to that, where the key to it is exploration and exploitation.

Rather than dealing with each action separately, we may want to explore sub-optimal actions in order to reach an overall optimum set of actions. Reinforcement learning is used in robotics, where a robot has a goal and it can only reach it through a sequence of steps—2 steps to the right, 5 steps forward, and so on. We can't tell whether a right versus left step is better on its own; the whole sequence must be found to reach the best outcome. Reinforcement learning is also used in gaming, as well as in recommendation engines. If Netflix only recommended to a user what matches their taste best, a user may end up with nothing but Star Wars movies on their home screen. Reinforcement learning is then needed to explore less-optimum matches to enrich the user's overall experience.

The model development life cycle

When asked to solve a problem using machine learning, data scientists achieve this by following a sequence of steps. In this section, we are going to discuss those iterative steps.

Understanding a problem

"All models are wrong, but some are useful."

– George Box

The first thing to do when developing a model is to understand the problem you are trying to solve thoroughly. This not only involves understanding what problem you are solving, but also why you are solving it, what impact are you expecting to have, and what the currently available solution is that you are comparing your new solution to. My understanding of what Box said when he stated that all models are wrong is that a model is just an approximation of reality by modeling one or more angles of it. By understanding the problem you are trying to solve, you can decide which angles of reality you need to model, and which ones you can tolerate ignoring.

You also need to understand the problem well to decide how to split your data for training and evaluation (more on that in the next section). You can then decide what kind of model to use. Is the problem suitable for supervised or unsupervised learning? Are we better off using classification or regression algorithms for this problem? What kind of classification algorithm will serve us best? Is a linear model good enough to approximate our reality? Do we need the most accurate model or one that we can easily explain to its users and to the business stakeholders?

Minimal exploratory data analysis can be done here, where you can check whether you have labels and check the cardinality of the labels, if present, to decide whether you are dealing with a classification or a regression problem. I would still save any further data analysis until after the dataset is split into training and test sets. It is important to limit advanced data analysis to the training set only to ensure your model's generalizability.

Finally, we need to understand what we are comparing our model to. What is the current baseline that we need to improve on? If there are already business rules in place, then our model has to be better at solving the problem at hand than these rules. To be able to decide how much better it is at solving the problem, we need to use evaluation metrics—metrics that are suitable for our model and also as close as possible to our business requirements. If our aim is to increase revenue, then our metric should be good at estimating the increase in revenue when our model is used, compared to the current status quo. If our aim is to increase repeat purchases regardless of the revenue, then other metrics may be more suitable.

Splitting our data

As we have seen in supervised learning, we train our model on a set of data where the correct answers (labels) are given. Learning, however, is only half of the problem. We also want to be able to tell whether the model we built is going to do a good job when used on future data. We cannot foresee the future, but we can use the data we already have to evaluate our model.

We do this by splitting our data into parts. We use one part of the data to train the model (the training set) and then use a separate part to evaluate the model (the test set). Since we want our test set to be as close as possible to the future data, there are two key points discussed in the following subsections to keep in mind when splitting our data:

- Finding the best manner to split the data
- Making sure the training and test datasets are separate

Finding the best manner to split the data

Say your users' data is sorted according to their country in alphabetical order. If you just take the first N records for training and the rest for testing, you will end up training the model on users from certain countries and will never let it learn anything about users from, say, Zambia and Zimbabwe. So, one common solution is to randomize your data before splitting it. Random split is not always the best option, however. Say we want to build a model to predict the stock prices or climate change phenomena a few years ahead. To be confident that our system will capture temporal trends such as global warming, we need to split our data based on time. We can train on earlier data and see whether the model can do a good job in predicting more recent data.

Sometimes, we just predict rare incidents. It can be that the number of fraud cases that occur in your payment system is 0.1%. If you randomly split your data, you may be unlucky and have the vast majority of the fraud cases in the training data and very few cases in the test data, or vice versa. So, it is advised that you use stratification when it comes to highly unbalanced data. Stratification makes sure that the distribution of your targets is more or less the same in both the training and test datasets.

A stratified sampling strategy is used to make sure that the different subgroups in our population are represented in our samples. If my dataset is made up of 99% males and 1% females, a random sample of the population may end up having only males in it. So, you should separate the male and female populations first, and then take a sample from each one of the two and combine them later to make sure they are both represented in the final sample. The same concept is applied here if we want to make sure all the class labels are present in our training and test sets. Later on in this book, we will be splitting our data using the `train_test_split()` function. This function uses the class labels to stratify its samples by default.

Making sure the training and the test datasets are separate

One of the most common mistakes new data scientists may fall prey to is the look-ahead bias. We use the test dataset to simulate the data we will see in the future, but usually, the test dataset contains information that we can only know after time has passed. Take the case of our example space vehicles; we may have two columns—one saying whether the vehicle returns, and the other saying how long the vehicle will take to return. If we are to build a classifier to predict whether a vehicle will return, we will use the former column as our target, but we will never use the latter column as a feature. We can only know how long a vehicle stayed in outer space once it is actually back. This example looks trivial, but believe me, look-ahead bias is a very common mistake, especially when dealing with less obvious cases than this one.

Besides training, you also learn things from the data in order to preprocess it. Say, instead of users' heights in centimeters, you want to have a feature stating whether a user's height is above or below the median. To do that, you need to go through the data and calculate the median. Now, since anything that we learn has to come from the training set itself, we also need to learn this median from the training set and not from the entire dataset. Luckily, in all the data preprocessing functions of scikit-learn, there are separate methods for the `fit()`, `predict()`, and `transform()` functions. This makes sure that anything learned from the data (via the `fit()` method) is only learned from the training dataset, and then it can be applied to the test set (via the `predict()` and/or `transform()` methods).

Development set

When developing a model, we need to try multiple configurations of the model to decide which configuration gives the best results. To be able to do so, we usually split the training dataset further into training and development sets. Having two new subsets allows us to try different configurations when training on one of the two subsets and evaluating the effect of those configuration changes on the other. Once we find the best configuration, we evaluate our model with its final configuration on the test set. In Chapter 2, *Making Decisions with Trees*, we will do all this in practice. Note that I will be using the terms *model configuration* and *hyperparameters* interchangeably.

Evaluating our model

Evaluating your model's performance is essential in picking the best algorithm for the job and to be able to estimate how your model will perform in real life. As Box said, a model that is wrong can still be useful. Take the example of a web start-up. They run an ad campaign where they are paid $1 for each view they get, and they know that for every 100 viewers, only one viewer signs up and buys stuff for $50. In other words, they have to spend $100 to make $50. Obviously, that's a bad **Return of Investment (ROI)** for their business. Now, what if you create a model for them that can pick users for them to target, but your new model is only correct 10% of the time? Is 10% precision good or bad, in this case? Well, of course, this model is wrong 90% of the time, which may sound like a very bad model, but if we calculate ROI now, then for every $100 they spend, they make $500. Well, I would definitely pay you to build me this model that is quite wrong, yet quite useful!

scikit-learn provides a large number of evaluation metrics that we will be using to evaluate the models we build in this book. But remember, a metric is only useful if you really understand the problem you are solving and its business impact.

Deploying in production and monitoring

The main reason that many data scientists use Python for machine learning instead of R, for example, is that it makes it easier to productionize your code. Python has plenty of web frameworks to build APIs with and put the machine learning models behind. It is also supported by all cloud providers. I find it important that the team developing a model is also responsible for deploying it in production. Building your model in one language and then asking another team to port it into another language is error-prone. Of course, having one person or team building and deploying models may not be feasible in larger companies or due to other implementation constraints.

However, keeping the two teams in close contact and making sure that the ones developing the model can still understand the production code is essential and helps to minimize errors on account of development and production code inconsistency.

We try our best not to have any look-ahead bias when training our models. We hope data doesn't change after our models are trained, and we want our code to be bug-free. However, we cannot guarantee any of this. We may overlook the fact that the user's credit score is only added to the database after they make their first purchase. We may not know that our developers decided to switch to the metric system to specify our inventory's weights while it was saved in pounds when the model was trained. Because of that, it is important to log all the predictions your model makes to be able to monitor its performance in real life and compare it to the test set's performance. You can also log the test set's performance every time you retrain the model or keep track of the target's distribution over time.

Iterating

Often, when you deploy a model, you end up with more data. Furthermore, the performance of your model is not guaranteed to be the same when deployed in production. This can be due to some implementation issues or mistakes that took place during the evaluation process. Those two points mean that the first version of your solution is always up for improvement. Starting with simple solutions (that can be improved via iterations) is an important concept for agile programming and is a paramount concept for machine learning.

This whole process, from understanding the problem to monitoring the ongoing improvements on the solution, requires tools that allow us to iterate quickly and efficiently. In the next section, we will introduce you to scikit-learn and explain why many machine learning practitioners consider it the right tool for the job.

When to use machine learning

> *"Pretty much anything that a normal person can do in less than 1 second, we can now automate with AI."*

> *– Andrew Ng*

One additional note before moving on to the next section is that when faced with a problem, you have to decide whether machine learning is apt for the task. Andrew Ng's 1-second rule is a good heuristic for you to estimate whether a machine learning-based solution will work. The main reason behind this is that computers are good with patterns. They are way better than humans at picking repeated patterns and acting on them.

Once they identify the same pattern over and over again, it is easy to codify them to make the same decisions every time. In the same manner, computers are also good with tactics. In 1908, Richard Teichmann stated that a game of chess is 99% based on tactics. Maybe that's why computers have beat humans in chess since 1997. If we are to believe Teichmann's statement, then the remaining 1% is strategy. Unlike tactics, strategy is the arena where humans beat machines. If the problem you want to solve can be formulated as a set of tactics, then go for machine learning and leave the strategic decisions for humans to make. In the end, most of our day-to-day decisions are tactical. Furthermore, one man's strategy is often someone else's tactics.

Introduction to scikit-learn

Since you have already picked up this book, you probably don't need me to convince you why machine learning is important. However, you may still have doubts about why to use scikit-learn in particular. You may encounter names such as TensorFlow, PyTorch, and Spark more often during your daily news consumption than scikit-learn. So, let me convince you of my preference for the latter.

It plays well with the Python data ecosystem

scikit-learn is a Python toolkit built on top of NumPy, SciPy, and Matplotlib. These choices mean that it fits well into your daily data pipeline. As a data scientist, Python is most likely your language of choice since it is good for both offline analysis and real-time implementations. You will also be using tools such as `pandas` to load data from your database, which allows you to perform a vast amount of transformation to your data. Since both `pandas` and scikit-learn are built on top of NumPy, they play very well with each other. Matplotlib is the *de facto* data visualization tool for Python, which means you can use its sophisticated data visualization capabilities to explore your data and unravel your model's ins and outs.

Since it is an open source tool that is heavily used in the community, it is very common to see other data tools use an almost identical interface to scikit-learn. Many of these tools are built on top of the same scientific Python libraries, and they are collectively known as **SciKits** (short for **SciPy Toolkits**)—hence, the *scikit* prefix in scikit-learn. For example, `scikit-image` is a library for image processing, while `categorical-encoding` and `imbalanced-learn` are separate libraries for data preprocessing that are built as add-ons to scikit-learn.

We are going to use some of these tools in this book, and you will notice how easy it is to integrate these different tools into your workflow when using scikit-learn.

Being a key player in the Python data ecosystem is what makes scikit-learn the *de facto* toolset for machine learning. This is the tool that you will most likely hand your job application assignment to, as well as use for Kaggle competitions and to solve most of your professional day-to-day machine learning problems for your job.

Practical level of abstraction

scikit-learn implements a vast amount of machine learning, data processing, and model selection algorithms. These implementations are abstract enough, so you only need to apply minor changes when switching from one algorithm to another. This is a key feature since you will need to quickly iterate between different algorithms when developing a model to pick the best one for your problem. Having that said, this abstraction doesn't shield you from the algorithms' configurations. In other words, you are still in full control of your hyperparameters and settings.

When not to use scikit-learn

Most likely, the reasons to not use scikit-learn will include combinations of deep learning or scale. scikit-learn's implementation of neural networks is limited. Unlike scikit-learn, TensorFlow and PyTorch allow you to use a custom architecture, and they support GPUs for a massive training scale. All of scikit-learn's implementations run in memory on a single machine. I'd say that way more than 90% of businesses are at a scale where these constraints are fine. Data scientists can still fit their data in memory in large enough machines thanks to the cloud options available. They can cleverly engineer workarounds to deal with scaling issues, but if these limitations become something that they can no longer deal with, then they will need other tools to do the trick for them.

 There are solutions being developed that allow scikit-learn to scale to multiple machines, such as Dask. Many scikit-learn algorithms allow parallel execution using `joblib`, which natively provides thread-based and process-based parallelism. Dask can scale these `joblib`-backed algorithms out to a cluster of machines by providing an alternative `joblib` backend.

Installing the packages you need

It's time to install the packages we will need in this book, but first of all, make sure you have Python installed on your computer. In this book, we will be using Python version 3.6. If your computer comes with Python 2.x installed, then you should upgrade Python to version 3.6 or later. I will show you how to install the required packages using `pip`, Python's *de facto* package-management system. If you use other package-management systems, such as Anaconda, you can easily find the equivalent installation commands for each of the following packages online.

To install `scikit-learn`, run the following command:

```
$ pip install --upgrade scikit-learn==0.22
```

I will be using version `0.22` of `scikit-learn` here. You can add the `--user` switch to the `pip` command to limit the installation to your own directories. This is important if you do not have root access to your machine or if you do not want to install the libraries globally. Furthermore, I prefer to create a virtual environment for each project I work on and install all the libraries I need for this project into that environment. You can check the documentation for Anaconda or Python's `venv` module to see how to create virtual environments.

Along with scikit-learn, we will need to install `pandas`. I will briefly introduce `pandas` in the next section, but for now, you can use the following command to install it:

```
$ pip install --upgrade pandas==0.25.3
```

Optionally, you may need to install **Jupyter**. Jupyter notebooks allow you to write code in your browser and run bits of it in whichever order you want. This makes it ideal for experimentation and trying different parameters without the need to rerun the entire code every time. You can also plot graphs in your notebooks with the help of Matplotlib. Use the following commands to install both Jupyter and Matplotlib:

```
$ pip install jupyter
$ pip install matplotlib
```

To start your Jupyter server, you can run `jupyter notebook` in your terminal, and then visit `http://localhost:8888/` in your browser.

We will make use of other libraries later on in the book. I'd rather introduce you to them when we need them and show you how to install each of them then.

Introduction to pandas

`pandas` is an open source library that provides data analysis tools for the Python programming language. If this definition doesn't tell you much, then you may think of `pandas` as Python's response to spreadsheets. I have decided to dedicate this section to `pandas` since you will be using it to create and load the data you are going to use in this book. You will also use `pandas` to analyze and visualize your data and alter the value of its columns before applying machine learning algorithms to it.

Tables in `pandas` are referred to as DataFrames. If you are an R programmer, then this name should be familiar to you. Now, let's start by creating a DataFrame for some polygon names and the number of sides each has:

```python
# It's customary to call pandas pd when importing it
import pandas as pd

polygons_data_frame = pd.DataFrame(
    {
        'Name': ['Triangle', 'Quadrilateral', 'Pentagon', 'Hexagon'],
        'Sides': [3, 4, 5, 6],
    }
)
```

You can then use the `head` method to print the first *N* rows of your newly created DataFrame:

```python
polygons_data_frame.head(3)
```

Here, you can see the first three rows of the DataFrame. In addition to the columns we specified, `pandas` add a default index:

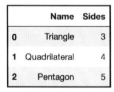

	Name	Sides
0	Triangle	3
1	Quadrilateral	4
2	Pentagon	5

Since we are programming in Python, we can also use the language's built-in function or even use our custom-built functions when creating a DataFrame. Here, we will use the `range` generator, rather than typing in all the possible side counts ourselves:

```python
polygons = {
    'Name': [
        'Triangle', 'Quadrilateral', 'Pentagon', 'Hexagon', 'Heptagon',
```

```
'Octagon', 'Nonagon', 'Decagon', 'Hendecagon', 'Dodecagon', 'Tridecagon',
'Tetradecagon'
    ],
    # Range parameters are the start, the end of the range and the step
    'Sides': range(3, 15, 1),
}
polygons_data_frame = pd.DataFrame(polygons)
```

You can also sort your DataFrame by column. Here, we will sort it by polygon name in alphabetical order, and then print the first five polygons:

```
polygons_data_frame.sort_values('Name').head(5)
```

This time, we can see the first five rows of the DataFrame after it has been ordered by the names of the polygons in alphabetical order:

	Name	Sides
7	Decagon	10
9	Dodecagon	12
8	Hendecagon	11
4	Heptagon	7
3	Hexagon	6

Feature engineering is the art of deriving new features by manipulating existing data. This is something that pandas is good at. In the following example, we are creating a new column, Length of Name, and adding the character lengths of each polygon's name:

```
polygons_data_frame[
    'Length of Name'
] = polygons_data_frame['Name'].str.len()
```

We use str to be able to access the string functions to apply them to the values in the Name column. We then use the len method of a string. One other way to achieve the same result is to use the apply() function. If you call apply() on a column, you can get access to the values in the column. You can then apply any Python built-in or custom functions there. Here are two examples of how to use the apply() function.

Example 1 is as follows:

```
polygons_data_frame[
    'Length of Name'
] = polygons_data_frame['Name'].apply(len)
```

Example 2 is as follows:

```
polygons_data_frame[
    'Length of Name'
] = polygons_data_frame['Name'].apply(lambda n: len(n))
```

The good thing about the `apply()` method is that it allows you to run your own custom code anywhere, which is something you will need to use a lot when performing complex feature engineering. Nevertheless, the code you run using the `apply()` method isn't as optimized as the code in the first example. This is a clear case of flexibility versus performance trade-off that you should be aware of.

Finally, we can use the plotting capabilities provided by `pandas` and Matplotlib to see whether there is any correlation between the number of sides a polygon has and the length of its name:

```
# We use the DataFrame's plot method here,
# where we specify that this is a scatter plot
# and also specify which columns to use for x and y
polygons_data_frame.plot(
    title='Sides vs Length of Name',
    kind='scatter',
    x='Sides',
    y='Length of Name',
)
```

Once we run the previous code, the following scatter plots will be displayed:

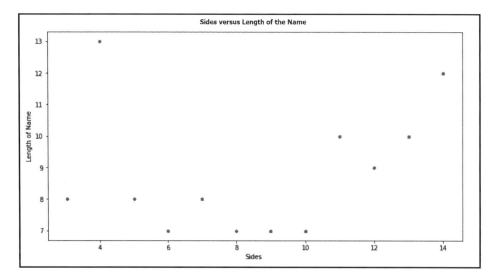

Scatter plots are generally useful for seeing correlations between two features. In the following plot, there is no clear correlation to be seen.

Python's scientific computing ecosystem conventions

Throughout this book, I will be using pandas, NumPy, SciPy, Matplotlib, and Seaborn. Any time you see the np, sp, pd, sns, and plt prefixes, you should assume that I have run the following import statements prior to the code:

```
import numpy as np
import scipy as sp
import pandas as pd
import seaborn as sns
import matplotlib.pyplot as plt
```

This is the *de facto* way of importing the scientific computing ecosystem into Python. If any of these libraries is missing on your computer, here is how to install them using pip:

```
$ pip install --upgrade numpy==1.17.3
$ pip install --upgrade scipy==1.3.1
$ pip install --upgrade pandas==0.25.3
$ pip install --upgrade scikit-learn==0.22
$ pip install --upgrade matplotlib==3.1.2
$ pip install --upgrade seaborn==0.9.0
```

Usually, you do not need to specify the versions for each library; running pip install numpy will just install the latest stable version of the library. Nevertheless, pinning the version is good practice for reproducibility. It ensures the same results from the same code when it runs on different machines.

The code used in this book is written in Jupyter notebooks. I advise you to do the same on your machine. In general, the code should run smoothly in any other environment with very few changes when it comes to printing and displaying the results. If the figures are not shown in your Jupyter notebook, you may need to run the following line at least once in any cell at the beginning of your notebook:

```
%matplotlib inline
```

Furthermore, randomness is quite common in many machine learning tasks. We may need to create random data to use with our algorithms. We may also randomly split this data into training and test sets. The algorithms themselves may use random values for initialization. There are tricks to make sure we all get the exact same results by using pseudo-random numbers. I will be using these tricks when needed sometimes, but other times, it would be better to make sure we get slightly different results to give you an idea of how things are not always deterministic and how to find ways to deal with underlying uncertainties. More on this later.

Summary

Mastering machine learning is a desirable skill nowadays given its vast application everywhere, from business to academia. Nevertheless, just understanding the theory of it will only take you so far since practitioners also need to understand their tools to be self-sufficient and capable.

In this chapter, we started with a high-level introduction to machine learning and learned when to use each of the machine learning types; from classification and regression to clustering and reinforcement learning. We then learned about scikit-learn and why practitioners recommend it when solving both supervised and unsupervised learning problems. To keep this book self-sufficient, we also covered the basics of data manipulation for those who haven't used libraries such as `pandas` and Matplotlib before. In the following chapters, we will continue to combine our understanding of the underlying theory of machine learning with more practical examples using scikit-learn.

The first two parts of this book will cover supervised machine learning algorithms. The first part will cover basic algorithms, as well as some other machine learning basics, such as data splitting and preprocessing. Then, we will move on to more advanced topics in the second part. The third and final part will cover unsupervised learning and topics such as anomaly detection and recommendation engines.

So that this book remains a practical guide, I have made sure to provide examples in each chapter. I also did not want to separate the data preparation from model creation. Although topics such as data splitting, feature selection, data scaling, and model evaluation are key concepts to know about, we usually deal with them as part of an overall whole solution. I also feel that those concepts are best understood in their correct context. That's why, within each chapter, I will be covering one main algorithm but will use some examples to shed light on some other concepts along the way.

This means that it is up to you whether you read this book from cover to cover or use it as a reference and jump straight to the algorithms you want to know about when you need them. Nevertheless, I advise that you skim through all the chapters, even if you already know about the algorithm covered there or don't need to know about it at the moment.

I hope that you are now ready for the next chapter, where we will start by looking at decision trees and learn how to use them to solve different classification and regression problems.

Further reading

For more information on the relative topics of this chapter, please refer to the following links:

- *Learn Python Programming – Second Edition,* by *Fabrizio Romano*: https://www.packtpub.com/application-development/learn-python-programming-second-edition

- *Hands-On Data Analysis with Pandas,* by *Stefanie Molin*: https://www.packtpub.com/big-data-and-business-intelligence/hands-data-analysis-pandas

Making Decisions with Trees 2

In this chapter, we are going to start by looking at our first supervised learning algorithm—decision trees. The decision tree algorithm is versatile and easy to understand. It is widely used and also serves as a building block for the numerous advanced algorithms that we will encounter later on in this book. In this chapter, we will learn how to train a decision tree and use it for either classification or regression problems. We will also understand the details of its learning process in order to know how to set its different hyperparameters. Furthermore, we will use a real-world dataset to apply what we are going to learn here in practice. We will start by getting and preparing the data and apply our algorithm to it. Along the way, we will also try to understand key machine learning concepts, such as cross-validation and model evaluation metrics. By the end of this chapter, you will have a very good understanding of the following topics:

- Understanding decision trees
- How do decision trees learn?
- Getting a more reliable score
- Tuning the hyperparameters for higher accuracy
- Visualizing the tree's decision boundaries
- Building decision tree regressors

Understanding decision trees

I chose to start this book with decision trees because I've noticed that the majority of new machine learning practitioners have previous experience in one of two fields—software development, or statistics and mathematics. Decision trees can conceptually resemble some of the concepts software developers are used to, such as nested `if-else` conditions and binary search trees. As for the statisticians, bear with me—soon, you will feel at home when we reach the chapter about linear models.

What are decision trees?

I think the best way to explain what decision trees are is by showing the rules they generate after they are trained. Luckily, we can access those rules and print them. Here is an example of how decision tree rules look:

```
Shall I take an umbrella with me?
|--- Chance of Rainy <= 0.6
|    |--- UV Index <= 7.0
|    |    |--- class: False
|    |--- UV Index >  7.0
|    |    |--- class: True
|--- Chance of Rainy >  0.6
|    |--- class: True
```

As you can see, it's basically a set of conditions. If the chance of rain falling is above `0.6` (60%), then I need to take an umbrella with me. If it is below `0.6`, then it all depends on the UV index. If the UV index is above `7`, then an umbrella is needed; otherwise, I will be fine without one. Now, you might be thinking *well, a few nested* `if-else` *conditions will do the trick.* True, but the main difference here is that I didn't write any of these conditions myself. The algorithm just learned the preceding conditions automatically after it went through the following data:

Chance of Rain	UV Index	Umbrella
0.1	11	True
0.9	1	True
0.3	3	False
0.1	2	False

Of course, for this simple case, anyone can manually go through the data and come up with the same conditions. Nevertheless, when dealing with a bigger dataset, the number of conditions we need to program will quickly grow with the number of columns and the values in each column. At such a scale, it is not possible to manually perform the same job, and an algorithm that can learn the conditions from the data is needed.

Conversely, it is also possible to map a constructed tree back to the nested `if-else` conditions. This means that you can use Python to build a tree from data, then export the underlying conditions to be implemented in a different language or even to put them in **Microsoft Excel** if you want.

Iris classification

scikit-learn comes loaded with a number of datasets that we can use to test new algorithms. One of these datasets is the Iris set. Iris is a genus of 260–300 species of flowering plants with showy flowers. However, in our dataset, just three species are covered—**Setosa**, **Versicolor**, and **Virginica**. Each example in our dataset has the length and the widths of the sepal and petal of each plant (the features), along with whether it is a Setosa, a Versicolor, or a Virginica (the target). Our task is to be able to identify the species of a plant given its sepal and petal dimensions. Clearly, this is a classification problem. It is a supervised learning problem since the targets are provided with the data. Furthermore, it is a classification problem since we take a limited number of predefined values (three species).

Loading the Iris dataset

Let's now start by loading the dataset:

1. We import the dataset's module from scikit-learn, and then load the Iris data into a variable, which we are going to call `iris` as well:

   ```
   from sklearn import datasets
   import pandas as pd
   iris = datasets.load_iris()
   ```

2. Using `dir`, we can see what methods and attributes the dataset provides:

   ```
   dir(iris)
   ```

   We get a list of the `DESCR`, `data`, `feature_names`, `filename`, `target`, and `target_names` methods.

   It's nice of the data creators to provide descriptions with each one, which we can access using `DESCR`. This is rarely the case with real-life data, however. Usually, in real life, we need to talk to the people who produced the data in the first place to understand what each value means, or at least use some descriptive statistics to understand the data before using it.

3. For now, let's print the Iris data's description:

   ```
   print(iris.DESCR)
   ```

Have a look at the description now and try to think of some of the main takeaways from it. I will list my own takeaways afterward:

```
.. _iris_dataset:
 Iris plants dataset
 --------------------

 Data Set Characteristics:
 :Number of Instances: 150 (50 in each of three classes)
   :Number of Attributes: 4 numeric, predictive attributes and the
 class
    :Attribute Information:
 - sepal length in cm
 - sepal width in cm
 - petal length in cm
 - petal width in cm
 - class:
      - Iris-Setosa
      - Iris-Versicolor
      - Iris-Virginica
 :Summary Statistics:
      =============== ==== ==== ======= ===== ====================
                      Min  Max  Mean    SD    Class  Correlation
      =============== ==== ==== ======= ===== ====================
 sepal length:        4.3  7.9  5.84    0.83  0.7826
 sepal width:         2.0  4.4  3.05    0.43  -0.4194
 petal length:        1.0  6.9  3.76    1.76  0.9490  (high!)
 petal length:        1.0  6.9  3.76    1.76  0.9490  (high!)
 petal width:         0.1  2.5  1.20    0.76  0.9565  (high!)
      =============== ==== ==== ======= ===== ====================
 :Missing Attribute Values: None
 :Class Distribution: 33.3% for each of 3 classes.

 :Creator: R.A. Fisher
```

This description holds some useful information for us, and I found the following points the most interesting:

- The data is composed of 150 rows (or 150 samples). This is a reasonably small dataset. Later on, we will see how to deal with this fact when evaluating our model.
- The class labels or targets take three values—Iris-Setosa, Iris-Versicolor, and Iris-Virginica. Some classification algorithms can only deal with two class labels; we call them binary classifiers. Luckily, the decision tree algorithm can deal with more than two classes, so we have no problems this time.

- The data is balanced; there are 50 samples for each class. This is something we need to keep in mind when training and evaluating our model later on.
- We have four features—`sepal length`, `sepal width`, `petal length`, and `petal width`—and all four features are numeric. In *Chapter 3, Preparing Your Data*, we will learn how to deal with non-numeric data.
- There are no missing attribute values. In other words, none of our samples contains null values. Later on in this book, we will learn how to deal with missing values if we encounter them.
- The petal dimensions correlate with the class values more than the sepal dimensions. I wish we had never seen this piece of information. Understanding your data is useful, but the problem here is that this correlation is calculated for the entire dataset. Ideally, we will only calculate it for our training data. Anyway, let's ignore this information for now and just use it for a sanity check later on.

4. It's time to put all the dataset information into one DataFrame.

The `feature_names` method returns the names of our features, while the `data` method returns their values in the form of a NumPy array. Similarly, the `target` variable has the values of the target in the form of zeros, ones, and twos, and `target_names` maps 0, 1, and 2 to `Iris-Setosa`, `Iris-Versicolor`, and `Iris-Virginica`, respectively.

NumPy arrays are efficient to deal with, but they do not allow columns to have names. I find column names to be useful for debugging purposes. I find `pandas` DataFrames to be more suitable here since we can use column names and combine the features and target into one DataFrame.

Here, we can see the first eight rows we get using `iris.data[:8]`:

```
array([[5.1, 3.5, 1.4, 0.2], [4.9, 3. , 1.4, 0.2], [4.7, 3.2, 1.3,
0.2], [4.6, 3.1, 1.5, 0.2], [5. , 3.6, 1.4, 0.2], [5.4, 3.9, 1.7,
0.4], [4.6, 3.4, 1.4, 0.3], [5. , 3.4, 1.5, 0.2]])
```

The following code uses the `data`, `feature_names`, and `target` methods to combine all the dataset information into one DataFrame and assign its column names accordingly:

```
df = pd.DataFrame(
    iris.data,
    columns=iris.feature_names
)
```

```
df['target'] = pd.Series(
  iris.target
)
```

 scikit-learn versions 0.23 and up support loading datasets as `pandas` DataFrames right away. You can do this by setting `as_frame=True` in `datasets.load_iris` and its similar data-loading methods. Nevertheless, this has not been tested in this book since version 0.22 is the most stable release at the time of writing.

5. The `target` column now has the class IDs. However, for more clarity, we can also create a new column called `target_names`, where we can map our numerical target values to the class names:

```
df['target_names'] = df['target'].apply(lambda y:
iris.target_names[y])
```

6. Finally, let's print a sample of six rows to see how our new DataFrame looks. Running the following code in a Jupyter notebook or a Jupyter lab will just print the contents of the DataFrame; otherwise, you need to surround your code with a `print` statement. I will assume that a Jupyter notebook environment is used in all later code snippets:

```
# print(df.sample(n=6))
df.sample(n=6)
```

This gave me the following random sample:

	sepal length (cm)	sepal width (cm)	petal length (cm)	petal width (cm)	target	target_names
26	5.0	3.4	1.6	0.4	0	setosa
101	5.8	2.7	5.1	1.9	2	virginica
113	5.7	2.5	5.0	2.0	2	virginica
52	6.9	3.1	4.9	1.5	1	versicolor
134	6.1	2.6	5.6	1.4	2	virginica
11	4.8	3.4	1.6	0.2	0	setosa

The sample methods picked six random rows to display. This means that you will get a different set of rows each time you run the same code. Sometimes, we need to get the same random results every time we run the same code. Then, we use a pseudo-random number generator with a preset seed. A pseudo-random number generator initialized with the same seed will produce the same results every time it runs.

So, set the `random_state` parameter in the `sample()` method to `42`, as follows:

```
df.sample(n=6, random_state=42)
```

You will get the exact same rows shown earlier.

Splitting the data

Let's split the DataFrame we have just created into two—70% of the records (that is, 105 records) should go into the training set, while 30% (45 records) should go into testing. The choice of 70/30 is arbitrary for now. We will use the `train_test_split()` function provided by scikit-learn and specify `test_size` to be `0.3`:

```
from sklearn.model_selection import train_test_split
df_train, df_test = train_test_split(df, test_size=0.3)
```

We can use `df_train.shape[0]` and `df_test.shape[0]` to check how many rows there are in the newly created DataFrames. We can also list the columns of the new DataFrames using `df_train.columns` and `df_test.columns`. They both have the same six columns:

- `sepal length (cm)`
- `sepal width (cm)`
- `petal length (cm)`
- `petal width (cm)`
- `target`
- `target_names`

The first four columns are our features, while the fifth column is our target (or label). The sixth column will not be needed for now. Visually, you could say that we have split our data vertically into training and test sets. Usually, it makes sense to further split each of our DataFrames horizontally into two parts—one part for the features, which we usually call x, and another part for the targets, which is usually called y. We will continue to use this x and y naming convention throughout the rest of this book.

Some prefer to use a capital *X* to illustrate that it is a two-dimensional array (or DataFrames) and use a small letter for *y* when it is a single-dimensional array (or series). I find it more practical to stick to a single case.

As you know, the `feature_names` method in `iris` contains a list of the corresponding column names to our features. We will use this information, along with the `target` label, to create our *x* and *y* sets, as follows:

```
x_train = df_train[iris.feature_names]
x_test = df_test[iris.feature_names]

y_train = df_train['target']
y_test = df_test['target']
```

Training the model and using it for prediction

To get a feel for how everything works, we will train our algorithm using its default configuration for now. Later on in this chapter, I will explain the details of the decision tree algorithms and how to configure them.

We need to import `DecisionTreeClassifier` first, and then create an instance of it, as follows:

```
from sklearn.tree import DecisionTreeClassifier

# It is common to call the classifier instance clf
clf = DecisionTreeClassifier()
```

One commonly used synonym for training is fitting. This is how an algorithm uses the training data (*x* and *y*) to learn its parameters. All scikit-learn models implement a `fit()` method that takes `x_train` and `y_train`, and `DecisionTreeClassifier` is no different:

```
clf.fit(x_train, y_train)
```

By calling the `fit()` method, the `clf` instance is trained and ready to be used for predictions. We then call the `predict()` method on `x_test`:

```
# If y_test is our truth, then let's call our predictions y_test_pred
y_test_pred = clf.predict(x_test)
```

When predicting, we usually don't know the actual targets (*y*) for our features (*x*). That's why we only provide the `predict()` method here with `x_test`. In this particular case, we happened to know `y_test`; nevertheless, we will pretend that we don't know it for now, and only use it later on for evaluation. As our actual targets are called `y_test`, we will call the predicted ones `y_test_pred` and compare the two later on.

Evaluating our predictions

As we have `y_test_predict`, all we need now is to compare it to `y_test` to check how good our predictions are. If you remember from the previous chapter, there are multiple metrics for evaluating a classifier, such as `precision`, `recall`, and `accuracy`. The Iris dataset is a balanced dataset; it has the same number of instances for each class. Therefore, it is apt to use the accuracy metric here.

Calculating the accuracy, as follows, gives us a score of `0.91`:

```
from sklearn.metrics import accuracy_score
accuracy_score(y_test, y_test_pred)
```

 Did you get a different score than mine? Don't worry. In the *Getting a more reliable score* section, I will explain why the accuracy score calculated here may vary.

Congratulations! You've just trained your first supervised learning algorithm. From now on, all the algorithms we are going to use in this book have a similar interface:

- The `fit()` method takes the *x* and *y* parts of your training data.
- The `predict()` method takes *x* only and returns a predicted *y*.

Which features were more important?

We may now ask ourselves, *Which features did the model find more useful in deciding the iris species?* Luckily, `DecisionTreeClassifier` has a method called `feature_importances_`, which is computed after the classifier is fitted and scores how important each feature is to the model's decision. In the following code snippet, we will create a DataFrames where we will put the features' names and their importance together and then sort the features by their importance:

```
pd.DataFrame(
    {
        'feature_names': iris.feature_names,
```

```
         'feature_importances': clf.feature_importances_
     }
).sort_values(
    'feature_importances', ascending=False
).set_index('feature_names')
```

This is the output we get:

feature_names	feature_importances
petal width (cm)	0.594961
petal length (cm)	0.405039
sepal length (cm)	0.000000
sepal width (cm)	0.000000

As you will recall, when we printed the dataset's description, the petal length and width values started to correlate highly with the target. They also have high feature importance scores here, which confirms what is stated in the description.

Displaying the internal tree decisions

We can also print the internal structure of the learned tree using the following code snippet:

```
from sklearn.tree import export_text
print(
    export_text(clf, feature_names=iris.feature_names, spacing=3, decimals=1)
)
```

This will print the following text:

```
|--- petal width (cm) <= 0.8
|   |--- class: 0
|--- petal width (cm) > 0.8
|   |--- petal width (cm) <= 1.8
|   |   |--- petal length (cm) <= 5.3
|   |   |   |--- sepal length (cm) <= 5.0
|   |   |   |   |--- class: 2
|   |   |   |--- sepal length (cm) > 5.0
|   |   |   |   |--- class: 1
```

```
| | |--- petal length (cm) > 5.3
| | | |--- class: 2
| |--- petal width (cm) > 1.8
| | |--- class: 2
```

If you print the complete dataset description, you will notice that toward the end, it says the following:

One class is linearly separable from the other two; the latter are NOT linearly separable from each other.

This means that one class is easier to separate from the other two, while the other two are harder to separate from each other. Now, look at the internal tree's structure. You may notice that in the first step, it decided that anything with a petal width below or equal to 0.8 belongs to class 0 (Setosa). Then, for petal widths above 0.8, the tree kept on branching, trying to differentiate between classes 1 and 2 (Versicolor and Virginica). Generally, the harder it is to separate classes, the deeper the branching goes.

How do decision trees learn?

It's time to find out how decision trees actually learn in order to configure them. In the internal structure we just printed, the tree decided to use a petal width of 0.8 as its initial splitting decision. This was done because decision trees try to build the smallest possible tree using the following technique.

It went through all the features trying to find a feature (petal width, here) and a value within that feature (0.8, here) so that if we split all our training data into two parts (one for petal width ≤ 0.8, and one for petal width > 0.8), we get the purest split possible. In other words, it tries to find a condition where we can separate our classes as much as possible. Then, for each side, it iteratively tries to split the data further using the same technique.

Splitting criteria

If we only had two classes, an ideal split would put members of one class on one side and members of the others on the other side. In our case, we succeeded in putting members of class 0 on one side and members of classes 1 and 2 on the other. Obviously, we are not always guaranteed to get such a pure split. As we can see in the other branches further down the tree, we always had a mix of samples from classes 1 and 2 on each side.

Having said that, we need a way to measure purity. We need a criterion based on if one split is purer than the other. There are two criteria that scikit-learn uses for classifiers' purity—`gini` and `entropy`—with the `gini` criterion as its default option. When it comes to decision tree regression, there are other criteria that we will come across later on.

Preventing overfitting

"If you look for perfection, you'll never be content."

– Leo Tolstoy

After the first split, the tree went on to try to separate between the remaining classes; the `Versicolor` and the `Virginica` irises. However, are we really sure that our training data is detailed enough to explain all the nuances that differentiate between the two classes? Isn't it possible that all those branches are driving the algorithm to learn things that happen to exist in the training data, but will not generalize well enough when faced with future data? Allowing a tree to grow so much results in what is called overfitting. The tree tries to perfectly fit the training data, forgetting that the data it may encounter in the future may be different. To prevent overfitting, the following settings may be used to limit the growth of a tree:

- `max_depth`: This is the maximum depth a tree can get to. A lower number means that the tree will stop branching earlier. Setting it to `None` means that the tree will continue to grow until all the leaves are pure or until all the leaves contain fewer than the `min_samples_split` samples.
- `min_samples_split`: The minimum number of samples needed in a level to allow further splitting there. A higher number means that the tree will stop branching earlier.
- `min_samples_leaf`: The minimum number of samples needed in a level to allow it to become a leaf node. A leaf node is a node where there are no further splits and where decisions are made. A higher number may have the effect of smoothing the model, especially in regression.

 One quick way to check for overfitting is to compare the classifier's accuracy on the test set to its accuracy on the training set. Having a much higher score for your training set compared to the test set is a sign of overfitting. A smaller and more pruned tree is recommended in this case.

If `max_depth` is not set at training time to limit the tree's growth, then alternatively, you can prune the tree after it has been built. Curious readers can check the `cost_complexity_pruning_path()` method of the decision tree and find out how to use it to prune an already-grown tree.

Predictions

At the end of the training process, nodes that aren't split any further are called leaf nodes. Within a leaf node, we may have five samples—four of them from class 1, one from class 2, and none from class 0. Then, at prediction time, if a sample ends up in the same leaf node, we can easily decide that the new sample belongs to class 1 since this leaf node had a 4:1 ratio of its training samples from class 1 compared to the other two classes.

When we make predictions on the test set, we can evaluate the classifier's accuracy versus the actual labels we have in the test set. Nevertheless, the manner in which we split our data may affect the reliability of the scores we get. In the next section, we will see how to get more reliable scores.

Getting a more reliable score

The Iris dataset is a small set of just 150 samples. When we randomly split it into training and test sets, we ended up with 45 instances in the test set. With such a small number, we may have variations in the distribution of our targets. For example, when I randomly split the data, I got 13 samples from class 0 and 16 samples from each one of the two other classes in my test set. Knowing that predicting class 0 is easier than the other two classes in this particular dataset, we can tell that if I was luckier and had more samples of class 0 in the test set, I'd have had a higher score. Furthermore, decision trees are very sensitive to data changes, and you may get a very different tree with every slight change in your training data.

What to do now to get a more reliable score

A statistician would say *let's run the whole process of data splitting, training, and predicting, more than once, and get the distribution of the different accuracy scores we get each time.* The following code does exactly that for 100 iterations:

```
import pandas as pd

from sklearn.model_selection import train_test_split
```

```
from sklearn.tree import DecisionTreeClassifier
from sklearn.metrics import accuracy_score

# A list to store the score from each iteration
accuracy_scores = []
```

After importing the required modules and defining an `accuracy_scores` list to store the scores we are going get with each iteration, it is time to write a `for` loop to freshly split the data and recalculate the classifier's accuracy with each iteration:

```
for _ in range(100):

    # At each iteration we freshly split our data
    df_train, df_test = train_test_split(df, test_size=0.3)
    x_train = df_train[iris.feature_names]
    x_test = df_test[iris.feature_names]

    y_train = df_train['target']
    y_test = df_test['target']
    # We then create a new classifier
    clf = DecisionTreeClassifier()
    # And use it for training and prediction
    clf.fit(x_train, y_train)
    y_pred = clf.predict(x_test)

    # Finally, we append the score to our list
    accuracy_scores.append(round(accuracy_score(y_test, y_pred), 3))

# Better convert accuracy_scores from a list into a series
# Pandas series provides statistical methods to use later
accuracy_scores = pd.Series(accuracy_scores)
```

The following snippet lets us plot the accuracy's distribution using a box plot:

```
accuracy_scores.plot(
    title='Distribution of classifier accuracy',
    kind='box',
)

print(
    'Average Score: {:.3} [5th percentile: {:.3} & 95th percentile:
{:.3}]'.format(
        accuracy_scores.mean(),
        accuracy_scores.quantile(.05),
        accuracy_scores.quantile(.95),
    )
)
```

This will give us the following graphical analysis of the accuracy. Your results might vary slightly due to the random split of the training and test sets and the random initial settings of the decision trees. Almost all of the scikit-learn modules support a pseudo-random number generator that can be initialized via a `random_state` hyperparameter. This can be used to enforce code reproducibility. Nevertheless, I deliberately ignored it this time to show how the model's results may vary from one run to the other, and to show the importance of estimating the distributions of your models' errors via iterations:

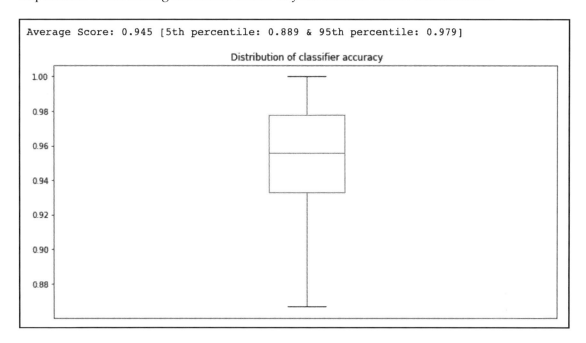

Box plots are good at showing distributions. Rather than having a single number, we now have an estimation of the best- and the worst-case scenarios of our classifier's performance.

 If, at any point, you do not have access to NumPy, you can still calculate a sample's mean and standard deviation using the `mean()` and `stdev()` methods provided by Python's built-in `statistics` module. It also provides functionalities for calculating the geometric and harmonic mean, as well as the median and quantiles.

ShuffleSplit

Generating different train and test splits is called cross-validation. This helps us have a more reliable estimation of our model's accuracy. What we did in the previous section is one of many cross-validation strategies called repeated random sub-sampling validation, or Monte Carlo cross-validation.

 In probability theory, the law of large numbers states that if we repeat the same experiment a large number of times, the average of the results obtained should be close to the expected outcome. The Monte Carlo methods make use of random sampling in order to repeat an experiment over and over to reach better estimates for the results, thanks to the law of large numbers. The Monte Carlo methods were made possible due to the existence of computers, and here we use the same method to repeat the training/test split over and over to reach a better estimation of the model's accuracy.

scikit-learn's `ShuffleSplit` module provides us with the functionality to perform Monte Carlo cross-validation. Rather than us splitting the data ourselves, `ShuffleSplit` gives us lists of indices to use for splitting our data. In the following code, we are going to use the DataFrame's `loc()` method and the indices we get from `ShuffleSplit` to randomly split the dataset into 100 training and test pairs:

```
import pandas as pd

from sklearn.model_selection import ShuffleSplit
from sklearn.tree import DecisionTreeClassifier
from sklearn.metrics import accuracy_score

accuracy_scores = []

# Create a shuffle split instance
rs = ShuffleSplit(n_splits=100, test_size=0.3)

# We now get 100 pairs of indices
for train_index, test_index in rs.split(df):

 x_train = df.loc[train_index, iris.feature_names]
 x_test = df.loc[test_index, iris.feature_names]

 y_train = df.loc[train_index, 'target']
 y_test = df.loc[test_index, 'target']

 clf = DecisionTreeClassifier()
```

```
clf.fit(x_train, y_train)
y_pred = clf.predict(x_test)

accuracy_scores.append(round(accuracy_score(y_test, y_pred), 3))

accuracy_scores = pd.Series(accuracy_scores)
```

Alternatively, we can simplify the preceding code even further by using scikit-learn's `cross_validate` functionality. This time, we are not event splitting the data into training and test sets ourselves. We will give `cross_validate` the x and y values for the entire set, and then give it our `ShuffleSplit` instance for it to use internally to split the data. We also give it the classifier and specify what kind of scoring metric to use. When done, it will give us back a list with the calculated test set scores:

```
import pandas as pd

from sklearn.model_selection import ShuffleSplit
from sklearn.tree import DecisionTreeClassifier
from sklearn.model_selection import cross_validate

clf = DecisionTreeClassifier()
rs = ShuffleSplit(n_splits=100, test_size=0.3)

x = df[iris.feature_names]
y = df['target']

cv_results = cross_validate(
    clf, x, y, cv=rs, scoring='accuracy'
)

accuracy_scores = pd.Series(cv_results['test_score'])
```

We can plot the resulting series of accuracy scores now to get the same box plot as earlier. Cross-validation is recommended when dealing with a small dataset since a group of accuracy scores will give us a better understanding of the classifier's performance compared to a single score calculated after a single trial.

Tuning the hyperparameters for higher accuracy

Now that we have learned how to evaluate the model's accuracy more reliably using the `ShuffleSplit` cross-validation method, it is time to test our earlier hypothesis: would a smaller tree be more accurate?

Here is what we are going to do in the following sub sections:

1. Split the data into training and test sets.
2. Keep the test side to one side now.
3. Limit the tree's growth using different values of `max_depth`.
4. For each `max_depth` setting, we will use the `ShuffleSplit` cross-validation method on the training set to get an estimation of the classifier's accuracy.
5. Once we decide which value to use for `max_depth`, we will train the algorithm one last time on the entire training set and predict on the test set.

Splitting the data

Here is the usual code for splitting the data into training and test sets:

```
from sklearn.model_selection import train_test_split

df_train, df_test = train_test_split(df, test_size=0.25)

x_train = df_train[iris.feature_names]
x_test = df_test[iris.feature_names]

y_train = df_train['target']
y_test = df_test['target']
```

Trying different hyperparameter values

If we allowed our earlier tree to grow indefinitely, we would get a tree depth of 4. You can check the depth of a tree by calling `clf.get_depth()` once it is trained. So, it doesn't make sense to try any `max_depth` values above 4. Here, we are going to loop over the maximum depths from 1 to 4 and use `ShuffleSplit` to get the classifier's accuracy:

```
import pandas as pd
from sklearn.model_selection import ShuffleSplit
from sklearn.tree import DecisionTreeClassifier
from sklearn.model_selection import cross_validate

for max_depth in [1, 2, 3, 4]:

    # We initialize a new classifier each iteration with different
max_depth
    clf = DecisionTreeClassifier(max_depth=max_depth)
    # We also initialize our shuffle splitter
```

```
rs = ShuffleSplit(n_splits=20, test_size=0.25)

cv_results = cross_validate(
    clf, x_train, y_train, cv=rs, scoring='accuracy'
)
accuracy_scores = pd.Series(cv_results['test_score'])

print(
    '@ max_depth = {}: accuracy_scores: {}~{}'.format(
        max_depth,
        accuracy_scores.quantile(.1).round(3),
        accuracy_scores.quantile(.9).round(3)
    )
)
```

We called the `cross_validate()` method as we did earlier, giving it the classifier's instance, as well as the `ShuffleSplit` instance. We also defined our evaluation score as `accuracy`. Finally, we print the scores we get with each iteration. We will look more at the printed values in the next section.

Comparing the accuracy scores

Since we have a list of scores for each iteration, we can calculate their mean, or, as we will do here, we will print their 10th and 90th percentiles to get an idea of the accuracy ranges versus each `max_depth` setting.

Running the preceding code gave me the following results:

```
@ max_depth = 1: accuracy_scores: 0.532~0.646
@ max_depth = 2: accuracy_scores: 0.925~1.0
@ max_depth = 3: accuracy_scores: 0.929~1.0
@ max_depth = 4: accuracy_scores: 0.929~1.0
```

One thing I am sure about now is that a single-level tree (usually called a stub) is not as accurate as deeper trees. In other words, having a single decision based on whether the petal width is less than `0.8` is not enough. Allowing the tree to grow further improves the accuracy, but I can't see many differences between trees of depths 2, 3, and 4. I'd conclude that contrary to my earlier speculations, we shouldn't worry too much about overfitting here.

Here, we tried different values for a single parameter, `max_depth`. That's why a simple `for` loop over its different values was feasible. In later chapters, we will see what to do when we need to tune multiple hyperparameters at once to reach a combination that gives the best accuracy.

Finally, you can train your model once more using the entire training set and a `max_depth` value of, say, 3. Then, use the trained model to predict the classes for the test set in order to evaluate your final model. I won't bore you with the code for it this time as you can easily do it yourself.

In addition to printing the classifier's decision and descriptive statistics about its accuracy, it is useful to also see its decision boundaries visually. Mapping those boundaries versus the data samples helps us understand why the classifier made certain mistakes. In the next section, we are going to check the decision boundaries we got for the Iris dataset.

Visualizing the tree's decision boundaries

To be able to pick the right algorithm for the problem, it is important to have a conceptual understanding of how an algorithm makes its decision. As we already know by now, decision trees pick one feature at a time and try to split the data accordingly. Nevertheless, it is important to be able to visualize those decisions as well. Let me first plot our classes versus our features, then I will explain further:

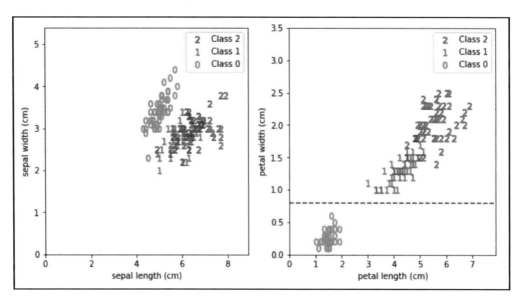

When the tree made a decision to split the data around a petal width of 0.8, you can think of it as drawing a horizontal line in the right-hand side graph at the value of 0.8. Then, with every later split, the tree splits the space further using combinations of horizontal and vertical lines. By knowing this, you should not expect the algorithm to use curves or 45-degree lines to separate the classes.

One trick to plot the decision boundaries that a tree has after it has been trained is to use contour plots. For simplicity, let's assume we only have two features—petal length and petal width. We then generate almost all the possible values for those two features and predict the class labels for our new hypothetical data. Then, we create a contour plot using those predictions to see the boundaries between the classes. The following function, created by Richard Johansson of the University of Gothenburg, does exactly that:

```python
import numpy as np
import pandas as pd
import matplotlib.pyplot as plt

def plot_decision_boundary(clf, x, y):

  feature_names = x.columns
  x, y = x.values, y.values

  x_min, x_max = x[:,0].min(), x[:,0].max()
  y_min, y_max = x[:,1].min(), x[:,1].max()

  step = 0.02

  xx, yy = np.meshgrid(
  np.arange(x_min, x_max, step),
  np.arange(y_min, y_max, step)
  )
  Z = clf.predict(np.c_[xx.ravel(), yy.ravel()])
  Z = Z.reshape(xx.shape)

  plt.figure(figsize=(12,8))
  plt.contourf(xx, yy, Z, cmap='Paired_r', alpha=0.25)
  plt.contour(xx, yy, Z, colors='k', linewidths=0.7)
  plt.scatter(x[:,0], x[:,1], c=y, edgecolors='k')
  plt.title("Tree's Decision Boundaries")
  plt.xlabel(feature_names[0])
  plt.ylabel(feature_names[1])
```

This time, we will train our classifier using two features only, and then call the preceding function using the newly trained model:

```
x = df[['petal width (cm)', 'petal length (cm)']]
y = df['target']

clf = DecisionTreeClassifier(max_depth=3)
clf.fit(x, y)

plot_decision_boundary(clf, x, y)
```

Richard Johansson's functions overlay the contour graph over our samples to give us the following graph:

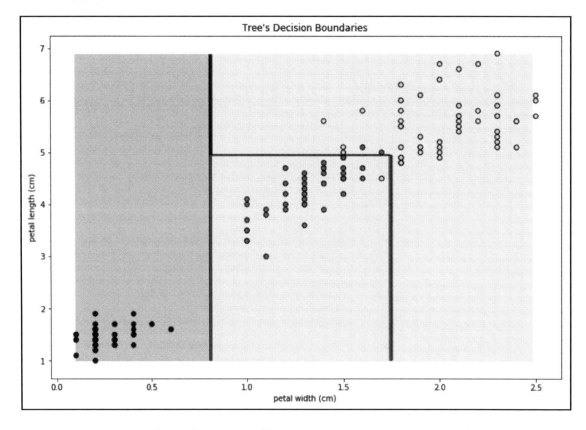

By seeing the decision boundaries as well as the data samples, you can make better decisions on whether one algorithm is good for the problem at hand.

Feature engineering

"Every man takes the limits of his own field of vision for the limits of the world."

– Arthur Schopenhauer

On seeing the class distribution versus the petal lengths and widths, you may wonder: *what if the decision trees could also draw boundaries that are at 40 degrees? Wouldn't 40-degree boundaries be more apt than those horizontal and vertical jigsaws?* Unfortunately, decision trees cannot do that, but let's put the algorithm aside for a moment and think about the data instead. How about creating a new axis where the class boundaries change their orientation?

Let's create two new columns—petal length x width (cm) and sepal length x width (cm)—and see how the class distribution will look:

```
df['petal length x width (cm)'] = df['petal length (cm)'] * df['petal width (cm)']
df['sepal length x width (cm)'] = df['sepal length (cm)'] * df['sepal width (cm)']
```

The following code will plot the classes versus the newly derived features:

```
fig, ax = plt.subplots(1, 1, figsize=(12, 6));

h_label = 'petal length x width (cm)'
v_label = 'sepal length x width (cm)'

for c in df['target'].value_counts().index.tolist():
    df[df['target'] == c].plot(
        title='Class distribution vs the newly derived features',
        kind='scatter',
        x=h_label,
        y=v_label,
        color=['r', 'g', 'b'][c], # Each class different color
        marker=f'${c}$', # Use class id as marker
        s=64,
        alpha=0.5,
        ax=ax,
    )

fig.show()
```

Running this code will produce the following graph:

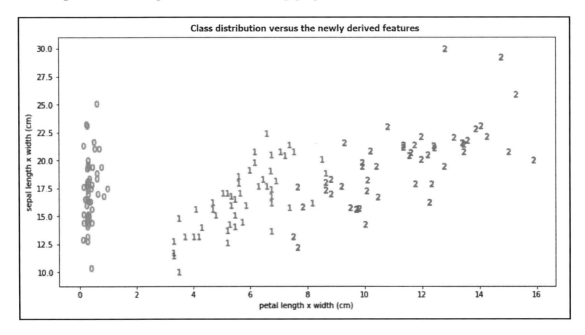

This new projection looks better; it makes the data more vertically separable. Nevertheless, the proof of the pudding is still in the eating. So, let's train two classifiers—one on the original features and one on the newly derived features—and see

how their accuracies compare. The following code goes through 500 iterations, each time splitting the data randomly, and then training both models, each with its own set of features, and storing the accuracy we get with each iteration:

```
features_orig = iris.feature_names
features_new = ['petal length x width (cm)', 'sepal length x width (cm)']

accuracy_scores_orig = []
accuracy_scores_new = []

for _ in range(500):

    df_train, df_test = train_test_split(df, test_size=0.3)

    x_train_orig = df_train[features_orig]
    x_test_orig = df_test[features_orig]

    x_train_new = df_train[features_new]
    x_test_new = df_test[features_new]
```

```
    y_train = df_train['target']
    y_test = df_test['target']

    clf_orig = DecisionTreeClassifier(max_depth=2)
    clf_new = DecisionTreeClassifier(max_depth=2)

    clf_orig.fit(x_train_orig, y_train)
    clf_new.fit(x_train_new, y_train)

    y_pred_orig = clf_orig.predict(x_test_orig)
    y_pred_new = clf_new.predict(x_test_new)

    accuracy_scores_orig.append(round(accuracy_score(y_test, y_pred_orig),
                                3))
    accuracy_scores_new.append(round(accuracy_score(y_test, y_pred_new),
                               3))

accuracy_scores_orig = pd.Series(accuracy_scores_orig)
accuracy_scores_new = pd.Series(accuracy_scores_new)
```

Then, we can use box plots to compare the accuracies of the two classifiers:

```
fig, axs = plt.subplots(1, 2, figsize=(16, 6), sharey=True);

accuracy_scores_orig.plot(
    title='Distribution of classifier accuracy [Original Features]',
    kind='box',
    grid=True,
    ax=axs[0]
)

accuracy_scores_new.plot(
    title='Distribution of classifier accuracy [New Features]',
    kind='box',
    grid=True,
    ax=axs[1]
)

fig.show()
```

Here, we put the top plots side by side to be able to compare them to each other:

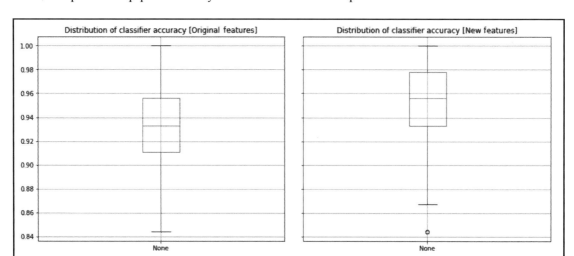

Clearly, the derived features helped a bit. Its accuracy is higher on average (0.96 versus 0.93), and its lower bound is also higher.

Building decision tree regressors

Decision tree regressors work in a similar fashion to their classifier counterparts. The algorithm splits the data recursively using one feature at a time. At the end of the process, we end up with leaf nodes—that is, nodes where there are no further splits. In the case of a classifier, if, at training time, a leaf node has three instances of class A and one instance of class B, then at prediction time, if an instance lands in the same leaf node, the classifier decides that it belongs to the majority class (class A). In the case of a regressor, if, at training time, a leaf node has three instances of values 12, 10, and 8, then, at prediction time, if an instance lands in the same leaf node, the regressor predicts its value to be 10 (the average of the three values at training time).

 Actually, picking the average is not always the best case. It rather depends on the splitting criterion used. In the next section, we are going to see this in more detail with the help of an example.

Predicting people's heights

Say we have two populations. Population 1 has an average height of 155 cm for females, with a standard deviation of 4, and an average height of 175 cm for males, with a standard deviation of 5. Population 2 has an average height of 165 cm for females, with a standard deviation of 15, and an average height of 185 cm for males, with a standard deviation of 12. We decide to take 200 males and 200 females from each population. To be able to simulate this, we can use a function provided by NumPy that draws random samples from a normal (Gaussian) distribution.

Here is the code for generating random samples:

```
# It's customary to call numpy np
import numpy as np

# We need 200 samples from each
n = 200

# From each population we get 200 male and 200 female samples
height_pop1_f = np.random.normal(loc=155, scale=4, size=n)
height_pop1_m = np.random.normal(loc=175, scale=5, size=n)
height_pop2_f = np.random.normal(loc=165, scale=15, size=n)
height_pop2_m = np.random.normal(loc=185, scale=12, size=n)
```

At the moment, we don't actually care about which population each sample comes from. So, we will use `concatenate` to group all the males and all the females together:

```
# We group all females together and all males together
height_f = np.concatenate([height_pop1_f, height_pop2_f])
height_m = np.concatenate([height_pop1_m, height_pop2_m])
```

We then put this data into a DataFrame (`df_height`) to be able to deal with it easily. There, we also give a label of 1 to females and 2 to males:

```
df_height = pd.DataFrame(
    {
        'Gender': [1 for i in range(height_f.size)] +
                  [2 for i in range(height_m.size)],
        'Height': np.concatenate((height_f, height_m))
    }
)
```

Let's plot our fictional data using histograms to see the height distributions among each gender:

```
fig, ax = plt.subplots(1, 1, figsize=(10, 5))

df_height[df_height['Gender'] == 1]['Height'].plot(
    label='Female', kind='hist',
    bins=10, alpha=0.7, ax=ax
)
df_height[df_height['Gender'] == 2]['Height'].plot(
    label='Male', kind='hist',
    bins=10, alpha=0.7, ax=ax
)

ax.legend()

fig.show()
```

The preceding code gives us the following graph:

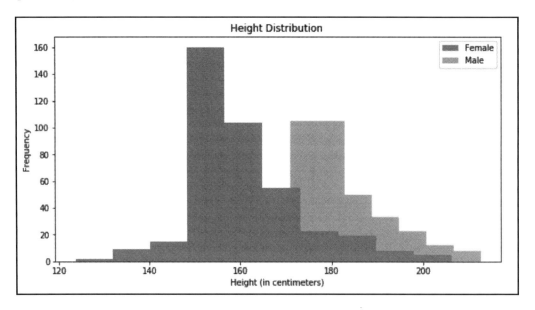

As you can see, the resulting distributions are not symmetrical. Although normal distributions are symmetrical, these artificial distributions are made of two sub-distributions combined. We can use this line of code to see that their mean and median values are not equal:

```
df_height.groupby('Gender')[['Height']].agg([np.mean, np.median]).round(1)
```

Here, we have the mean and median heights for each group:

		Height	
		mean	**median**
Gender			
	1	160.5	157.3
	2	180.5	178.4

Now, we want to predict people's heights using one feature—their gender. Therefore, we are going to split our data into training and test sets and create our x and y sets, as follows:

```
df_train, df_test = train_test_split(df_height, test_size=0.3)
x_train, x_test = df_train[['Gender']], df_test[['Gender']]
y_train, y_test = df_train['Height'], df_test['Height']
```

Remember that in the case of classifications, the trees use either `gini` or `entropy` to decide the best split at each step during the training process. The goal for these criteria was to find a split where each of the two resulting sub-groups is as pure as possible. In the case of regression, we have a different goal. We want the members of each group to have target values that are as close as possible to the predictions they make. scikit-learn implements two criteria to achieve this goal:

- **Mean squared error** (**MSE or L2**): Say after the split, we get three samples in one group with targets of 5, 5, and 8. We calculate the mean value of these three numbers (6). Then, we calculate the squared differences between each sample and the calculated mean—1, 1, and 4. We then take the mean of these squared differences, which is 2.
- **Mean absolute error** (**MAE or L1**): Say after the split, we get three samples in one group with targets of 5, 5, and 8. We calculate the median value of these three numbers (5). Then, we calculate the absolute differences between each sample and the calculated median—0, 0, and 3. We then take the mean of these absolute differences, which is 1.

For each possible split at training time, the tree calculates either L1 or L2 for each of the expected sub-groups after the split. A split with the minimum L1 or L2 is then chosen at this step. L1 may be preferred sometimes due to its robustness to outliers. The other important difference to keep in mind is that L1 uses median while L2 uses mean in its calculations.

If, at training time, we see 10 samples with almost identical features but different targets, they may all end up together in one leaf node. Now, if we use L1 as the splitting criterion when building our regressor, then if we get a sample at prediction time with identical features to the 10 training samples, we should expect the prediction to be close to the median value of the targets of the 10 training samples. Likewise, if L2 is used for building the regressor, we should then expect the prediction of the new sample to be close to the mean value of the targets of the 10 training samples.

Let's now compare the effect of the splitting criteria on our height dataset:

```
from sklearn.tree import export_text
from sklearn.tree import DecisionTreeRegressor

for criterion in ['mse', 'mae']:
    rgrsr = DecisionTreeRegressor(criterion=criterion)
    rgrsr.fit(x_train, y_train)

    print(f'criterion={criterion}:\n')
    print(export_text(rgrsr, feature_names=['Gender'], spacing=3,
decimals=1))
```

We get the following two trees depending on the chosen criterion:

```
criterion=mse:

|--- Gender <= 1.5
|    |--- value: [160.2]
|--- Gender > 1.5
|    |--- value: [180.8]

criterion=mae:

|--- Gender <= 1.5
|    |--- value: [157.5]
|--- Gender > 1.5
|    |--- value: [178.6]
```

As expected, when MSE was used, the predictions were close to the mean of each gender, while for MAE, the predictions were close to the median.

Of course, we only had one binary feature in our dataset—gender. That's why we had a very shallow tree with a single split (a **stub**). Actually, in this case, we do not even need to train a decision tree; we could have easily calculated the mean heights for males and females and used them as our expected values right away. The decisions made by such a shallow tree are called biased decisions. If we would have allowed each individual to express themselves using more information, rather than just their gender, then we would have been able to make more accurate predictions for each individual.

Finally, just as in the classification trees, we have the same knobs, such as `max_depth`, `min_samples_split`, and `min_samples_leaf`, to control the growth of a regression tree.

Regressor's evaluation

The very same MSE and MAE scores can also be used to evaluate a regressor's accuracy. We use them to compare the regressor's predictions to the actual targets in the test set. Here is the code predicting and evaluating the predictions made:

```
from sklearn.metrics import mean_squared_error, mean_absolute_error

y_test_pred = rgrsr.predict(x_test)
print('MSE:', mean_squared_error(y_test, y_test_pred))
print('MAE:', mean_absolute_error(y_test, y_test_pred))
```

Using MSE as a splitting criterion gives us an MSE of `117.2` and an MAE of `8.2`, while using MAE as a splitting criterion gives us an MSE of `123.3` and an MAE of `7.8`. Clearly, using MAE as the splitting criterion gives a lower MAE at test time, and vice versa. In other words, if your aim is to reduce the error of your predictions based on a certain metric, it is advised to use the same metric when growing your tree at the time of training.

Setting sample weights

Both the decision tree classifiers and the regressors allow us to give more or less emphasis to the individual training samples via setting their weights while fitting. This is a common feature in many estimators, and decision trees are no exception here. To see the effect of sample weights, we are going to give 10 times more weight to users above 150 cm versus the remaining users:

```
rgrsr = DecisionTreeRegressor(criterion='mse')
sample_weight = y_train.apply(lambda h: 10 if h > 150 else 1)
rgrsr.fit(x_train, y_train, sample_weight=sample_weight)
```

Conversely, we can also give more weights to users who are 150 cm and below by changing the `sample_weight` calculations, as follows:

```
sample_weight = y_train.apply(lambda h: 10 if h <= 150 else 1)
```

By using the `export_text()` function, as we did in the previous section, we can display the resulting trees. We can see how `sample_weight` affected their final structures:

```
Emphasis on "below 150":

|--- Gender <= 1.5
|     |--- value: [150.7]
|--- Gender > 1.5
|     |--- value: [179.2]

Emphasis on "above 150":

|--- Gender <= 1.5
|     |--- value: [162.4]
|--- Gender > 1.5
|     |--- value: [180.2]
```

By default, all samples are given the same weight. Weighting individual samples differently is useful when dealing with imbalanced data or imbalanced business decisions; maybe you can tolerate delaying a shipment for a new customer more than you can do for your loyal ones. In `Chapter 8`, *Ensembles – When One Model Is Not Enough*, we will also see how sample weights are an integral part of how the AdaBoost algorithm learns.

Summary

Decision trees are intuitive algorithms that are capable of performing classification and regression tasks. They allow users to print out their decision rules, which is a plus when communicating the decisions you made to business personnel and non-technical third parties. Additionally, decision trees are easy to configure since they have a limited number of hyperparameters. The two main decisions you need to make when training a decision tree are your splitting criterion and how to control the growth of your tree to have a good balance between *overfitting* and *underfitting*. Your understanding of the limitations of the tree's decision boundaries is paramount in deciding whether the algorithm is good enough for the problem at hand.

In this chapter, we looked at how decision trees learn and used them to classify a well-known dataset. We also learned about the different evaluation metrics and how the size of our data affects our confidence in a model's accuracy. We then learned how to deal with the evaluation's uncertainties using different data-splitting strategies. We saw how to tune the algorithm's hyperparameters for a good balance between overfitting and underfitting. Finally, we built on the knowledge we gained to build decision tree regressors and learned how the choice of a splitting criterion affects our resulting predictions.

I hope this chapter has served as a good introduction to scikit-learn and its consistent interface. With this knowledge at hand, we can move on to our next algorithm and see how it compares to this one. In the next chapter, we will learn about linear models. This set of algorithms has its roots back in the 18th century, and it is still one of the most commonly used algorithms today.

3
Making Decisions with Linear Equations

The method of least squares regression analysis dates back to the time of Carl Friedrich Gauss in the 18th century. For over two centuries, many algorithms have been built on top of it or have been inspired by it in some form. These linear models are possibly the most commonly used algorithms today for both regression and classification. We will start this chapter by looking at the basic least squares algorithm, then we will move on to more advanced algorithms as the chapter progresses.

Here is a list of the topics covered in this chapter:

- Understanding linear models
- Predicting house prices in Boston
- Regularizing the regressor
- Finding regression intervals
- Additional linear regressors
- Using logistic regression for classification
- Additional linear classifiers

Understanding linear models

To be able to explain linear models well, I would like to start with an example where the solution can be found using a system of linear equations—a technique we all learned in school when we were around 12 years old. We will then see why this technique doesn't always work with real-life problems, and so a linear regression model is needed. Then, we will apply the regression model to a real-life regression problem and learn how to improve our solution along the way.

Linear equations

"Mathematics is the most beautiful and most powerful creation of the human spirit."

– Stefan Banach

In this example, we have five passengers who have taken a taxi trip. Here, we have a record of the distance each taxi covered in kilometers and the fair displayed on its meter at the end of each trip:

Kilometres	Meter
1	7.5
2	10.0
3	12.5
4	15.0
5	17.5

We know that taxi meters usually start with a certain amount and then they add a fixed charge for each kilometer traveled. We can model the meter using the following equation:

$$Meter = A + B \times Distance$$

Here, A is the meter's starting value and B is the charge added per kilometer. We also know that with two unknowns—A and B—we just need two data samples to figure out that A is 5 and B is 2.5. We can also plot the formula with the values for A and B, as follows:

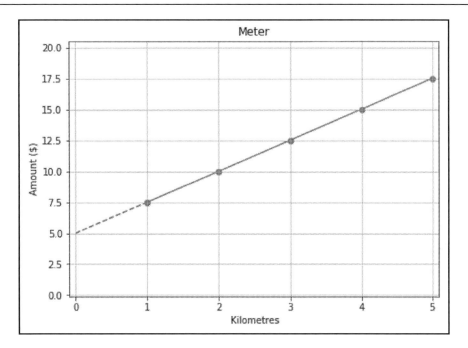

We also know that the blue line will meet the *y*-axis at the value of *A* (5). So, we call *A* the **intercept**. We also know that the slope of the line equals *B* (2.5).

The passengers didn't always have change, so they sometimes rounded up the amount shown on the meter to add a tip for the driver. Here is the data for the amount each passenger ended up paying:

Kilometres	Meter	Paid (incl. tips)
1	7.5	8
2	10.0	10
3	12.5	14
4	15.0	15
5	17.5	20

After we add the tips, it's clear that the relationship between the distance traveled and the amount paid is no longer linear. The plot on the right-hand side shows that a straight line cannot be drawn to capture this relationship:

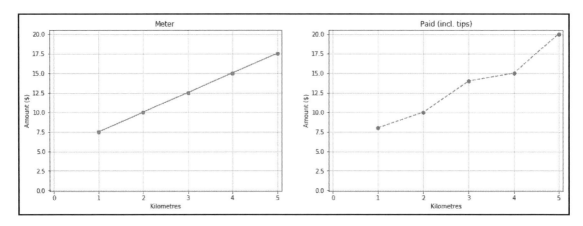

We now know that our usual method of solving equations will not work this time. Nevertheless, we can tell that there is still a line that can somewhat approximate this relationship. In the next section, we will use a linear regression algorithm to find this approximation.

Linear regression

Algorithms are all about objectives. Our objective earlier was to find a single line that goes through all the points in the graph. We have seen that this objective is not feasible if a linear relationship does not exist between the points. Therefore, we will use the linear regression algorithm since it has a different objective. The linear regression algorithm tries to find a line where the mean of the squared errors between the estimated points on the line and the actual points is minimal. Visually speaking, in the following graph, we want a dotted line that makes the average squared lengths of the vertical lines minimal:

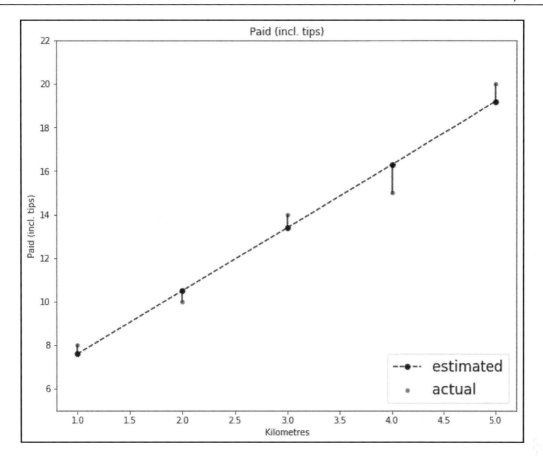

The method used here to find a line that minimizes the **Mean Squared Error (MSE)** is known as ordinary least squares. Often, linear regression just means ordinary least squares. Nevertheless, throughout this chapter, I will be using the term `LinearRegression` (as a single word) to refer to scikit-learn's implementation of ordinary least squares, and I will reserve the term *linear regression* (as two separate words) for referring to the general concept of linear regression, whether the ordinary least squares method is used or a different method is being employed.

The method of ordinary least squares is about two centuries old and it uses simple mathematics to estimate the parameters. That's why some may argue that this algorithm is not actually a machine learning one. Personally, I follow a more liberal approach when categorizing what is machine learning and what is not. As long as the algorithm automatically learns from data and we use that data to evaluate it, then for me, it falls within the machine learning paradigm.

Estimating the amount paid to the taxi driver

Now that we know how linear regression works, let's take a look at how to estimate the amount paid to the taxi driver.

1. Let's use scikit-learn to build a regression model to estimate the amount paid to the taxi driver:

```
from sklearn.linear_model import LinearRegression

# Initialize and train the model
reg = LinearRegression()
reg.fit(df_taxi[['Kilometres']], df_taxi['Paid (incl. tips)'])

# Make predictions
df_taxi['Paid (Predicted)'] = reg.predict(df_taxi[['Kilometres']])
```

Clearly, scikit-learn has a consistent interface. We have used the same `fit()` and `predict()` methods as in the previous chapter, but this time with the `LinearRegression` object.

We only have one feature this time, `Kilometres`; nevertheless, the `fit()` and `predict()` methods expect a two-dimensional `ax`, which is why we enclosed `Kilometers` in an extra set of square brackets—`df_taxi[['Kilometres']]`.

2. We put our predictions in the same DataFrame under `Paid (Predicted)`. We can then plot the actual values versus the estimated ones using the following code:

```
fig, axs = plt.subplots(1, 2, figsize=(16, 5))

df_taxi.set_index('Kilometres')['Meter'].plot(
    title='Meter', kind='line', ax=axs[0]
)

df_taxi.set_index('Kilometres')['Paid (incl. tips)'].plot(
    title='Paid (incl. tips)', label='actual', kind='line',
ax=axs[1]
)
df_taxi.set_index('Kilometres')['Paid (Predicted)'].plot(
    title='Paid (incl. tips)', label='estimated', kind='line',
ax=axs[1]
)

fig.show()
```

I cut out the formatting parts of the code to keep it short and to the point. Here is the final result:

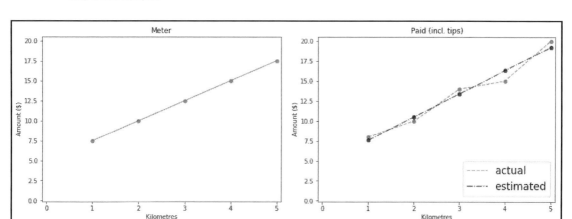

3. Once a linear model is trained, you can get its intercept and coefficients using the `intercept_` and `coef_` parameters. So, we can use the following code snippet to create the linear equations of the estimated line:

```
print(
    'Amount Paid = {:.1f} + {:.1f} * Distance'.format(
        reg.intercept_, reg.coef_[0],
    )
)
```

The following equation is then printed:

$$AmountPaid = 4.7 + 2.9 \times Distance$$

Getting the parameters for the linear equation can be handy in cases where you want to build a model in scikit-learn and then use it in another language or even in your favorite spreadsheet software. Knowing the coefficient also helps us understand why the model made certain decisions. More on this later in this chapter.

In software, the input to functions and methods is referred to as parameters. In machine learning, the weights learned for a model are also referred to as parameters. When setting a model, we pass its configuration to its `__init__` method. Thus, to prevent any confusion, the model's configurations are called hyperparameters.

Predicting house prices in Boston

Now that we understand how linear regression works, let's move on to looking at a real dataset where we can demonstrate a more practical use case.

The Boston dataset is a small set representing the house prices in the city of Boston. It contains 506 samples and 13 features. Let's load the data into a DataFrame, as follows:

```
from sklearn.datasets import load_boston

boston = load_boston()

df_dataset = pd.DataFrame(
    boston.data,
    columns=boston.feature_names,
)
df_dataset['target'] = boston.target
```

Data exploration

It's important to make sure you do not have any null values in your data; otherwise, scikit-learn will complain about it. Here, I will count the sum of the null values in each column, then take the sum of it. If I get 0, then I am a happy man:

```
df_dataset.isnull().sum().sum() # Luckily, the result is zero
```

For a regression problem, the most important thing to do is to understand the distribution of your target. If a target ranges between 1 and 10, and after training our model we get a mean absolute error of 5, we can tell that the error is large in this context.

However, the same error for a target that ranges between 500,000 and 1,000,000 is negligible. Histograms are your friend when you want to visualize distributions. In addition to the target's distribution, let's also plot the mean values for each feature:

```
fig, axs = plt.subplots(1, 2, figsize=(16, 8))

df_dataset['target'].plot(
    title='Distribution of target prices', kind='hist', ax=axs[0]
)
df_dataset[boston.feature_names].mean().plot(
    title='Mean of features', kind='bar', ax=axs[1]
)

fig.show()
```

This gives us the following graphs:

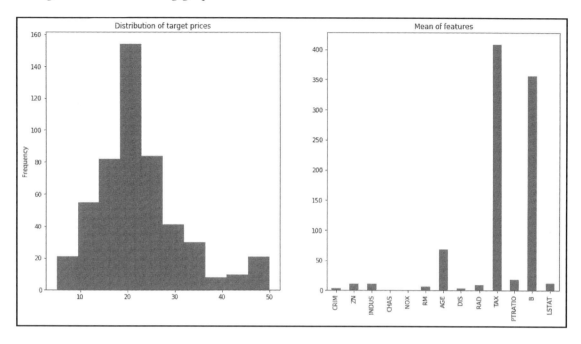

In the preceding graph, it is observed that:

- The prices range between 5 and 50. Obviously, these are not real prices, probably normalized values, but this doesn't matter for now.
- Furthermore, we can tell from the histogram that most of the prices are below 35. We can use the following code snippet to see that 90% of the prices are below 34.8:

```
df_dataset['target'].describe(percentiles=[.9, .95, .99])
```

You can always go deeper with your data exploration, but we will stop here on this occasion.

Splitting the data

When it comes to small datasets, it's advised that you allocate enough data for testing. So, we will split our data into 60% for training and 40% for testing using the `train_test_split` function:

```
from sklearn.model_selection import train_test_split

df_train, df_test = train_test_split(df_dataset, test_size=0.4)

x_train = df_train[boston.feature_names]
x_test = df_test[boston.feature_names]
y_train = df_train['target']
y_test = df_test['target']
```

Once you have the training and test sets, split them further into *x* sets and *y* sets. Then, we are ready to move to the next step.

Calculating a baseline

The distribution of the target gave us an idea of what level of error we can tolerate. Nevertheless, it is always useful to compare our final model to something. If we were in the real estate business and human agents were used to estimate house prices, then we would most likely be expected to build a model that can do better than the human agents. Nevertheless, since we do not know any real estimations to compare our model to, we can come up with our own baseline instead. The mean house price is 22.5. If we build a dummy model that returns the mean price regardless of the data given to it, then it would make a reasonable baseline.

Keep in mind that the value of 22.5 is calculated for the entire dataset, but since we are pretending to only have access to the training data, then it makes sense to calculate the mean price for the training set only. To save us all this effort, scikit-learn has dummy regressors available that do all this work for us.

Here, we will create a dummy regressor and use it to calculate baseline predictions for the test set:

```
from sklearn.dummy import DummyRegressor

baselin = DummyRegressor(strategy='mean')
baselin.fit(x_train, y_train)

y_test_baselin = baselin.predict(x_test)
```

There are other strategies that we can use, such as finding the median (the 50th quantile) or any other N^{th} quantile. Keep in mind that for the same data, using the mean as an estimation gives a lower MSE compared to when the median is used. Conversely, the median gives a lower **Mean Absolute Error (MAE)**. We want our model to beat the baseline for both the MAE and MSE.

Training the linear regressor

Isn't the code for the baseline model almost identical to the one for the actual models? That's the beauty of scikit-learn's API. It means that when we decide to try a different algorithm—say, the decision tree algorithm from the previous chapter—we only need to change a few lines of code. Anyway, here is the code for the linear regressor:

```
from sklearn.linear_model import LinearRegression

reg = LinearRegression()
reg.fit(x_train, y_train)

y_test_pred = reg.predict(x_test)
```

We are going to stick to the default configuration for now.

Evaluating our model's accuracy

There are three commonly used metrics for regression: R^2, *MAE*, and *MSE*. Let's first write the code that calculates the three metrics and prints the results:

```
from sklearn.metrics import r2_score
from sklearn.metrics import mean_absolute_error
from sklearn.metrics import mean_squared_error

print(
    'R2 Regressor = {:.2f} vs Baseline = {:.2f}'.format(
```

```
            r2_score(y_test, y_test_pred),
            r2_score(y_test, y_test_baselin)
        )
    )
print(
    'MAE Regressor = {:.2f} vs Baseline = {:.2f}'.format(
        mean_absolute_error(y_test, y_test_pred),
        mean_absolute_error(y_test, y_test_baselin)
    )
)
print(
    'MSE Regressor = {:.2f} vs Baseline = {:.2f}'.format(
        mean_squared_error(y_test, y_test_pred),
        mean_squared_error(y_test, y_test_baselin)
    )
)
```

Here are the results we get:

```
R2 Regressor = 0.74 vs Baseline = -0.00
MAE Regressor = 3.19 vs Baseline = 6.29
MSE Regressor = 19.70 vs Baseline = 76.11
```

By now, you should already know how *MAE* and *MSE* are calculated. Just keep in mind that *MSE* is more sensitive to outliers than *MAE*. That's why the mean estimations for the baseline scored badly there. As for the R^2, let's look at its formula:

$$R^2 = 1 - \frac{\sum(Y_{actual} - Y_{predict})^2}{\sum(Y_{actual} - Y_{mean})^2}$$

Here's an explanation of the preceding formula:

- The numerator probably reminds you of *MSE*. We basically calculate the squared differences between all the predicted values and their corresponding actual values.
- As for the denominator, we use the mean of the actual values as pseudo estimations.

- Basically, this metric tells us how much better our predictions are compared to using the target's mean as an estimation.
- An R^2 score of 1 is the best we could get, and a score of 0 means that we offered no additional value in comparison to using a biased model that just relies on the mean as an estimation.
- A negative score means that we should throw our model in the trash and use the target's mean instead.
- Obviously, in the baseline model, we already used the target's mean as the prediction. That's why its R^2 score is 0.

> For *MAE* and *MSE*, the smaller their values, the better the model is. Conversely, for R^2, the higher its values, the better the model is. In scikit-learn, the names of metric functions, where higher values correlate with better results, end with _score, while for functions ending with _error or _loss, the lower the value, the better.

Now, if we compare the scores, it is clear that our model scored better than the baseline in all of the three scores used. Congratulations!

Showing feature coefficients

We know that a linear model multiplies each of the features by a certain coefficient, and then gets the sum of these products as its final prediction. We can use the regressor's coef_ method after the model is trained to print these coefficients:

```
df_feature_importance = pd.DataFrame(
    {
        'Features': x_train.columns,
        'Coeff': reg.coef_,
        'ABS(Coeff)': abs(reg.coef_),
    }
).set_index('Features').sort_values('Coeff', ascending=False)
```

As we can see in these results, some coefficients are positive and others are negative. A positive coefficient means that the feature correlates positively with the target and vice versa. I also added another column for the absolute values of the coefficients:

Features	Coeff	ABS(Coeff)
RM	3.771080	3.771080
CHAS	2.300030	2.300030
RAD	0.306593	0.306593
INDUS	0.048167	0.048167
ZN	0.041997	0.041997
B	0.010654	0.010654
AGE	0.008924	0.008924
TAX	-0.010705	0.010705
CRIM	-0.080001	0.080001
LSTAT	-0.646811	0.646811
PTRATIO	-1.036784	1.036784
DIS	-1.314393	1.314393
NOX	-15.325464	15.325464

In the preceding screenshot, the following is observed :

- Ideally, the value for each coefficient should tell us how important each feature is. A higher absolute value, regardless of its sign, reflects high importance.
- However, I made a mistake here. If you check the data, you will notice that the maximum value for NOX is 0.87, while TAX goes up to 711. This means that if NOX has just marginal importance, its coefficient will still be high to balance its small value, while for TAX , its coefficient will always be small compared to the high values of the feature itself.
- So, we want to scale the features to keep them all in the comparable ranges. In the next section, we are going to see how to scale our features.

Scaling for more meaningful coefficients

scikit-learn has a number of scalers. We are going to use `MinMaxScaler` for now. Using it with its default configuration will squeeze out all the values for all the features between 0 and 1. The scaler needs to be fitted first to learn the features' ranges. Fitting should be done on the training *x* set only. Then, we use the scaler's `transform` function to scale both the training and test *x* sets:

```python
from sklearn.linear_model import LinearRegression
from sklearn.preprocessing import MinMaxScaler

scaler = MinMaxScaler()
reg = LinearRegression()

scaler.fit(x_train)
x_train_scaled = scaler.transform(x_train)
x_test_scaled = scaler.transform(x_test)

reg.fit(x_train_scaled, y_train)
y_test_pred = reg.predict(x_test_scaled)
```

There is a shorthand version of this code for fitting one dataset and then transforming it. In other words, the following uncommented line takes the place of the two commented ones:

```python
# scaler.fit(x_train)
# x_train_scaled = scaler.transform(x_train)
x_train_scaled = scaler.fit_transform(x_train)
```

We will be using the `fit_transform()` function a lot from now on where needed.

It's important to scale your features if you want meaningful coefficients. Furthermore, scaling helps gradient-based solvers converge quicker (more on this later). In addition to scaling, you should also make sure you don't have highly correlated features for more meaningful coefficients and a stable linear regression model.

Now that we have scaled our features and retrained the model, we can print the features and their coefficients again:

Features	Coeff	ABS(Coeff)
RM	19.473855	19.473855
RAD	7.051632	7.051632
B	4.200840	4.200840
ZN	4.199695	4.199695
CHAS	2.300030	2.300030
INDUS	1.313999	1.313999
AGE	0.866509	0.866509
TAX	-5.598546	5.598546
CRIM	-5.882282	5.882282
NOX	-7.340897	7.340897
PTRATIO	-9.331056	9.331056
DIS	-12.592804	12.592804
LSTAT	-22.800083	22.800083

Notice how NOX is less important now than before.

Adding polynomial features

Now that we know what the most important features are, we can plot the target against them to see how they correlate with them:

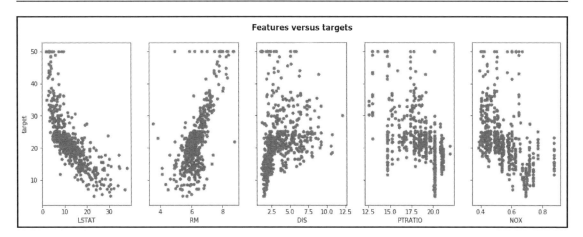

In the preceding screenshot, the following is observed:

- These plots don't seem to be very linear to me, and a linear model will not be able to capture this non-linearity.
- Although we cannot turn a linear model into a non-linear one, we can still transform the data instead.
- Think of it this way: if y is a function of x^2, we can either use a non-linear model—one that is capable of capturing the quadratic relation between x and y—or we can just calculate x^2 and give it to a linear model instead of x. Furthermore, linear regression algorithms do not capture feature interactions.
- The current model cannot capture interactions between multiple features.

A polynomial transformation can solve both the non-linearity and feature interaction issues for us. Given the original data, scikit-learn's polynomial transformer will transform the features into higher dimensions (for example, it will add the quadratic and cubic values for each feature). Additionally, it will also add the products to each feature-pair (or triplets). `PolynomialFeatures` works in a similar fashion to the scaler we used earlier in this chapter. We are going to use its `fit_transform` variable and a `transform()` method, as follows:

```
from sklearn.preprocessing import PolynomialFeatures

poly = PolynomialFeatures(degree=3)
x_train_poly = poly.fit_transform(x_train)
x_test_poly = poly.transform(x_test)
```

To get both the quadratic and cubic feature transformation, we set the `degree` parameter to 3.

One annoying thing about `PolynomialFeatures` is that it doesn't keep track of the DataFrame's column names. It replaces the feature names with x0, x1, x2, and so on. However, with our Python skills at hand, we can reclaim our column names. Let's do exactly that using the following block of code:

```
feature_translator = [
    (f'x{i}', feature) for i, feature in enumerate(x_train.columns, 0)
]

def translate_feature_names(s):
    for key, val in feature_translator:
        s = s.replace(key, val)
    return s

poly_features = [
    translate_feature_names(f) for f in poly.get_feature_names()
]

x_train_poly = pd.DataFrame(x_train_poly, columns=poly_features)
x_test_poly = pd.DataFrame(x_test_poly, columns=poly_features)
```

We can now use the newly derived polynomial features instead of the original ones.

Fitting the linear regressor with the derived features

"When I was six, my sister was half my age. Now I am 60 years old, how old is my sister?"

This is a puzzle found on the internet. If your answer is 30, then you forgot to fit an intercept into your linear regression model.

Now, we are ready to use our linear regressor with the newly transformed features. One thing to keep in mind is that the `PolynomialFeatures` transformer adds one additional column where all the values are 1. The coefficient this column gets after training is equivalent to the intercept. So, we will not fit an intercept by setting `fit_intercept=False` when training our regressor this time:

```
from sklearn.linear_model import LinearRegression

reg = LinearRegression(fit_intercept=False)
```

```
reg.fit(x_train_poly, y_train)

y_test_pred = reg.predict(x_test_poly)
```

Finally, as we print the R^2, *MAE*, and *MSE* results, we face the following unpleasant surprise:

```
R2 Regressor = -84.887 vs Baseline = -0.0
MAE Regressor = 37.529 vs Baseline = 6.2
MSE Regressor = 6536.975 vs Baseline = 78.1
```

The regressor is way worse than before and even worse than the baseline. What did the polynomial features do to our model?

One major problem with the ordinary least squares regression algorithm is that it doesn't work well with highly correlated features (multicollinearity).

The polynomial feature transformation's kitchen-sink approach—where we add features, their squared and cubic values, and the product of the features' pairs and triples—will very likely give us multiple correlated features. This multi-collinearity harms the model's performance. Furthermore, if you print the shape of x_train_poly, you will see that it has 303 samples and 560 features. This is another problem known as the curse of dimensionality.

The **curse of dimensionality** is when you have too many features compared to your samples. If you imagine your DataFrame as a rectangle with the features as its base and the samples as its height, you always want your rectangle to have a much bigger height than its base. Imagine having two binary columns—x1 and x2. They can take four possible value combinations—(0, 0), (0, 1), (1, 0), and (1, 1). Similarly, for n columns, they can take 2^n combinations. As you can see, the number of possibilities increases exponentially with the number of features. For a supervised learning algorithm to work well, it needs enough samples to cover a reasonable number of all these possibilities. This problem is even more drastic when we have non-binary features, as is our case here.

Thankfully, two centuries is long enough for people to find solutions to these two problems. Regularization is the solution we are going to have fun with in the next section.

Regularizing the regressor

"It is vain to do with more what can be done with fewer."

– William of Occam

Originally, our objective was to minimize the MSE value of the regressor. Later on, we discovered that too many features are an issue. That's why we need a new objective. We still need to minimize the MSE value of the regressor, but we also need to incentivize the model to ignore the useless features. This second part of our objective is what regularization does in a nutshell.

Two algorithms are commonly used for regularized linear regression—**lasso** and **ridge**. Lasso pushes the model to have fewer coefficients—that is, it sets as many coefficients as possible to 0—while ridge pushes the model to have as small values as possible for its coefficients. Lasso uses a form of regularization called L1, which penalizes the absolute values of the coefficients, while ridge uses L2, which penalizes the squared values of the coefficients. These two algorithms have a hyperparameter (alpha), which controls how strongly the coefficients will be regularized. Setting alpha to 0 means no regularization at all, which brings us back to an ordinary least squares regressor. While larger values for alpha specify stronger regularization, we will start with the default value for alpha, and then see how to set it correctly later on.

 The standard approach used in the ordinary least squares algorithm does not work here. We now have an objective function that aims to minimize the size of the coefficients, in addition to minimizing the predictor's MSE values. So, a solver is used to find the optimum coefficients to minimize the new objective functions. We will look further at solvers later in this chapter.

Training the lasso regressor

Training lasso is no different to training any other model. Similar to what we did in the previous section, we will set `fit_intercept` to `False` here:

```
from sklearn.linear_model import Ridge, Lasso

reg = Lasso(fit_intercept=False)
reg.fit(x_train_poly, y_train)

y_test_pred = reg.predict(x_test_poly)
```

Once done, we can print the R², MAE, and MSE:

```
R2 Regressor = 0.787 vs Baseline = -0.0
MAE Regressor = 2.381 vs Baseline = 6.2
MSE Regressor = 16.227 vs Baseline = 78.
```

Not only did we fix the problems introduced by the polynomial features, but we also have better performance than the original linear regressor. *MAE* is 2.4 here, compared to 3.6 before, *MSE* is 16.2, compared to 25.8 before, and R^2 is 0.79, compared to 0.73 before.

Now that we have seen promising results after applying regularization, it's time to see how to set an optimum value for the regularization parameter.

Finding the optimum regularization parameter

Ideally, after splitting the data into training and test sets, we would further split the training set into N folds. Then, we would make a list of all the values of alpha that we would like to test and loop over them one after the other. With each iteration, we would apply N-fold cross-validation to find the value for alpha that gives the minimal error. Thankfully, scikit-learn has a module called LassoCV (CV stands for cross-validation). Here, we are going to use this module to find the best value for alpha using five-fold cross-validation:

```
from sklearn.linear_model import LassoCV

# Make a list of 50 values between 0.000001 & 1,000,000
alphas = np.logspace(-6, 6, 50)

# We will do 5-fold cross validation
reg = LassoCV(alphas=alphas, fit_intercept=False, cv=5)
reg.fit(x_train_poly, y_train)

y_train_pred = reg.predict(x_train_poly)
y_test_pred = reg.predict(x_test_poly)
```

Once done, we can use the model for predictions. You may want to predict for both the training and test sets and see whether the model overfits on the training set. We can also print the chosen alpha, as follows:

```
print(f"LassoCV: Chosen alpha = {reg.alpha_}")
```

I got an `alpha` value of `1151.4`.

Furthermore, we can also see, for each value of alpha, what the *MSE* value for each of the five folds was. We can access this information via `mse_path_`.

Since we have five values for *MSE* for each value of alpha, we can plot the mean of these five values, as well as the confidence interval around the mean.

 The confidence interval is used to show the expected range that observed data may take. A 95% confidence interval means that we expect 95% of our values to fall within this range. Having a wide confidence interval means that the data may take a wide range of values, while a narrower confidence interval means that we can almost pinpoint exactly what value the data will take.

A 95% confidence interval is calculated as follows:

$$ConfidenceInterval = Mean \pm 1.96 \times StandardError$$

Here, the standard error is equal to the standard deviation divided by the square root of the number of samples ($\sqrt{5}$, since we have five folds here).

 The equation for the confidence interval here is not 100% accurate. Statistically speaking, when dealing with small samples, and their underlying variance is not known, a t-distribution should be used instead of a z-distribution. Thus, given the small number of folds here, the 1.96 coefficient should be replaced by a more accurate value from the t-distribution table, where its degrees of freedom are inferred from the number of folds.

The following code snippets calculate and plot the confidence intervals for MSE versus alpha:

1. We start by calculating the descriptive statistics of the *MSE* values returned:

```
# n_folds equals to 5 here
n_folds = reg.mse_path_.shape[1]

# Calculate the mean and standard error for MSEs
mse_mean = reg.mse_path_.mean(axis=1)
mse_std = reg.mse_path_.std(axis=1)
# Std Error = Std Deviation / SQRT(number of samples)
mse_std_error = mse_std / np.sqrt(n_folds)
```

2. Then, we put our calculations into a data frame and plot them using the default line chart:

```
fig, ax = plt.subplots(1, 1, figsize=(16, 8))

# We multiply by 1.96 for a 95% Confidence Interval
pd.DataFrame(
    {
        'alpha': reg.alphas_,
        'Mean MSE': mse_mean,
        'Upper Bound MSE': mse_mean + 1.96 * mse_std_error,
        'Lower Bound MSE': mse_mean - 1.96 * mse_std_error,
    }
).set_index('alpha')[
    ['Mean MSE', 'Upper Bound MSE', 'Lower Bound MSE']
].plot(
    title='Regularization plot (MSE vs alpha)',
    marker='.', logx=True, ax=ax
)

# Color the confidence interval
plt.fill_between(
    reg.alphas_,
    mse_mean + 1.96 * mse_std_error,
    mse_mean - 1.96 * mse_std_error,
)

# Print a vertical line for the chosen alpha
ax.axvline(reg.alpha_, linestyle='--', color='k')
ax.set_xlabel('Alpha')
ax.set_ylabel('Mean Squared Error')
```

Here is the output of the previous code:

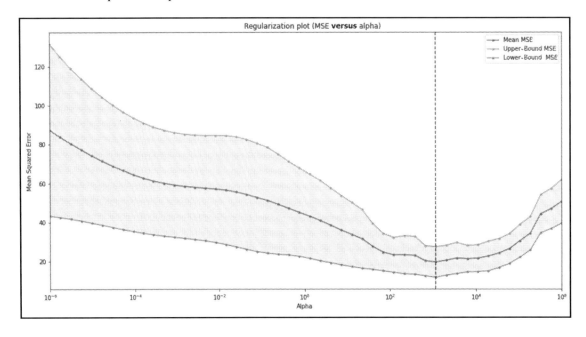

The MSE value is lowest at the chosen alpha value. The confidence interval is also narrower there, which reflects more confidence in the expected *MSE* result.

Finally, setting the model's alpha value to the one suggested and using it to make predictions for the test data gives us the following results:

	Baseline	Linear Regression	Lasso at Alpha = 1151.4
R^2	0.00	0.73	0.83
MAE	7.20	3.56	2.76
MSE	96.62	25.76	16.31

Clearly, regularization fixed the issues caused by the curse of dimensionality earlier. Furthermore, we were able to use cross-validation to find the optimum regularization parameter. We plotted the confidence intervals of errors to visualize the effect of alpha on the regressor. The fact that I have been talking about the confidence intervals in this section inspired me to dedicate the next section to regression intervals.

Finding regression intervals

"Exploring the unknown requires tolerating uncertainty."

– *Brian Greene*

It's not always guaranteed that we have accurate models. Sometimes, our data is inherently noisy and we cannot model it using a regressor. In these cases, it is important to be able to quantify how certain we are in our estimations. Usually, regressors make point predictions. These are the expected values (typically the mean) of the target (y) at each value of x. A Bayesian ridge regressor is capable of returning the expected values as usual, yet it also returns the standard deviation of the target (y) at each value of x.

To demonstrate how this works, let's create a noisy dataset, where $y = x + Noise$:

```
import numpy as np
import pandas as pd

df_noisy = pd.DataFrame(
    {
        'x': np.random.random_integers(0, 30, size=150),
        'noise': np.random.normal(loc=0.0, scale=5.0, size=150)
    }
)

df_noisy['y'] = df_noisy['x'] + df_noisy['noise']
```

Then, we can plot it in the form of a scatter plot:

```
df_noisy.plot(
    kind='scatter', x='x', y='y'
)
```

Plotting the resulting data frame will give us the following plot:

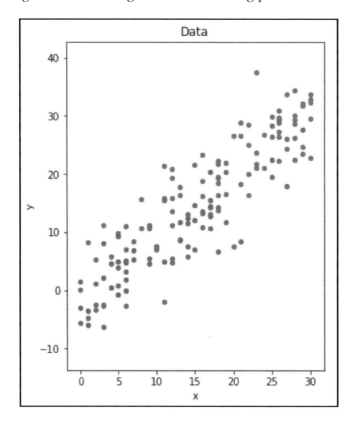

Now, let's train two regressors on the same data—LinearRegression and BayesianRidge. I will stick to the default values for the Bayesian ridge hyperparameters here:

```
from sklearn.linear_model import LinearRegression
from sklearn.linear_model import BayesianRidge

lr = LinearRegression()
br = BayesianRidge()

lr.fit(df_noisy[['x']], df_noisy['y'])
df_noisy['y_lr_pred'] = lr.predict(df_noisy[['x']])

br.fit(df_noisy[['x']], df_noisy['y'])
df_noisy['y_br_pred'], df_noisy['y_br_std'] = br.predict(df_noisy[['x']],
return_std=True)
```

Notice how the Bayesian ridge regressor returns two values when predicting.

The Bayesian approach to linear regression differs from the aforementioned algorithms in the way that it sees its coefficients. For all the algorithms we have seen so far, each coefficient takes a single value after training, but for a Bayesian model, a coefficient is rather a distribution with an estimated mean and standard deviation. A coefficient is initialized using a prior distribution, which gets updated by the training data to reach a posterior distribution via Bayes' theorem. The Bayesian ridge regressor is a regularized Bayesian regressor.

The predictions made by the two models are very similar. Nevertheless, we can use the standard deviation returned to calculate a range around the values that we expect most of the future data to fall into. The following code snippet creates plots for the two models and their predictions:

```
fig, axs = plt.subplots(1, 3, figsize=(16, 6), sharex=True, sharey=True)

# We plot the data 3 times
df_noisy.sort_values('x').plot(
    title='Data', kind='scatter', x='x', y='y', ax=axs[0]
)
df_noisy.sort_values('x').plot(
    kind='scatter', x='x', y='y', ax=axs[1], marker='o', alpha=0.25
)
df_noisy.sort_values('x').plot(
    kind='scatter', x='x', y='y', ax=axs[2], marker='o', alpha=0.25
)

# Here we plot the Linear Regression predictions
df_noisy.sort_values('x').plot(
    title='LinearRegression', kind='scatter', x='x', y='y_lr_pred',
    ax=axs[1], marker='o', color='k', label='Predictions'
)

# Here we plot the Bayesian Ridge predictions
df_noisy.sort_values('x').plot(
    title='BayesianRidge', kind='scatter', x='x', y='y_br_pred',
    ax=axs[2], marker='o', color='k', label='Predictions'
)

# Here we plot the range around the expected values
# We multiply by 1.96 for a 95% Confidence Interval
axs[2].fill_between(
    df_noisy.sort_values('x')['x'],
    df_noisy.sort_values('x')['y_br_pred'] - 1.96 *
```

```
                    df_noisy.sort_values('x')['y_br_std'],
        df_noisy.sort_values('x')['y_br_pred'] + 1.96 *
                    df_noisy.sort_values('x')['y_br_std'],
        color="k", alpha=0.2, label="Predictions +/- 1.96 * Std Dev"
    )

    fig.show()
```

Running the preceding code gives us the following graphs. In the `BayesianRidge` case, the shaded area shows where we expect 95% of our targets to fall:

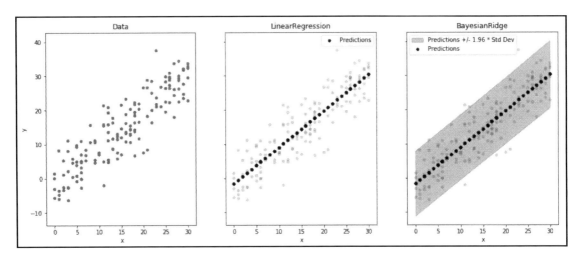

Regression intervals are handy when we want to quantify our uncertainties. In `Chapter 8`, *Ensembles – When One Model Is Not Enough*, we will revisit regression intervals

Getting to know additional linear regressors

Before moving on to linear classifiers, it makes sense to also add the following additional linear regression algorithms to your toolset:

- **Elastic-net** uses a mixture of L1 and L2 regularization techniques, where `l1_ratio` controls the mix of the two. This is useful in cases when you want to learn a sparse model where few of the weights are non-zero (as in **lasso**) while keeping the benefits of **ridge** regularization.
- **Random Sample Consensus** (**RANSAC**) is useful when your data has outliers. It tries to separate the outliers from the inlier samples. Then, it fits the model on the inliers only.
- **Least-Angle Regression** (**LARS**) is useful when dealing with high-dimensional data—that is, when there is a significant number of features compared to the number of samples. You may want to try it with the polynomial features example we saw earlier and see how it performs there.

Let's move on to the next section of the book where you will learn to use logistic regression to classify data.

Using logistic regression for classification

"You can tell whether a man is clever by his answers. You can tell whether a man is wise by his questions."

– Naguib Mahfouz

One day, when applying for a job, an interviewer asks: *So tell me, is logistic regression a classification or a regression algorithm?* The short answer to this is that it is a classification algorithm, but a longer and more interesting answer requires a good understanding of the logistic function. Then, the question may end up having a different meaning altogether.

Understanding the logistic function

The logistic function is a member of the sigmoid (s-shaped) functions, and it is represented by the following formula:

$$y = \frac{1}{1 + e^{-\theta}}$$

Don't let this equation scare you. What actually matters is how this function looks visually. Luckily, we can use our computer to generate a bunch of values for theta—for example, between −10 and 10. Then, we can plug these values into the formula and plot the resulting y values versus the theta values, as we have done in the following code:

```
import numpy as np
import pandas as pd

fig, ax = plt.subplots(1, 1, figsize=(16, 8))

theta = np.arange(-10, 10, 0.05)
y = 1 / (1 + np.exp(-1 * theta))

pd.DataFrame(
    {
        'theta': theta,
        'y': y
    }
).plot(
    title='Logistic Function',
    kind='scatter', x='theta', y='y',
    ax=ax
)

fig.show()
```

Running this code gives us the following graph:

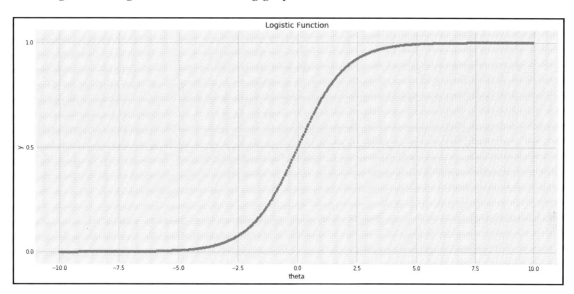

Two key characteristics to notice in the logistic function are as follows:

- y only goes between 0 and 1. It approaches 1 as theta approaches infinity, and approaches 0 as theta approaches negative infinity.
- y takes the value of 0.5 when theta is 0.

Plugging the logistic function into a linear model

"Probability is not a mere computation of odds on the dice or more complicated variants; it is the acceptance of the lack of certainty in our knowledge and the development of methods for dealing with our ignorance."

– Nassim Nicholas Taleb

For a line model with a couple of features, x_1 and x_2, we can have an intercept and two coefficients. Let's call them β_0, β_1, and β_2. Then, the linear regression equation will be as follows:

$$y = \beta_0 + \beta_1 x_1 + \beta_2 x_2$$

Separately, we can also plug the right-hand side of the preceding equation into the logistic function in place of θ. This will give the following equation for y:

$$y = \frac{1}{1 + e^{-(\beta_0 + \beta 1 x_1 + \beta_2 x_2)}}$$

In this case, the variation in the values of x will move y between 0 and 1. Higher values for the products of x and its coefficients will move y closer to 1, and lower values will move it toward 0. We also know that probabilities take values between 0 and 1. So, it makes sense to interpret y as the probability of y belonging to a certain class, given the value of x. If we don't want to deal with probabilities, we can just specify $y \geq 0.5$; then, our sample belongs to class 1, and it belongs to class 0 otherwise.

This was a brief look at how logistic regression works. It is a classifier, yet it is called *regression* since it's basically a regressor returning a value between 0 and 1, which we interpret as probabilities.

To train the logistic regression model, we need an objective function, as well as a solver that tries to find the optimal coefficients to minimize this function. In the following sections, we will go through all of these in more detail.

Objective function

During the training phase, the algorithm loops through the data trying to find the coefficients that minimize a predefined objective (loss) function. The loss function we try to minimize in the case of logistic regression is called log loss. It measures how far the predicted probabilities (p) are from the actual class labels (y) using the following formula:

-log(p) if y = 1 else -log(1 - p)

Mathematicians use a rather ugly way to express this formula due to their lack of `if-else` conditions. So, I chose to display the Python form here for its clarity. Jokes aside, the mathematical formula will turn out to be beautiful once you know its informational theory roots, but that's not something we'll look at now.

Regularization

Furthermore, scikit-learn's implementation of logistic regression algorithms uses regularization by default. Out of the box, it uses L2 regularization (as in the ridge regressor), but it can also use L1 (as in lasso) or a mixture of L1 and L2 (as in elastic-net).

Solvers

Finally, how do we find the optimal coefficients to minimize our loss function? A naive approach would be to try all the possible combinations of the coefficients until the minimal loss is found. Nevertheless, since an exhaustive search is not feasible given the infinite combinations, solvers are there to efficiently search for the best coefficients. scikit-learn implements about half a dozen solvers.

The choice of solver, along with the regularization method used, are the two main decisions to take when configuring the logistic regression algorithm. In the next section, we are going to see how and when to pick each one.

Configuring the logistic regression classifier

Before talking about solvers, let's go through some of the common hyperparameters used:

- `fit_intercept`: Usually, in addition to the coefficient for each feature, there is a constant intercept in your equation. Nevertheless, there are cases where you might not need an intercept—for example, if you know for sure that the value of y is supposed to be 0.5 when all the values of x are 0. One other case is when your data already has an additional constant column with all values set to 1. This usually occurs if your data has been processed in an earlier stage, as in the case of the polynomial processor. The coefficient for the `constant` column will be interpreted as the intercept in this case. The same configuration exits for the linear regression algorithms explained earlier.

- `max_iter`: For the solver to find the optimum coefficients, it loops over the training data more than once. These iterations are also called epochs. You usually set a limit on the number of iterations to prevent overfitting. The same hyperparameter is used by the lasso and ridge regressors explained earlier.
- `tol`: This is another way to stop the solver from iterating too much. If you set this to a high value, it means that only high improvements between one iteration and the next are tolerated; otherwise, the solver will stop. Conversely, a lower value will keep the solver going for more iterations until it reaches `max_iter`.
- `penalty`: This picks the regularization techniques to be used. This can be either L1, L2, elastic-net, or none for no regularization. Regularization helps to prevent overfitting, so it is important to use it when you have a lot of features. It also mitigates the overfitting effect when `max_iter` and `tol` are set to high values.
- `C` or `alpha`: These are parameters for setting how strong you want the regularization to be. Since we are going to use two different implementations of the logistic regression algorithm here, it is important to know that each of these two implementations uses a different parameter (`C` versus `alpha`). `alpha` is basically the inverse of `C`—($\frac{1}{C}$). This means that smaller values for `C` specify stronger regularization, while for `alpha`, larger values are needed for stronger regularization.
- `l1_ratio`: When using a mixture of L1 and L2, as in elastic-net, this fraction specifies how much weight to give to L1 versus L2.

The following are some of the solvers we can use:

- `liblinear`: This solver is implemented in `LogisticRegression` and is recommended for smaller datasets. It supports L1 and L2 regularization, but you cannot use it if you want to use elastic-net, nor if you do not want to use regularization at all.
- `sag` or `saga`: These solvers are implemented in `LogisticRegression` and `RidgeClassifier`. They are faster for larger datasets. However, you need to scale your features for them to converge. We used `MinMaxScaler` earlier in this chapter to scale our features. Now, it is not only needed for more meaningful coefficients, but also for the solver to find a solution earlier. `saga` supports all four penalty options.

- `lbfgs`: This solver is implemented in `LogisticRegression`. It supports the L2 penalty or no regularization at all.

- **Stochastic Gradient Descent (SGD)**: There are dedicated implementations for SGD—`SGDClassifier` and `SGDRegressor`. This is different to `LogisticRegression`, where the focus is on performing logistic regression by optimizing the one-loss function—log loss. The focus of `SGDClassifier` is on the SGD solver itself, which means that the same classifier allows different loss functions to be used. If `loss` is set to `log`, then it is a logistic regression model. However, setting `loss` to `hinge` or `perceptron` turns it into a **Support Vector Machine (SVM)** or perceptron, respectively. These are two other linear classifiers.

> **Gradient descent** is an optimization algorithm that aims to find a local minimum in a function by iteratively moving in the direction of steepest descent. The direction of the steepest descent is found using calculus, hence the term *gradient*. If you imagine the objective (loss) function as a curve, the gradient descent algorithm blindly lands on a random point on this curve and uses the gradient at the point it is on as a guiding stick to move to a local minimum step by step. Usually, the loss function is chosen to be a convex one so that its local minima is also its global one. In the **stochastic** version of **gradient descent**, rather than calculating the gradient for the entire training data, the estimator's weights are updated with each training sample. Gradient descent is covered in more detail in `Chapter 7`, *Neural Networks – Here Comes the Deep Learning*.

Classifying the Iris dataset using logistic regression

We will load the Iris dataset into a data frame. The following is a similar block of code to the one used in `Chapter 2`, *Making Decisions with Trees*, to load the dataset:

```
from sklearn import datasets
iris = datasets.load_iris()

df = pd.DataFrame(
    iris.data,
    columns=iris.feature_names
)
```

```
df['target'] = pd.Series(
    iris.target
)
```

Then, we will use `cross_validate` to evaluate the accuracy of the `LogisticRegression` algorithm using six-fold cross-validation, as follows:

```
from sklearn.linear_model import LogisticRegression
from sklearn.model_selection import cross_validate

num_folds = 6

clf = LogisticRegression(
    solver='lbfgs', multi_class='multinomial', max_iter=1000
)
accuracy_scores = cross_validate(
    clf, df[iris.feature_names], df['target'],
    cv=num_folds, scoring=['accuracy']
)

accuracy_mean = pd.Series(accuracy_scores['test_accuracy']).mean()
accuracy_std = pd.Series(accuracy_scores['test_accuracy']).std()
accuracy_sterror = accuracy_std / np.sqrt(num_folds)

print(
    'Logistic Regression: Accuracy ({}-fold): {:.2f} ~ {:.2f}'.format(
        num_folds,
        (accuracy_mean - 1.96 * accuracy_sterror),
        (accuracy_mean + 1.96 * accuracy_sterror),
    )
)
```

Running the preceding code will give us a set of accuracy scores with a 95% confidence interval that ranges between `0.95` and `1.00`. Running the same code for the decision tree classifier gives us a confidence interval that ranges between `0.93` and `0.99`.

Since we have three classes here, the coefficients calculated for each class boundary are separate from the others. After we train the logistic regression algorithm once more without the `cross_validate` wrapper, we can access the coefficients via `coef_`. We can also access the intercepts via `intercept_`.

In the next code snippet, I will be using a dictionary comprehension. In Python, one way to create the `[0, 1, 2, 3]` list is by using the `[i for i in range(4)]` list comprehension. This basically executes the loop to populate the list. Similarly, the `['x' for i in range(4)]` list comprehension will create the `['x', 'x', 'x, 'x']` list. Dictionary comprehension works in the same fashion. For example, the `{str(i): i for i in range(4)}` line of code will create the `{'0': 0, '1': 1, '2': 2, '3': 3}` dictionary.

The following code puts the coefficients into a data frame. It basically creates a dictionary whose keys are the class IDs and maps each ID to a list of its corresponding coefficients. Once the dictionary is created, we convert it into a data frame and add the intercepts to the data frame before displaying it:

```
# We need to fit the model again before getting its coefficients
clf.fit(df[iris.feature_names], df['target'])

# We use dictionary comprehension instead of a for-loop
df_coef = pd.DataFrame(
    {
        f'Coef [Class {class_id}]': clf.coef_[class_id]
        for class_id in range(clf.coef_.shape[0])
    },
    index=iris.feature_names
)
df_coef.loc['intercept', :] = clf.intercept_
```

Don't forget to scale your features before training. Then, you should get a coefficient data frame that looks like this:

	Coef [Class 0]	Coef [Class 1]	Coef [Class 2]
sepal length (cm)	-1.404926	0.261358	1.143569
sepal width (cm)	1.560021	-1.437230	-0.122791
petal length (cm)	-2.860633	0.418396	2.442238
petal width (cm)	-2.787136	-0.478438	3.265574
intercept	2.203698	1.229151	-3.432848

The table in the preceding screenshot shows the following:

- From the first row, we can tell that the increase in sepal length is correlated with classes 1 and 2 more than the remaining class, based on the positive sign of classes 1 and class 2's coefficients.
- Having a linear model here means that the class boundaries will not be limited to horizontal and vertical lines, as in the case of decision trees, but they will take linear forms.

To better understand this, in the next section, we will draw the logistic regression classifier's decision boundaries and compare them to those of decision trees.

Understanding the classifier's decision boundaries

By seeing the decision boundaries visually, we can understand why the model makes certain decisions. Here are the steps for plotting those boundaries:

1. We start by creating a function that takes the classifier's object and data samples and then plots the decision boundaries for that particular classifier and data:

```
def plot_decision_boundary(clf, x, y, ax, title):

    cmap='Paired_r'
    feature_names = x.columns
    x, y = x.values, y.values

    x_min, x_max = x[:,0].min(), x[:,0].max()
    y_min, y_max = x[:,1].min(), x[:,1].max()

    step = 0.02

    xx, yy = np.meshgrid(
        np.arange(x_min, x_max, step),
        np.arange(y_min, y_max, step)
    )
    Z = clf.predict(np.c_[xx.ravel(), yy.ravel()])
    Z = Z.reshape(xx.shape)
    ax.contourf(xx, yy, Z, cmap=cmap, alpha=0.25)
    ax.contour(xx, yy, Z, colors='k', linewidths=0.7)
    ax.scatter(x[:,0], x[:,1], c=y, edgecolors='k')
    ax.set_title(title)
    ax.set_xlabel(feature_names[0])
    ax.set_ylabel(feature_names[1])
```

2. Then, we split our data into training and test sets:

```
from sklearn.model_selection import train_test_split
df_train, df_test = train_test_split(df, test_size=0.3,
random_state=22)
```

3. To be able to visualize things easily, we are going to use two features. In the following code, we will train a logistic regression model and a decision tree model, and then compare their decision boundaries when trained on the same data:

```
from sklearn.metrics import accuracy_score
from sklearn.linear_model import LogisticRegression
from sklearn.tree import DecisionTreeClassifier

fig, axs = plt.subplots(1, 2, figsize=(12, 6))

two_features = ['petal width (cm)', 'petal length (cm)']

clf_lr = LogisticRegression()
clf_lr.fit(df_train[two_features], df_train['target'])
accuracy = accuracy_score(
    df_test['target'],
    clf_lr.predict(df_test[two_features])
)
plot_decision_boundary(
    clf_lr, df_test[two_features], df_test['target'], ax=axs[0],
    title=f'Logistic Regression Classifier\nAccuracy:
{accuracy:.2%}'
)

clf_dt = DecisionTreeClassifier(max_depth=3)
clf_dt.fit(df_train[two_features], df_train['target'])
accuracy = accuracy_score(
    df_test['target'],
    clf_dt.predict(df_test[two_features])
)
plot_decision_boundary(
    clf_dt, df_test[two_features], df_test['target'], ax=axs[1],
    title=f'Decision Tree Classifier\nAccuracy: {accuracy:.2%}'
)

fig.show()
```

Running this code will give us the following graphs:

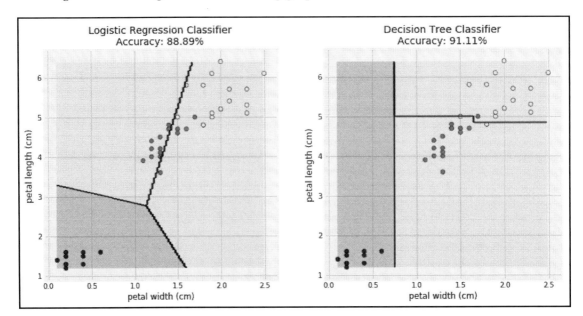

In the preceding graph, the following is observed:

- The logistic regression model did not perform well this time when only two features were used. Nevertheless, what we care about here is the shape of the boundaries.
- It's clear that the boundaries on the left are not horizontal and vertical lines as on the right. While the ones on the right can be composed of multiple line fragments, the ones on the left can only be made of continuous lines.

Getting to know additional linear classifiers

Before ending this chapter, it is useful to highlight some additional linear classification algorithms:

- **SGD** is a versatile solver. As mentioned earlier, it can perform a logistic regression classification in addition to SVM and perceptron classification, depending on the loss function used. It also allows regularized penalties.

- **The ride classifier** converts class labels into 1 and −1 and treats the problem as a regression task. It also deals well with non-binary classification tasks. Due to its design, it uses a different set of solvers, so it's worth trying as it may be quicker to learn when dealing with a large number of classes.
- **Linear Support Vector Classification (LinearSVC)** is another linear model. Rather than log loss, it uses the `hinge` function, which aims to find class boundaries where the samples of each class are as far as possible from the boundaries. This is not to be confused with SVMs. Contrary to their linear cousins, SVMs are non-linear algorithms, due to what is known as the kernel trick. SVMs are not as commonly used as they used to be a couple of decades ago, and they are beyond the scope of this book.

Summary

Linear models are found everywhere. Their simplicity, as well as the capabilities they offer—such as regularization—makes them popular among practitioners. They also share many concepts with neural networks, which means that understanding them will help you in later chapters.

Being linear isn't usually a limiting factor as long as we can get creative with our feature transformation. Furthermore, in higher dimensions, the linearity assumption may hold more often than we think. That's why it is advised to always start with a linear model and then decide whether you need to go for a more advanced model.

Having that said, it can sometimes be tricky to figure out the best configurations for your linear model or decide on which solver to use. In this chapter, we learned about using cross-validation to fine-tune a model's hyperparameters. We have also seen the different hyperparameters and solvers available, with tips for when to use each one.

So far, for all the datasets that we have dealt with in the first two chapters, we were lucky to have the data in the correct format. We have dealt only with numerical data with no missing values. Nevertheless, in real-world scenarios, this is rarely the case.

In the next chapter, we are going to learn more about data preprocessing so that we can seamlessly continue working with more datasets and more advanced algorithms later on.

4

Preparing Your Data

In the previous chapter, we dealt with clean data, where all the values were available to us, all the columns had numeric values, and when faced with too many features, we had a regularization technique on our side. In real life, it will often be the case that the data is not as clean as you would like it to be. Sometimes, even clean data can still be preprocessed in ways to make things easier for our machine learning algorithm. In this chapter, we will learn about the following data preprocessing techniques:

- Imputing missing values
- Encoding non-numerical columns
- Changing the data distribution
- Reducing the number of features via selection
- Projecting data into new dimensions

Imputing missing values

"It is a capital mistake to theorize before one has data."

– Sherlock Holmes

To simulate a real-life scenario where the data has missing values, we will create a dataset with people's weights as a function of their height. Then, we will randomly remove 75% of the values in the height column and set them to NaN:

```
df = pd.DataFrame(
    {
        'gender': np.random.binomial(1, .6, 100),
        'height': np.random.normal(0, 10, 100),
        'noise': np.random.normal(0, 2, 100),
    }
)
```

```
df['height'] = df['height'] + df['gender'].apply(
    lambda g: 150 if g else 180
)
df['height (with 75% NaN)'] = df['height'].apply(
    lambda x: x if np.random.binomial(1, .25, 1)[0] else np.nan
)
df['weight'] = df['height'] + df['noise'] - 110
```

We used a random number generator with an underlying **binomial/Bernoulli** distribution here to decide whether each sample will be removed. The distribution's *n* value is set to 1—that is, it is a Bernoulli distribution—and its *p* value is set to 0.25—that is, each sample has a 25% chance of staying. Whenever the returned value of the generator is 0, the sample is set to NaN. As you can see, due to the nature of the random generator, the final percentage of NaN values may be slightly more or less than 75%.

Here are the first four rows of the DataFrame that we have just created. Only the height column, with the missing values, and the weights are shown here:

	height (with 75% NaN)	weight
0	NaN	30.417204
1	172.458316	59.818478
2	NaN	47.255345
3	NaN	50.682057

We can also check what percentage of each column has missing values by using the following code:

```
df.isnull().mean()
```

When I ran the previous line, 77% of the values were missing. Note that you may get a different ratio of missing values than the ones I've got here, thanks to the random number generator used.

None of the regressors we have seen so far will accept this data with all the NaN values in it. Therefore, we need to convert those missing values into something. Deciding on which values to fill in place of the missing values is the job of the data imputation process.

There are different kinds of imputation techniques. We are going to try them here and observe their effect on our weight estimations. Keep in mind that we happen to know the original height data without any missing values, and we know that using a ridge regressor on the original data gives us an MSE value of 3.4. Let's keep this piece of information as a reference for now.

Setting missing values to 0

One simple approach would be to set all the missing values to 0. The following code will make our data usable once more:

```
df['height (75% zero imputed)'] = df['height (with 75% NaN)'].fillna(0)
```

Fitting a ridge regressor on the newly imputed column will give us an MSE value of 365:

```
from sklearn.linear_model import Ridge
from sklearn.metrics import mean_squared_error

reg = Ridge()
x, y = df[['height (75% zero imputed)']], df['weight']
reg.fit(x, y)
mean_squared_error(y, reg.predict(x))
```

Although we were able to use the regressor, its error is huge compared to our reference scenario. To understand the effect of zero imputation, let's plot the imputed data and use the regressor's coefficients to see what kind of line it created after training. Let's also plot the original data for comparison. I am sure the code for generating the following graph is straightforward to you by now, so I'll skip it:

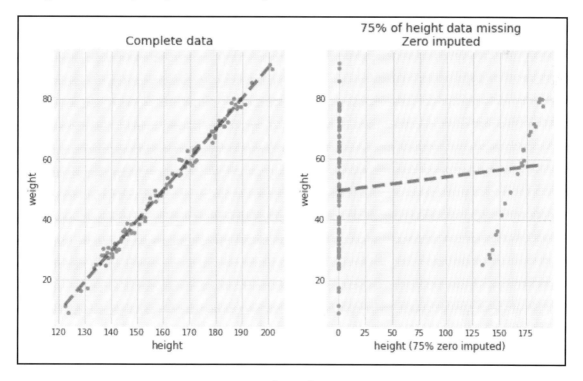

We already know by now that a linear model is only capable of fitting a continuous straight line onto the data (or a hyperplane, in the case of higher dimensions). We also know that 0 is not a reasonable height for anyone. Nevertheless, with zero imputation, we introduced a bunch of values where the heights are 0 and the weights range between 10 and 90 or so. This obviously confused our regressor, as we can see in the right-hand side graph.

A non-linear regressor, such as a decision tree, will be able to deal with this problem much better than its linear counterpart. Actually, for tree-based models, I'd suggest you try replacing the missing values in *x* with values that don't exist in your data. For example, you may experiment with setting the height to –1, in this case.

Setting missing values to the mean

Another name for statistical mean is *expected value*. That's because the mean serves as a biased estimation of the data. Having that said, replacing missing values with the column's mean values sounds like a plausible idea.

In this chapter, I am fitting a regressor on the entire dataset. I am not concerned about splitting the data into training and test sets here since I am mainly bothered with how the regressor behaves with imputation. Nevertheless, in real life, you will just want to learn the mean value of the training set and use it to impute the missing values for both the training and test sets.

scikit-learn's `SimpleImputer` feature makes it possible to find out the mean value from the training set and use it to impute both the training and test sets. It does so by using our favorite `fit()` and `transform()` methods. But let's stick to a one-step `fit_transform()` function here since we only have one set:

```
from sklearn.impute import SimpleImputer
imp = SimpleImputer(missing_values=np.nan, strategy='mean')
df['height (75% mean imputed)'] = imp.fit_transform(
    df[['height (with 75% NaN)']]
)[:, 0]
```

We have a single column to impute here, which is why I used `[:, 0]` to access its values after imputation.

A ridge regressor will give us an MSE value of 302. To understand where this improvement came from, let's plot the model's decision and compare it to the previous one with zero imputation:

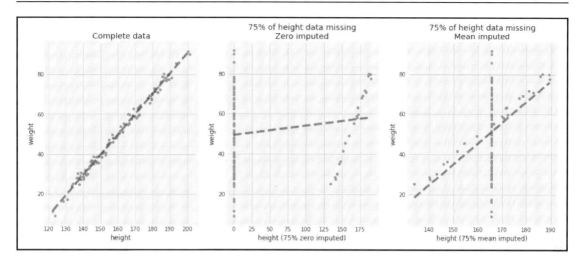

Clearly, the model's decisions make more sense now. You can see how the dotted line coincides with the actual non-imputed data points.

In addition to using **mean** as a strategy, the algorithm can also find the **median** of the training data. The median is usually a better option if your data has outliers. In the case of non-numerical features, you should instead use the `most_frequent` option as your strategy.

Using informed estimations for missing values

Using a single value for all missing values may not be ideal. For example, we know here that our data includes male and female samples and each sub-sample has a different average height. The `IterativeImputer()` method is an algorithm that can use neighboring features to estimate the missing values in a certain feature. Here, we use the gender information to infer values to use when imputing the missing heights:

```
# We need to enable the module first since it is an experimental one
from sklearn.experimental import enable_iterative_imputer
from sklearn.impute import IterativeImputer
imp = IterativeImputer(missing_values=np.nan)
df['height (75% iterative imputed)'] = imp.fit_transform(
    df[['height (with 75% NaN)', 'gender']]
)[:, 0]
```

We now have two values to be used for imputation:

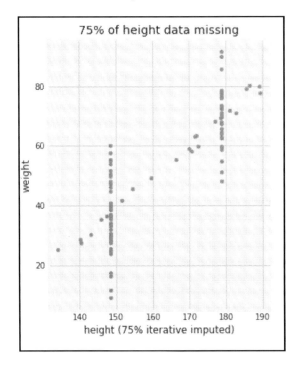

The MSE value is 96 this time. This strategy is the clear winner here.

We only had one feature with missing values here. In the case of multiple features, the IterativeImputer() method loops over all the features. It uses all the features but one to predict the missing values of the remaining one via regression. Once it is done looping over all the features, it may repeat the entire process more than once until the values converge. There are parameters to decide which regression algorithm to use, what order to use when looping over the features, and what the maximum number of iterations allowed is. Clearly, this strategy may be computationally expensive with bigger datasets and a higher number of incomplete features. Furthermore, the IterativeImputer() implementation is still experimental, and its API might change in the future.

A column with too many missing values carries too little information for our estimate to use. We can try our best to impute those missing values; but nevertheless, dropping the entire column and not using it at all is sometimes the best option, especially if the majority of the values are missing.

Encoding non-numerical columns

"Every decoding is another encoding."

– David Lodge

Non-numeric data is another issue that algorithm implementations cannot deal with. In addition to the core scikit-learn implementation, `scikit-learn-contrib` has a list of satellite projects. These projects provide additional tools to our data arsenal, and here is how they describe themselves:

> *"scikit-learn-contrib is a GitHub organization for gathering high-quality, scikit-learn - compatible projects. It also provides a template for establishing new scikit-learn compatible projects."*

We are going to use one of these projects here—`category_encoders`. This allows us to encode non-numerical data into different forms. First, we will install the library using the `pip` installer, as follows:

```
pip install category_encoders
```

Before jumping into the different encoding strategies, let's first create a fictional dataset to play with:

```
df = pd.DataFrame({
    'Size': np.random.choice(['XS', 'S', 'M', 'L', 'XL', 'XXL'], 10),
    'Brand': np.random.choice(['Nike', 'Puma', 'Adidas', 'Le Coq',
'Reebok'], 10),
})
```

We will then split it into two equal halves:

```
from sklearn.model_selection import train_test_split
df_train, df_test = train_test_split(df, test_size=0.5)
```

 Keep in mind that the core scikit-learn library implements two of the encoders we are going to see here—`preprocessing.OneHotEncoder` and `preprocessing.OrdinalEncoder`. Nevertheless, I prefer the `category_encoders` implementation for its richness and versatility.

Now, on to our first, and most popular, encoding strategy—one-hot encoding.

One-hot encoding

One-hot encoding, also known as dummy encoding, is the most common method for dealing with categorical features. If you have a column containing the red, green, and blue values, it sounds logical to convert them into three columns—is_red, is_green, and is_blue—and fill these columns with ones and zeroes, accordingly.

Here is the code for decoding our datasets using OneHotEncoder:

```
from category_encoders.one_hot import OneHotEncoder
encoder = OneHotEncoder(use_cat_names=True, handle_unknown='return_nan')
x_train = encoder.fit_transform(df_train)
x_test = encoder.transform(df_test)
```

I set use_cat_names=True to use the encoded values when assigning column names. The handle_unknown parameter tells the encoder how to deal with values in the test set that don't exist in the training set. For example, we have no clothing of the XS or S sizes in our training set. We also don't have any Adidas clothing in there. That's why these records in the test set are converted to NaN:

	Size_XL	Size_L	Size_XXL	Size_M	Brand_Reebok	Brand_Le Coq	Brand_Puma	Brand_Nike
4	1.0	0.0	0.0	0.0	0.0	0.0	0.0	1.0
5	NaN	NaN	NaN	NaN	1.0	0.0	0.0	0.0
1	NaN	NaN	NaN	NaN	1.0	0.0	0.0	0.0
2	NaN	NaN	NaN	NaN	0.0	1.0	0.0	0.0
8	0.0	0.0	1.0	0.0	NaN	NaN	NaN	NaN

You still have to impute those NaN values. Otherwise, we can just set those values to 0 by setting handle_unknown to value.

One-hot encoding is recommended for linear models and **K-Nearest Neighbor (KNN)** algorithms. Nevertheless, due to the fact that one column may be expanded into too many columns and some of them may be inter-dependent, regularization or feature selection are recommended here. We will look further at feature selection later in this chapter, and the KNN algorithm will be discussed later in this book.

Ordinal encoding

Depending on your use case, you may need to encode your categorical values in a way that reflects their order. If I am going to use this data to predict the level of demand for the items, then I know that it isn't the case that the larger the item's size, the higher the demand for it. So, one-hot encoding may still be apt for the sizes here. However, if we are to predict the amount of material needed to create each item of clothing, then we need to encode the sizes in a way that implies that XL needs more material than L. In this case, we are concerned with the order of those values and so we use OrdinalEncoder, as follows:

```
from category_encoders.ordinal import OrdinalEncoder

oencoder = OrdinalEncoder(
  mapping= [
    {
      'col': 'Size',
      'mapping': {'XS': 1, 'S': 2, 'M': 3, 'L': 4, 'XL': 5}
    }
  ]
)

df_train.loc[
  :, 'Size [Ordinal Encoded]'
] = oencoder.fit_transform(
  df_train['Size']
)['Size'].values
df_test.loc[
  :, 'Size [Ordinal Encoded]'
] = oencoder.transform(
  df_test['Size']
)['Size'].values
```

Note that we have to specify the mapping by hand. We want XS to be encoded as 1, S as 2, and so on. As a result, we get the following DataFrame:

	Size	Brand	Size [Ordinal Encoded]
4	XL	Nike	5.0
5	S	Reebok	2.0
1	S	Reebok	2.0
2	XS	Le Coq	1.0
8	XXL	Adidas	-1.0

This time, the encoded data fits into just one column, and the values missing from the training set are encoded as -1.

> This encoding method is recommended for non-linear models, such as decision trees. As for linear models, they may interpret XL (encoded as 5) to be five times the size of XS (encoded as 1). That's why one-hot encoding is still preferred for linear models. Furthermore, coming up with meaningful mappings and setting it by hand can be time-consuming.

Target encoding

One obvious way to encode categorical features, in a supervised learning scenario, is to base the encoding on the target values. Say we want to estimate the price of an item of clothing. We can replace the brand names with the average price for all items of the same brand in our training dataset. Nevertheless, there is one obvious problem here. Say one brand happens to appear only once or twice in our training set. There is no guarantee that these few appearances are good representations of the brand's price. In another world, using the target values just like that may result in overfitting, and the resulting model may not generalize well when dealing with new data. That's why the category_encoders library has multiple variations of target encoding; they all have the same underlying objective, but each of them has a different method for dealing with the aforementioned overfitting issue. Here are some examples of these implementations:

- Leave-one-out cross-validation
- The target encoder
- The catboost encoder
- The M-estimator

Leave-one-out is probably the most well-known implementation of the ones listed. In the training data, it replaces the categorical value in raw data with the mean of the corresponding target values of all the rows with the same categorical value except for this particular raw data. For the test data, it just uses the mean of the corresponding targets of each category value learned from the training data. Furthermore, the encoder also has a parameter called sigma, which allows you to add noise to the learned mean to prevent even more overfitting.

Homogenizing the columns' scale

Different numerical columns may have different scales. One column's age is in the tens, while its salary is typically in the thousands. As we saw earlier, putting different columns into a similar scale helps in some cases. Here are some of the cases where scaling is recommended:

- It allows gradient-descent solvers to converge quicker.
- It is needed for algorithms such as KNN and **Principle Component Analysis (PCA)**
- When training an estimator, it puts the features on a comparable scale, which helps when juxtaposing their learned coefficients.

In the next sections, we are going to examine the most commonly used scalers.

The standard scaler

This converts the features into normal distribution by setting their mean to 0 and their standard deviation to 1. This is done using the following operation, where a column's mean value is subtracted from each value in it, and then the result is divided by the column's standard deviation value:

$$Scaler(x_i) = \frac{(x_i - x_{mean})}{x_{std}}$$

The scaler's implementation can be used as follows:

```
from sklearn.preprocessing import StandardScaler

scaler = StandardScaler()
x_train_scaled = scaler.fit_transform(x_train)
x_test_scaled = scaler.transform(x_test)
```

Once fitted, you can also find out the mean and variance for each column in the training data via the `mean_` and `var_` attributes. In the presence of outliers, the standard scaler does not guarantee balanced feature scales.

The MinMax scaler

This squeezes the features into a certain range, typically between 0 and 1. If you need to use a different range, you can set it using the `feature_range` parameter. This scaler works as follows:

```
from sklearn.preprocessing import MinMaxScaler

scaler = MinMaxScaler(feature_range=(0,1))
x_train_scaled = scaler.fit_transform(x_train)
x_test_scaled = scaler.transform(x_test)
```

Once fitted, you can also find out the minimum and maximum values for each column in the training data with the `data_min_` and `data_max_` attributes. Since all samples are limited to a predefined range, outliers may force inliers to be squeezed into a small subset of this range.

RobustScaler

This is similar to the standard scaler, but uses the data quantiles instead to be more robust to the outliers' effect on the mean and standard deviation. It's advised that you use this if your data has outliers, and it can be used as follows:

```
from sklearn.preprocessing import RobustScaler

scaler = RobustScaler()
x_train_scaled = scaler.fit_transform(x_train)
x_test_scaled = scaler.transform(x_test)
```

Other scalers also exist; however, I have covered the most commonly used scalers here. Throughout this book, we will be using the aforementioned scalers. All scalers have an `inverse_transform()` method, so you can restore a feature's original scales if needed. Furthermore, if you cannot load all training data into memory at once, or if the data comes in batches, you can then call the scaler's `partial_fit()` method with each batch instead of calling the `fit()` method for the entire dataset once.

Selecting the most useful features

"More data, such as paying attention to the eye colors of the people around when crossing the street, can make you miss the big truck."

— Nassim Nicholas Taleb

We have seen, in previous chapters, that too many features can degrade the performance of our models. What is known as the curse of dimensionality may negatively impact an algorithm's accuracy, especially if there aren't enough training samples. Furthermore, it can also lead to more training time and higher computational requirements. Luckily, we have also learned how to regularize our linear models or limit the growth of our decision trees to combat the effect of feature abundance. Nevertheless, we may sometimes end up using models where regularization is not an option. Additionally, we may still need to get rid of some pointless features to reduce the algorithm's training time and computational needs. In these situations, feature selection is wise to use as a first step.

Depending on whether we are dealing with labeled or unlabeled data, we can choose different methods for feature selection. Furthermore, some methods are more computationally expensive than others, and some lead to more accurate results. In the following sections, we are going to see how those different methods can be used and, to demonstrate that, we will load scikit-learn's `wine` dataset:

```
from sklearn import datasets

wine = datasets.load_wine()
df = pd.DataFrame(
    wine.data,
    columns=wine.feature_names
)
df['target'] = pd.Series(
    wine.target
)
```

We then split the data as we usually do:

```
from sklearn.model_selection import train_test_split
df_train, df_test = train_test_split(df, test_size=0.4)

x_train = df_train[wine.feature_names]
x_test = df_test[wine.feature_names]

y_train = df_train['target']
y_test = df_test['target']
```

The `wine` dataset has 13 features and is used for classification tasks. In the following sections, we are going to discover which features are less important than the others.

VarianceThreshold

If you recall, when we used the `PolynomialFeatures` transformer, it added a column where all the values were set to `1`. Additionally, categorical encoders, such as one-hot encoding, can result in columns where almost all of the values are `0`. It's also common, in real-life scenarios, to have columns where all the data in it is identical or almost identical. Variance is the most obvious way to measure the amount of variation in a dataset, so `VarianceThreshold` allows us to set a minimum threshold for an accepted variance in each feature. In the following code, we will set the variance threshold to `0`. It then goes through the training set to learn which features deserve to stay:

```
from sklearn.feature_selection import VarianceThreshold
vt = VarianceThreshold(threshold=0)
vt.fit(x_train)
```

Like all of our other modules, this one also provides the usual `fit()`, `transform()`, and `fit_transform()` methods. However, I prefer not to use them here since we already gave our columns names, and the `transform()` functions don't honor the names we have given. That's why I prefer to use another method called `get_support()`. This method returns a list of Booleans, where any `False` values correspond to columns that ought to be removed based on the threshold we set. Here is how I remove unnecessary features using the `pandas` library's `iloc` function:

```
x_train = x_train.iloc[:, vt.get_support()]
x_test = x_test.iloc[:, vt.get_support()]
```

We can also print the feature names and sort them according to their variance, as follows:

```
pd.DataFrame(
    {
        'Feature': wine.feature_names,
        'Variance': vt.variances_,
    }
).sort_values(
    'Variance', ascending=True
)
```

This gives us the following table:

	Feature	Variance
7	nonflavanoid_phenols	0.013845
10	hue	0.055709
2	ash	0.068327
8	proanthocyanins	0.306081
5	total_phenols	0.369353
11	od280/od315_of_diluted_wines	0.478116
0	alcohol	0.679757
6	flavanoids	0.925865
1	malic_acid	0.987016
9	color_intensity	5.612742
3	alcalinity_of_ash	8.914152
4	magnesium	92.000000
12	proline	1402.000000

We can see that none of our features have zero variance; therefore, none of them are removed. You may decide to use a higher threshold—for example, setting the threshold to `0.05` will get rid of `nonflavanoid_phenols`. However, let me list the key advantages and disadvantages of this module to help you decide when and how to use it:

- Unlike the other feature selection methods we are going to see in a bit, this one does not use data labels when selecting features. This is useful when dealing with unlabeled data, as in unsupervised learning scenarios.
- The fact that it is label-agnostic also means that a low variance feature might still correlate well with our labels and removing it is a mistake.
- The variance, just like the mean, is scale-dependent. A list of numbers from `1` to `10` has a variance of `8.25`, while the list of `10, 20, 30, ...100` has a variance of `825.0`. We can clearly see this in the variance of `proline`. This makes the numbers in our table incomparable and makes it hard to pick a correct threshold. One idea may be to scale your data before calculating its variance. However, keep in mind that you cannot use `StandardScaler` since it deliberately unifies the variance of all features. So, I would find `MinMaxScaler` more meaningful here.

In summary, I find the variance threshold handy in removing zero-variance features. As for the remaining features, I'd let the next feature selection algorithms deal with them, especially when dealing with labeled data.

Filters

Now that our data comes with labels, it makes sense to use the correlation between each feature and the labels to decide which features are more useful for our model. This category of feature-selection algorithms deals with each individual feature and measures its usefulness in relation to the label; this algorithm is called *filters*. In other words, the algorithm takes each column in x and uses some measure to evaluate how useful it is in predicting y. Useful columns stay, while the rest are removed. The way that usefulness is measured is what differentiates one filter selector from the other. For the sake of clarity, I am going to focus on two selectors here since each one has its roots in a different scientific field, and understanding them both serves as a good foundation for future concepts. The two concepts are **ANOVA (F-values)** and **mutual information**.

f-regression and f-classif

As its name suggests, `f_regression` is used for feature selection in regression tasks. `f_classif` is its classification cousin. `f_regression` has its roots in the field of statistics. Its scikit-learn implementation uses the Pearson correlation coefficient to calculate the correlation between each column in x and y. The results are then converted into F-values and P-values, but let's keep that conversion aside since the correlation coefficient is the key here. We start by subtracting the mean values for each column from all the values in the same column, which is similar to what we did in `StandardScaler`, but without dividing the values by their standard deviation. Then, we calculate the correlation coefficient using the following formula:

$$r_{xy} = \frac{\sum x * y}{\sum x^2 * \sum y^2}$$

Since the mean is subtracted, the values for the x and y values are positive when an instance is above its column's mean value, and negative when it is below. So, this equation is maximized so that every time x is above average, y is also above average, and whenever x is below average, y follows suit. The maximum value for this equation is 1. We can then say that x and y are perfectly correlated. The equation is -1 when x and y stubbornly go opposite ways, in other words negatively correlated. A zero result means that x and y are uncorrelated (that is, independent or orthogonal).

Usually, statisticians write this equation differently. The fact that the mean is subtracted from x and y is usually written down as a part of the equation. Then, the numerator is clearly the covariance and the denominator is the product of the two variances. Nevertheless, I deliberately chose not to follow the statistical convention here so that our natural language processing friends feel at home once they realize that this is the exact same equation as for cosine similarity. There, x and y are seen as vectors, the numerator is their dot product, and the denominator is the product of their magnitudes. Consequently, the two vectors are perfectly correlated (go in the same direction) when the angle between them is 0 (cosine $0 = 1$). Conversely, they are independent when they are perpendicular to each other, hence the term *orthogonal*. One takeaway from this visual interpretation is that this metric only considers the linear relationship between x and y.

 For the case of classification, a one-way ANOVA test is performed. This compares the variance between the different class labels to the variance within each class. Just like its regression cousin, it measures the linear dependence between the features and the class labels.

Enough theory for now; let's use `f_classif` to pick the most useful features in our dataset:

```
from sklearn.feature_selection import f_classif
f, p = f_classif(x_train, y_train)
```

Let's keep the resulting f and p values to one side for now. After explaining the mutual information approach for feature selection, we will use these values to contrast the two approaches.

Mutual information

This approach has its roots in a different scientific field called **information theory**. This field was introduced by Claude Shannon to solve issues relating to signal processing and data compression. When we send a message made up of zeros and ones, we may know the exact content of this message, but can we actually quantify the amount of information this very message carries? Shannon solved this problem by borrowing the concept of **entropy** from thermodynamics. Further down the line comes the concept of **mutual information**. It quantifies the amount of information obtained about one variable when observing another variable. The formula for mutual information is as follows:

$$MI = \sum \sum P(x, y) * log \frac{P(x, y)}{P(x) * P(y)}$$

Before dissecting this equation, keep the following in mind:

- $P(x)$ is the probability of x taking a certain value, as is $P(y)$ for y.
- $P(x, y)$ is known as joint probability, which is the probability of both x and y taking a specific pair of values.
- $P(x, y)$ only equals the product of $P(x) * P(y)$ if x and y are independent. Otherwise, its value is more or less than their product, depending on whether x and y are positively or negatively correlated.

The double summation and the first part of the equation, $P(x, y)$, are our way of calculating a weighted average for all possible values of x and y. The logarithmic part is what we care about, and it is known as point-wise mutual information. If x and y are independent, the fraction is equal to 1 and its logarithm is 0. In other words, we get 0 when the two variables are uncorrelated. Otherwise, the sign of the outcome points to whether x and y are positively or negatively correlated.

Here is how we get the mutual information coefficient for each feature:

```
from sklearn.feature_selection import mutual_info_classif
mi = mutual_info_classif(x_train, y_train)
```

Unlike Pearson's correlation coefficient, mutual information captures any kind of correlation, whether it is linear or not.

Comparing and using the different filters

Let's now compare our mutual information scores to the F-values. To do so, we will put them both into one DataFrame and use the `pandas` styling feature to plot bar charts within the DataFrame, as follows:

```
pd.DataFrame(
  {
    'Feature': wine.feature_names,
    'F': f,
    'MI': mi,
  }
).sort_values(
  'MI', ascending=False
).style.bar(
  subset=['F', 'MI'], color='grey'
)
```

This gives us the following DataFrame:

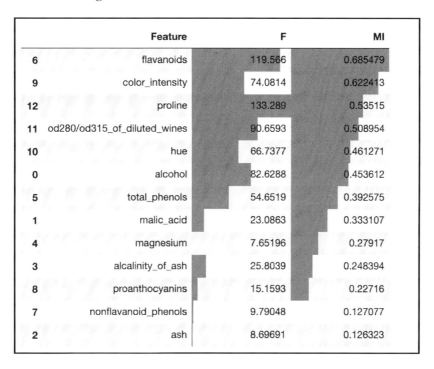

	Feature	F	MI
6	flavanoids	119.566	0.685479
9	color_intensity	74.0814	0.622413
12	proline	133.289	0.53515
11	od280/od315_of_diluted_wines	90.6593	0.508954
10	hue	66.7377	0.461271
0	alcohol	82.6288	0.453612
5	total_phenols	54.6519	0.392575
1	malic_acid	23.0863	0.333107
4	magnesium	7.65196	0.27917
3	alcalinity_of_ash	25.8039	0.248394
8	proanthocyanins	15.1593	0.22716
7	nonflavanoid_phenols	9.79048	0.127077
2	ash	8.69691	0.126323

As you can see, they mostly agree on the order of feature importance, yet they still disagree sometimes. I used each of the two methods to select the top four features, then compared the accuracy of a **logistic regression** classifier to that of a decision tree classifier with each feature selection method. Here are the results of the training set:

	Logistic Regression	Decision Tree Classifier
SelectKBest(f_classif)	0.97	0.89
SelectKBest(mutual_info_classif)	0.9	0.93

As you can tell, each of the two selection methods worked better for one of the two classifiers here. It seems that f_classif served the linear model better due to its linear nature, while the non-linear model favored an algorithm that captures non-linear correlations. I have not found any literature confirming the generality of this speculation, however.

It is hard not to see the underlying theme that links the two measures. The numerator calculates some intra-variable information—the covariance, dot product, or join probability. The denominator calculates the product of inter-variable information—the variance, norms, or probability. This very theme will continue to appear in different topics in the future. One day, we might use cosine similarity to compare two documents; another day, we might use mutual information to evaluate a clustering algorithm.

Evaluating multiple features at a time

The feature selection methods shown in the *Filters* section of this chapter are also regarded as univariate feature selection methods since they check each feature separately before deciding whether to keep it. This can result in any of the two following issues:

- If two features are highly correlated, we only want to keep one of them. However, due to the nature of the univariate feature selection, they will both still be selected.
- If two features are not very useful on their own, yet their combination is useful. They will still be removed due to the way the univariate feature selection methods work.

To deal with these issues, we may decide to use one of the following solutions:

- **Using estimators for feature selection**: Typically, regressors and classifiers assign values to the features used after training, signifying their importance. So, we can use an estimator's coefficients (or feature importance) to add or remove features from our initial feature set. scikit-learn's **Recursive Feature Elimination (RFE)** algorithm starts with an initial set of features. Then, it iteratively removes features with each iteration using the trained model's coefficients. The `SelectFromModel` algorithm is a meta-transformer that can make use of a regularized model to remove features with zero or near-zero coefficients.
- **Using estimators with built-in feature selection**: In other words, this means using a regularized estimator such as lasso, where feature selection is part of the estimator's objectives.

In summary, methods such as using variance thresholds and filters are quick to perform but have their drawbacks when it comes to feature correlation and interaction. More computationally expensive methods, such as wrappers, deal with these issues but are prone to overfitting.

If you ask me about my recommendations for feature selection, personally, my go-to method would be regularization after removing the zero-variance features, unless I am dealing with a huge amount of features where training on the entire set is unfeasible. In these cases, I'd use a univariate feature selection method while being careful about removing features that might end up being useful. I'd still use a regularized model afterward to deal with any multicollinearity.

In the end, the proof of the pudding is in the eating, and empirical results via trial and error may trump my recommendations. Furthermore, besides improving the final model's accuracy, feature selection can still be used to understand the data at hand. The feature importance scores can still be used to inform business decisions. For example, if our label states whether a user is going to churn, we can come up with a hypothesis that the top-scoring features affect the churn rate the most. Then, we can run experiments by changing the relevant parts of our product to see whether we can decrease the churn rate.

Summary

Pursuing a data-related career requires a tendency to deal with imperfections. Dealing with missing values is one step that we cannot progress without. So, we started this chapter by learning about different data imputation methods. Additionally, suitable data for one task may not be perfect for another. That's why we learned about feature encoding and how to change categorical and ordinal data to fit into our machine learning needs. Helping algorithms to perform better can require rescaling the numerical features. Therefore, we learned about three scaling methods. Finally, data abundance can be a curse on our models, so feature selection is one prescribed way to deal with the curse of dimensionality, along with regularization.

One main theme that ran through this entire chapter is the trade-off between simple and quick methods versus more informed and computationally expensive methods that may result in overfitting. Knowing which methods to use requires an understanding of their underlying theories, in addition to a willingness to experiment and use iterations. So, I decided to go a bit deeper into the theoretical background where needed, not only so that it helps you pick your methods wisely, but also so that it allows you to come up with your own methods in the future.

Now that we have the main data preprocessing tools on our side, we are ready to move on to our next algorithm—KNN.

5
Image Processing with Nearest Neighbors

In this chapter and the following one, we are going to take a different approach. The nearest neighbors algorithm will take a supporting role here, while image processing will be the main protagonist of the chapter. We will start by loading images and we will use Python to represent them in a suitable format for the machine learning algorithms to work with. We will be using the nearest neighbors algorithm for classification and regression. We will also learn how to compress information in images into a smaller space. Many of the concepts explained here are transferable and can be used with other algorithms with slight tweaks. Later, in `Chapter 7`, *Neural Networks - Here Comes the Deep Learning*, we will build on the knowledge acquired here and continue with image processing by using neural networks. In this chapter, we are going to cover the following topics:

- Nearest neighbors
- Loading and displaying images
- Image classification
- Using custom distances
- Using nearest neighbors for regression
- Reducing the dimensions of our image data

Nearest neighbors

"We learn by example and by direct experience because there are real limits to the adequacy of verbal instruction."

– Malcolm Gladwell

It feels as if Malcolm Gladwell is explaining the K-nearest neighbors algorithm in the preceding quote; we only need to replace "*verbal instruction*" with "*mathematical equation.*" In cases such as linear models, training data is used to learn a mathematical equation that models the data. Once a model is learned, we can easily put the training data aside. Here, in the nearest neighbors algorithm, the data itself is the model. Whenever we encounter a new data sample, we compare it to the training dataset. We locate the K-nearest samples in the training set to the newly encountered sample, and then we use the class labels of the K samples in the training set to assign a label to the new sample.

A few things should be noted here:

- The concept of training doesn't really exist here. Unlike other algorithms, where the training time is dependent on the amount of training data, the computational cost is mostly spent in the nearest neighbors algorithm at prediction time.
- Most of the recent research done on the nearest neighbors algorithm is focused on finding the optimum ways to quickly search through the training data during prediction time.
- What does *nearest* mean? In this chapter, we will learn about the different distance measures used to compare different data points to each other. Two data points are deemed near to each other depending on the distance metric used.
- What is K? We can compare a new data point to 1, 2, 3, or 50 other samples in the training set. The number of samples we decide to compare to is K, and we are going to see how different values of K affect the behavior of the algorithms.

Before using the nearest neighbors algorithm for image classification, we need to first learn how to deal with images. In the next section, we will load and display one of the most commonly used image datasets in the field of machine learning and image processing.

When finding the nearest neighbors of a sample, you can compare it to all the other training samples. This is a naive brute-force approach that doesn't scale well with the size of the training data. A more efficient approach for larger datasets requires the training samples to be stored in a specific data structure that is optimized for search. K-D tree and ball tree are two available data structures. These two data structures are parameterized by `leaf_size`. As its value approaches the size of the training set, the K-D tree and ball tree turn into a brute-force search. Conversely, setting the leaf size to 1 introduces lots of overhead when traversing the trees. A default leaf size of 30 is good middle ground for many sample sizes.

Loading and displaying images

"Photographs are two-dimensional. I work in four dimensions."

– Tino Sehgal

When asked about the number of dimensions that an image has, photographers, painters, illustrators, and almost everyone else on this planet will agree that images are two-dimensional objects. Only machine learning practitioners see images differently. For us, every pixel in a black and white image is a separate dimension. Dimensions expand even more with colored images, but that's something for later. We see each pixel as a separate dimension so that we can deal with each pixel and its value as a unique feature that defines the image, along with the other pixels (features). So, unlike Tino Sehgal, we can sometimes end up working with 4,000 dimensions.

The **Modified National Institute of Standards and Technology** (**MNIST**) dataset is a collection of handwritten digits that is commonly used in image processing. Due to its popularity, it is included in `scikit-learn`, and we can load it as we usually do with other datasets:

```
from sklearn.datasets import load_digits
digits = load_digits()
```

The dataset has digits from 0 to 9. We can access their targets (labels) as follows:

```
digits['target']
# Output: array([0, 1, 2, ..., 8, 9, 8])
```

Similarly, we can load the pixel values, as follows:

```
digits['data']
# Output:
# array([[ 0., 0., 5., ..., 0., 0., 0.],
#        [ 0., 0., 0., ..., 10., 0., 0.],
#        ...,
#        [ 0., 0., 2., ..., 12., 0., 0.],
#        [ 0., 0., 10., ..., 12., 1., 0.]])
```

Each line is a picture and each integer is a pixel value. In this dataset, the pixels take values between 0 and 16. The shape of the dataset (`digits['data'].shape`) is *1,797 x 64*. In other words, we have 1,797 square-shaped pictures, and each of them has 64 pixels (width = height = 8).

Knowing this information, we can create the following function to display an image. It takes an array of 64 values and reshapes it into a two-dimensional array with 8 rows and 8 columns. It also uses the corresponding target of the image to show on top of the digit. The `matplotlib` axis (`ax`) is given so that we can display the image on it:

```
def display_img(img, target, ax):
    img = img.reshape((8, 8))
    ax.imshow(img, cmap='gray')
    ax.set_title(f'Digit: {str(target)}')
    ax.grid(False)
```

We can now use the function we just created to display the first eight digits of our dataset:

```
fig, axs = plt.subplots(1, 8, figsize=(15, 10))

for i in range(8):
    display_img(digits['data'][i], digits['target'][i], axs[i])

fig.show()
```

The digits look as follows:

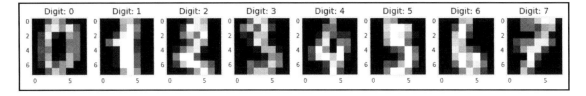

Being able to display the digits is a good first step. Next, we need to convert them into our usual training and test formats. This time, we want to keep each image as one row, so there is no need to reshape it into *8 x 8* matrices:

```
from sklearn.model_selection import train_test_split
x, y = digits['data'], digits['target']
x_train, x_test, y_train, y_test = train_test_split(x, y)
```

At this point, the data is ready to be used with an image classification algorithm. By learning to predict the targets when given a bunch of pixels, we are already one step closer to making our computer understand the handwritten text.

Image classification

Now that we have our data ready, we can predict the digits using the nearest neighbors classifier, as follows:

```
from sklearn.neighbors import KNeighborsClassifier

clf = KNeighborsClassifier(n_neighbors=11, metric='manhattan')
clf.fit(x_train, y_train)
y_test_pred = clf.predict(x_test)
```

For this example, I set `n_neighbors` to 11 and `metric` to `manhattan`, meaning at prediction time, we compare each new sample to the 11 nearest training samples, using the Manhattan distance to evaluate how near they are. More on these parameters in a bit. This model made predictions with an accuracy of 96.4% on the test set. This might sound reasonable, but I'm sorry to break it to you; this isn't a fantastic score for this particular dataset. Anyway, let's keep on dissecting the model's performance further.

Using a confusion matrix to understand the model's mistakes

When dealing with a dataset with 10 class labels, a single accuracy score can only tell us so much. To better understand what digits were harder to guess than others, we can print the model's confusion matrix. This is a square matrix where the actual labels are shown as rows and the predicted labels are shown as columns. Then, the numbers in each cell show the testing instances that fell into it. Let me create it now, and it will become clearer in a moment. The `plot_confusion_matrix` function needs the classifier's instance, along with the test's `x` and `y` values, to display the matrix:

```
from sklearn.metrics import plot_confusion_matrix
plot_confusion_matrix(clf, x_test, y_test, cmap='Greys')
```

Once called, the function runs the model internally on the test data and displays the following matrix:

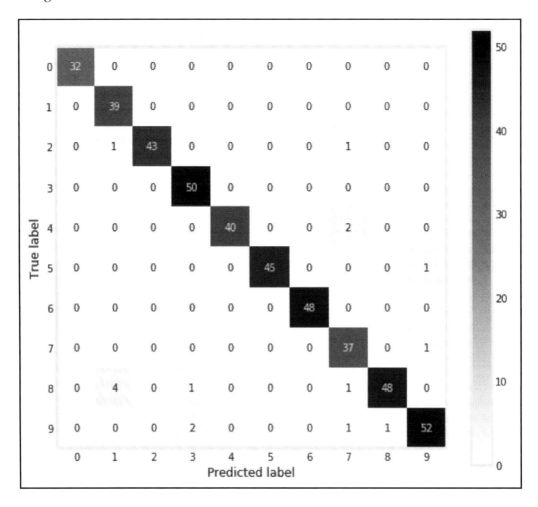

Ideally, all the cells should have zeros, except for the diagonal cells. Falling into a diagonal cell means that a sample is correctly labeled. However, there are only a few non-zero cells here. The four samples at the intersection of row 8 and column 1 signify that our model has classified four samples as 1, while their actual label was 8. Most likely, those were too-skinny eights that looked like ones to the algorithm. The same conclusions can be made for the remaining non-diagonal non-zero cells.

Picking a suitable metric

The images we are using are just lists of numbers (vectors). The distance metric decides whether one image is close to another. This also applies to non-image data, where distance metrics are used to decide whether one sample is close to another. Two commonly used metrics are the **Manhattan** and **Euclidean** distances:

Name	Manhattan (L1 norm)	Euclidean (L2 norm)
Formula	$d(x_1, x_2) = \sum_{i=1}^{n} \lvert x_{1i} - x_{2i} \rvert$	$d(x_1, x_2) = \sqrt[2]{\sum_{i=1}^{n}(x_{1i} - x_{2i})^2}$

Most likely, the equation for the Manhattan distance will remind you of the mean absolute error and L1 regularization, while the Euclidean distance resembles the mean squared error and L2 regularization. This resemblance is a nice reminder of how many concepts stem from common ideas:

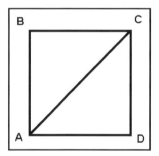

For the **Manhattan** distance, the distance between **A** and **C** is calculated by going from **A** to **D**, and then from **D** to **C**. It gets its name from Manhattan Island in New York, where its landscape is divided into blocks. For the **Euclidean** distance, the distance between **A** and **C** is calculated via the diagonal line between the two points. There is a generalized form for the two metrics, called the **Minkowski** distance, and here is its formula:

$$d(x_1, x_2) = \sqrt[2]{\sum_{i=1}^{\frac{1}{p}}(\lvert x_{1i} - x_{2i} \rvert)^p}$$

Setting p to 1 gives us the Manhattan distance, and we can get the Euclidean distance by setting it to 2. I am sure you can tell now where 1 and 2 in the L1 and L2 norms come from. To be able to compare the different values of p, we can run the following code. Here, we calculate the Minkowski distance for the two points—(1, 2) and (4, 6)—for different values of p:

```
from sklearn.neighbors import DistanceMetric

points = pd.DataFrame(
    [[1, 2], [4, 6]], columns=['x1', 'x2']
)

d = [
    (p, DistanceMetric.get_metric('minkowski', p=p).pairwise(points)[0][-1])
    for p in [1, 2, 10, 50, 100]
]
```

Plotting the results shows us how the Minkowski distance changes with p:

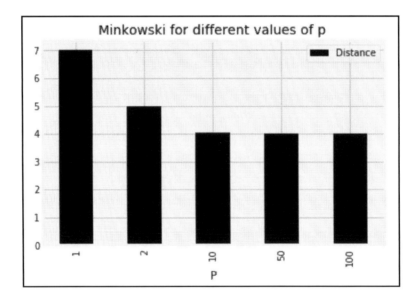

Clearly, the Minkowski distance decreases with an increase in p. For p = 1, the distance is 7, (4 - 1) + (6 - 2), and for p = 2, the distance is 5, the square root of (9 + 16). For higher values of p, the distance calculated approaches 4, which is (6 - 2) only. In other words, as p approaches infinity, the distance is just the maximum of all the spans between the points on all the axes, which is known as the Chebyshev distance.

The term *metric* is used to describe a distance measure that follows the following criteria:

It cannot be negative: $d(x_1, x_2) \geq 0$, and it is symmetric: $d(x_1, x_2) = d(x_2, x_1)$. The distance from one point to itself is 0. It follows the following triangle inequality criterion: $d(x_1, x_3) \leq d(x_1, x_2) + d(x_2, x_3)$.

Another common metric is the **cosine** distance, and its formula is as follows:

$$d(x1, x2) = \frac{\sum_i x_{1i} x_{2i}}{\sqrt{\sum_i x_{1i}} \sqrt{\sum_i x_{2i}}}$$

Unlike the Euclidean distance, the cosine distance is scale-insensitive. I think it would be better to show the difference between the two metrics with the following example.

Here, we take one digit and multiply each pixel value by 2:

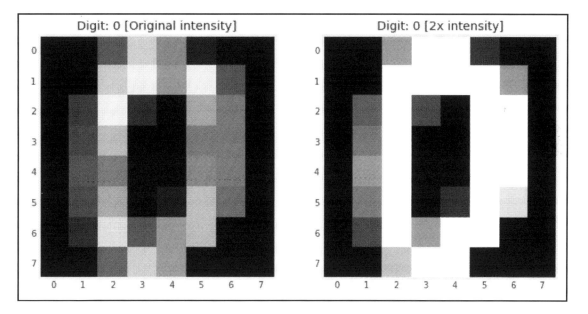

Now, let's calculate the distances between the original image and the intensified one:

```
from sklearn.metrics.pairwise import (
    euclidean_distances,
    manhattan_distances,
    cosine_distances
)

d0 = manhattan_distances(
  [1.0 * digits['data'][0], 2.0 * digits['data'][0]]
)[0,1]

d1 = euclidean_distances(
  [1.0 * digits['data'][0], 2.0 * digits['data'][0]]
)[0,1]

d2 = cosine_distances(
  [1.0 * digits['data'][0], 2.0 * digits['data'][0]]
)[0,1]
```

Running the preceding code gives us the values for each distance—Manhattan = 294, Euclidean = 55.41, and cosine = 0. As expected, the cosine distance does not care about the constant we used to multiply the pixels with, and it considers the two versions of the same images as one. The other two metrics, on the other hand, saw the two versions as further apart.

Setting the correct K

Equally important to metric selection is knowing how many neighbors to listen to when making a decision. You don't want to ask too few neighbors as maybe they don't know enough. You also don't want to ask everyone as the very distant neighbors probably don't know much about the sample at hand. To put it formally, a decision made based on too few neighbors introduces variance since any slight changes in the data will result in different neighborhoods and different results. Conversely, a decision made based on too many neighbors is a biased decision as it is less sensitive to the differences between the neighborhoods. Keep this in mind. Here, I used the model with different settings for *K* and plotted the resulting accuracy:

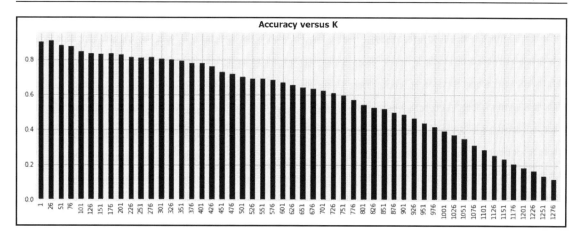

 The concept of bias-variance trade-off will follow us throughout this book. When it comes to picking sides, we usually opt to use a biased model when we have smaller training sets. A high-variance model will overfit if there isn't enough data to learn from. The most biased model is one where K is set to the number of training samples. Then, all the new data points will get the same prediction and will be assigned to the same label as the majority class. Conversely, when we have a good amount of data, the few closest neighbors within a smaller radius are a better choice to consult, as it's more likely that they will belong to the same class as our new sample.

Now, we have two hyperparameters to set: the number of neighbors and the distance metrics. In the next section, we are going to use a grid search to find the optimum values for these parameters.

Hyperparameter tuning using GridSearchCV

GridSearchCV is a method for looping over all the possible hyperparameter combinations and employing cross-validation to pick the optimum hyperparameters. For each hyperparameter combination, we do not want to limit ourselves to just one accuracy score. So, to get a better understanding of the estimator's accuracy of each combination, we make use of K-fold cross-validation. Then, the data is split into a number of folds, and for each iteration, all folds but one are used for training, and the remaining one is used for testing. This method for hyperparameter tuning performs an exhaustive search over all possible parameter combinations, hence the Grid prefix. In the following code, we give GridSearchCV a Python dictionary with all the parameter values we want to loop over, as well as the estimator we want to tune. We also specify the number of folds to split the data into, and then we call the grid search's fit method with the training data. Remember, it is bad practice to learn anything from the test dataset, which should be kept aside for now. Here is the code to do this:

```python
from sklearn.model_selection import GridSearchCV
from sklearn.neighbors import KNeighborsClassifier

parameters = {
    'metric':('manhattan','euclidean', 'cosine'),
    'n_neighbors': range(1, 21)
}

knn = KNeighborsClassifier()
gscv = GridSearchCV(knn, param_grid=parameters, scoring='accuracy')

gscv.fit(x_train, y_train)
```

Once done, we can show the best parameters found via gscv.best_params_. We can also show the accuracy achieved when using the chosen parameter via gscv.best_score_. Here, the euclidean distance was chosen as metric and n_neighbors was set to 3. I also got an accuracy score of 98.7% when using the chosen hyperparameters.

We can now use the resulting classifier to make predictions for the test set:

```python
from sklearn.metrics import accuracy_score

y_test_pred = gscv.predict(x_test)
accuracy_score(y_test, y_test_pred)
```

This gave me an accuracy of 98.0% on the test set. Luckily, the grid search helped us improve the accuracy of our estimator by picking the optimum hyperparameters.

GridSearchCV can become computationally expensive if we have too many hyperparameters to search through and too many values for each one. When facing a problem like this, RandomizedSearchCV may be an alternative solution since it randomly picks hyperparameter values while searching. Both hyperparameter tuning algorithms use the accuracy score by default for classifiers and R^2 for regressors. We can override this and specify different metrics to pick the best configuration.

Using custom distances

The digits here are written in white pixels over a black background. I don't think anyone would have a problem with identifying a digit if it was written in black pixels over a white background instead. As for a computer algorithm, things are a little different. Let's train our classifier as usual and see whether it will have any issues if the colors are inverted. We will start by training the algorithm on the original images:

```
clf = KNeighborsClassifier(n_neighbors=3, metric='euclidean')
clf.fit(x_train, y_train)
y_train_pred = clf.predict(x_train)
```

We then create an inverted version of the data we have just used for training:

```
x_train_inv = x_train.max() - x_train
```

The nearest neighbors implementation has a method called kneighbors. When given a sample, it returns a list of the K-nearest samples to it from the training set, as well as their distances from the given sample. We are going to give this method one of the inverted samples and see which samples it will consider as its neighbors:

```
img_inv = x_train_inv[0]

fig, axs = plt.subplots(1, 8, figsize=(14, 5))

display_img(img_inv, y_train[0], axs[0])

_, kneighbors_index_inv = clf.kneighbors(
    [x_train_inv[0]],
    n_neighbors=7,
    return_distance=True
)

for i, neighbor_index in enumerate(kneighbors_index_inv[0], 1):
```

```
display_img(
    x_train[neighbor_index],
    y_train[neighbor_index],
    axs[i]
)
```

Just to make things clearer, I ran the code twice—once with the original sample and its seven neighbors, and once with the inverted sample and its neighbors. The output of the two runs is displayed here. As you can see, unlike us humans, the algorithm got totally confused by the adversarial example where the colors were inverted:

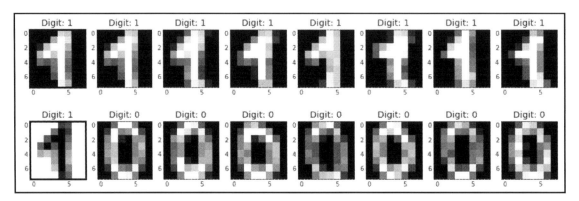

If you think about it, according to the distance we use, a sample and its inverted version cannot be too much further from each other. Although we visually see the two as one, the model sees them as different as day and night. Having that said, it is clear that we need to come up with a different way to evaluate distances. Since pixels take values between 0 and 16, in an inverted sample, all of the 16s are turned into 0s, the 15s are turned into 1s, and so on. Therefore, a distance that compares samples in relation to how far their pixels are from the midpoint between 0 and 16 (8) can help us solve our problem here. Here is how to create this custom distance. Let's call our new distance contrast_distance:

```
from sklearn.metrics.pairwise import euclidean_distances

def contrast_distance(x1, x2):
    _x1, _x2 = np.abs(8 - x1), np.abs(8 - x2)
    d = euclidean_distances([_x1], [_x2])
    return d[0][0]
```

Once defined, we can use the custom metric in our classifier, as follows:

```
clf = KNeighborsClassifier(n_neighbors=3, metric=contrast_distance)
clf.fit(x_train, y_train)
```

After this tweak, the inversion doesn't bother the model anymore. For the original and the inverted sets, we get the exact same accuracy of 89.3%. We can also print the seven nearest neighbors according to the new metric to validate the fact that the new model is already smarter and no longer discriminates against the black digits:

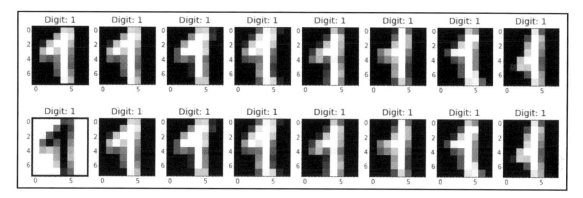

One thing to keep in mind when writing your own custom distances is that they are not as optimized as the built-in ones, and running the algorithm will be more computationally expensive at prediction time.

Using nearest neighbors for regression

At the end of the day, the targets we predict in the MNIST dataset are just numbers between 0 and 9. So, we can alternatively use a regressor algorithm for the same problem. In this case, our predictions will not be integers anymore, but rather floats. Training the regressor isn't much different from training the classifier:

```
from sklearn.neighbors import KNeighborsRegressor
clf = KNeighborsRegressor(n_neighbors=3, metric='euclidean')
clf.fit(x_train, y_train)
y_test_pred = clf.predict(x_test)
```

Here are some of the incorrectly made predictions:

	y_test	y_test_pred
117	3	3.666667
215	8	8.333333
304	7	7.666667

The first item's three nearest neighbors are 3, 3, and 5. So, the regressor used their mean (3.67) as the prediction. The second and third items' neighbors are 8, 9, 8 and 7, 9, 7, respectively. Remember to round these predictions and convert them into integers if you want to use a classifier's evaluation metric to evaluate this model.

More neighborhood algorithms

There are other variations of K-nearest neighbors that I'd like to quickly go through before moving on to the next section. These algorithms are less commonly used, although they have their merits as well as certain disadvantages.

Radius neighbors

Contrary to the K-nearest neighbors algorithm, where a certain number of neighbors are allowed to vote, in radius neighbors, all the neighbors within a certain radius participate in the voting process. By setting a predefined radius, the decisions in sparser neighborhoods are based on fewer neighbors than the ones made in denser neighborhoods. This can be useful when dealing with imbalanced classes. Furthermore, by using the haversine formula as our metric, we can use this algorithm to recommend nearby venues or gas stations on a map to the users. Both radius neighbors and K-nearest neighbors can give closer data points more voting power than distant ones by specifying the algorithm's `weights` parameter.

Nearest centroid classifier

As we have seen, the K-nearest neighbors algorithm compares the test samples to all of the samples in the training set. This exhaustive search causes the model to become slower at prediction time. To deal with this, the nearest centroid classifier summarizes all the training samples from each class into a pseudo-sample that represents this class. This pseudo-sample is called the centroid as it is typically created by calculating the mean value for each of the features in a class. At prediction time, a test sample is compared to all the centroids and is classified based on the class whose centroid is closest to it.

In the next section, we are going to use the centroid algorithm for training and prediction, but for now, we are going to use it to generate new digits just for fun. The algorithm is trained as follows:

```
from sklearn.neighbors import NearestCentroid
clf = NearestCentroid(metric='euclidean')
clf.fit(x_train, y_train)
```

The learned centroids are stored in `centroids_`. The following code displays these centroids, along with the class labels:

```
fig, axs = plt.subplots(1, len(clf.classes_), figsize=(15, 5))

for i, (centroid, label) in enumerate(zip(clf.centroids_, clf.classes_)):
    display_img(centroid, label, axs[i])

fig.show()
```

The generated digits are shown here:

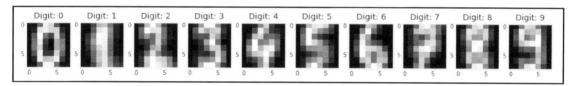

These digits do not exist in our dataset. They are just combinations of all the samples in each class.

The nearest centroid classifier is fairly simple, and I am sure you can implement it from scratch using a few lines of code. Its accuracy is not as good as nearest neighbors for the MNIST dataset, though. The centroid algorithm is more commonly used in natural language processing, where it's better known as Rocchio (pronounced like "we will rock you").

Finally, the centroid algorithm also has a hyperparameter called `shrink_threshold`. When set, this can help to remove the irrelevant features.

Reducing the dimensions of our image data

Earlier, we realized that the dimensionality of an image is equal to the number of pixels in it. So, there is no way to visualize our 43-dimensional MNIST dataset. It is true that we can display each digit separately, yet we cannot see where each image falls in our feature space. This is important to understand the classifier's decision boundaries. Furthermore, an estimator's memory requirements grow in proportion to the number of features in the training data. As a result, we need a way to reduce the number of features in our data to deal with the aforementioned issues.

In this section, we are going to discover two dimensionality-reduction algorithms: **Principal Component Analysis (PCA)** and **Neighborhood Component Analysis (NCA)**. After explaining them, we will use them to visualize the MNIST dataset and generate additional samples to add to our training set. Finally, we will also use **feature selection** algorithms to remove non-informative pixels from our images.

Principal component analysis

"A good photograph is knowing where to stand."

–Ansel Adams

Imagine having the following set of data with two features—x1 and x2:

	x1	x2
0	9.259916	28.129327
1	7.021191	23.122587
2	9.744407	29.393867
3	15.047500	44.300523
4	1.782589	6.445454
5	9.014174	26.074613
6	16.200623	48.464456
7	17.430507	52.386115

You can generate a previous data frame by using the following code snippet, keeping in mind that the numbers may vary on your machine, given their randomness:

```
df = pd.DataFrame(
    {
        'x1': np.random.normal(loc=10.0, scale=5.0, size=8),
        'noise': np.random.normal(loc=0.0, scale=1.0, size=8),
    }
)

df['x2'] = 3 * df['x1'] + df['noise']
```

When we plot the data, we realize that x1 and x2 take the following form:

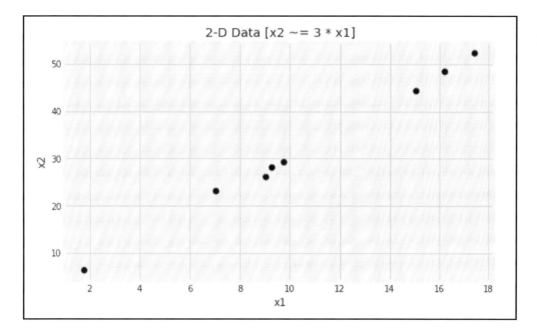

If you want, you can tilt your head to the left. Now, imagine we did not have the x1 and x2 axes, but instead had one diagonal axis that goes through the data. Wouldn't that axis be enough to represent our data? Then, we would have reduced it from a two-dimensional dataset into a one-dimensional dataset. That's exactly what PCA tries to achieve.

This new axis has one main characteristic—the distances between the points on it are more than their distances on the x1 or x2 axes. Remember, the hypotenuse of a triangle is always bigger than any of the two other sides. In conclusion, PCA tries to find a set of new axes (principal components) where the data variance is maximized.

Just like in the case of the correlation coefficient equation discussed in `Chapter 4`, *Preparing Your Data*, PCA also needs the data to be centered. For each column, we subtract the mean of the column from each value in it. We can use the `with_std =False` standard scaler to achieve this. Here is how to calculate the PCA and convert our data into the new dimensions:

```
from sklearn.preprocessing import StandardScaler
from sklearn.decomposition import PCA

scaler = StandardScaler(with_std=False)
x = scaler.fit_transform(df[['x1', 'x2']])

pca = PCA(n_components=1)
x_new = pca.fit_transform(x)
```

The resulting `x_new` value is a single column data frame instead of two. We can also access the newly created component via `pca.components_`. Here, I plotted the new component over the original data:

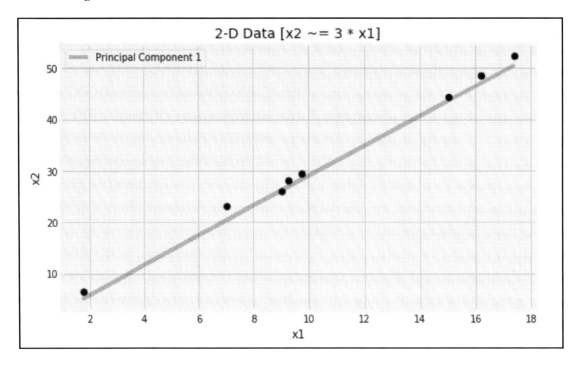

As you can see, we were able to use the PCA algorithm to reduce the number of features here from two to one. Since the dots don't fall exactly on the line, some information is lost by only using one component. This information is stored in the second component that we did not retrieve. You can transform your data into any number of components from one up to the original number of features. The components are ordered descendingly according to the amount of information they carry. Therefore, ignoring the latter components may help to remove any noisy and less-useful information. After transforming the data, it can also be transformed back (inverse transformation). The resulting data after the two operations only matches the original data if all the components are retained; otherwise, we can limit ourselves to the first few (principal) components to denoise the data.

In the PCA assumption, the directions in the feature space with the highest variance are expected to carry more information than the directions with lower variance. This assumption may hold in some cases, but it is not guaranteed to always be true. Remember that in PCA, the target is not used, only the features. This makes it more suitable for unlabeled data.

Neighborhood component analysis

In the nearest neighbors algorithms, the choice of the distance measure is paramount, yet it is only set empirically. We used K-fold cross-validation earlier in this chapter to decide which distance metric is better for our problem. This can be time-consuming, which triggers many researchers to look for better solutions. The main aim of NCA is to learn the distance metric from the data using gradient descend. The distances it tries to learn are usually represented by a square matrix. For N samples, we have $N \times N$ sample pairs to compare, hence the square matrix. Nevertheless, this matrix can be restricted to become a rectangular one, $N \times n$, where the small n is a lower number than N and represents the reduced components. These reduced components are the building blocks of NCA.

The nearest neighbors algorithms belong to a class of learners called instance-based learners. We use instances of the training set to make decisions. So, the matrix that carries the distances between the instances is an essential part of it. This matrix inspired many researchers to do research on it. For example, learning the distances from data is what NCA and large-margin nearest neighbors do; other researchers converted this matrix into a higher dimensional space—for example, with the kernel trick—and others tried to embed feature selection into the instance-based learners via regularization.

In the next section, we will visually compare the two dimensionality-reduction methods by using them to plot the MNIST dataset onto a two-dimensional graph.

Comparing PCA to NCA

We will reduce the dimensionality of the data by projecting it into a smaller space. We will use **PCA** and **NCA** in addition to random projection. We will start by importing the required models and putting the three algorithms into a Python dictionary to loop over them later on:

```
from sklearn.preprocessing import StandardScaler
from sklearn.random_projection import SparseRandomProjection
from sklearn.decomposition import PCA
from sklearn.neighbors import NeighborhoodComponentsAnalysis

methods = {
    'Rand': SparseRandomProjection(n_components=2),
    'PCA': PCA(n_components=2),
    'NCA': NeighborhoodComponentsAnalysis(n_components=2, init='random'),
}
```

Then, we will create three plots side by side for the three algorithms, as follows:

```
fig, axs = plt.subplots(1, 3, figsize=(15, 5))

for i, (method_name, method_obj) in enumerate(methods.items()):

    scaler = StandardScaler(with_std=False)
    x_train_scaled = scaler.fit_transform(x_train)

    method_obj.fit(x_train_scaled, y_train)
    x_train_2d = method_obj.transform(x_train_scaled)

    for target in set(y_train):
        pd.DataFrame(
            x_train_2d[
                y_train == target
            ], columns=['y', 'x']
        ).sample(n=20).plot(
            kind='scatter', x='x', y='y',
            marker=f'${target}$', s=64, ax=axs[i]
        )
        axs[i].set_title(f'{method_name} MNIST')
```

It is important to center your data before applying PCA. We used `StandardScaler` to do this. Other algorithms shouldn't mind the centering, anyway. Running the code gives us the following graphs:

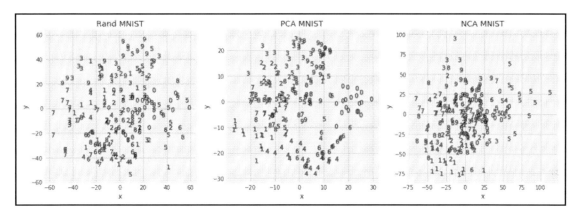

PCA and NCA do a better job than random projection in clustering the same digits together. In addition to the visual analysis, we can run the nearest neighbors algorithm on the reduced data to judge which transformation represents the data better. We can use similar code to the preceding one and replace the part inside the `for` loop with the following two chunks of code:

1. First, we need to scale and transform our data:

```
from sklearn.preprocessing import StandardScaler
from sklearn.preprocessing import MinMaxScaler

scaler = StandardScaler(with_std=False)

x_train_scaled = scaler.fit_transform(x_train)
x_test_scaled = scaler.fit_transform(x_test)

method_obj.fit(x_train_scaled, y_train)
x_train_2d = method_obj.transform(x_train_scaled)
x_test_2d = method_obj.transform(x_test_scaled)

scaler = MinMaxScaler()
x_train_scaled = scaler.fit_transform(x_train_2d)
x_test_scaled = scaler.transform(x_test_2d)
```

2. Then, we use cross-validation to set the optimum hyperparameters:

```
from sklearn.neighbors import KNeighborsClassifier
from sklearn.model_selection import GridSearchCV
from sklearn.metrics import accuracy_score

parameters = {'metric':('manhattan','euclidean'), 'n_neighbors':
range(3, 9)}

knn = KNeighborsClassifier()
clf = GridSearchCV(knn, param_grid=parameters, scoring='accuracy',
cv=5)

clf.fit(x_train_scaled, y_train)
y_test_pred = clf.predict(x_test_scaled)

print(
    'MNIST test accuracy score: {:.1%} [k={}, metric={} -
{}]'.format(
        accuracy_score(y_test, y_test_pred),
        clf.best_params_['n_neighbors'],
        clf.best_params_['metric'],
        method_name
    )
)
```

Since we do not need to visualize the data this time, we can set the number of components to 6. This gives us the following accuracy scores. Keep in mind that your results may vary due to the random split of the data and the estimator's initial values:

Projection	Accuracy
Sparse random projection	73%
PCA	93%
NCA	95%

 In PCA, the class labels are not needed. I just passed them in the preceding code for consistency, but they were simply ignored by the algorithm. In comparison, in NCA, the class labels are used by the algorithm.

Picking the most informative components

After fitting PCA, `explained_variance_ratio_` contains the percentage of variance explained by each of the selected components. According to the principal components hypothesis, higher ratios should reflect more information. We can put this information into a data frame, as follows:

```
df_explained_variance_ratio = pd.DataFrame(
    [
        (component, explained_variance_ratio)
        for component, explained_variance_ratio in
enumerate(pca.explained_variance_ratio_[:32], 1)
    ], columns=['component', 'explained_variance_ratio']
)
```

Then, plot it to get the following graph. I am sure plotting data via bar charts is becoming second nature to you by now:

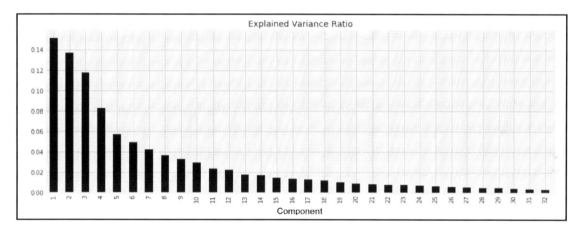

From the graph, we can tell that starting from the eighth component, the remaining components carry less than 5% of the information.

We can also loop through different values for `n_components`, and then train a model on the reduced data and see how the accuracy changes with the number of components used. I'd trust this approach more than relying on the explained variance since it is independent of the principal components assumption and evaluates the feature reduction algorithm and the classifier as a single black box. This time, I am going to use a different algorithm: nearest centroid.

Using the centroid classifier with PCA

In the following code, we will try the centroid algorithm with a different number of principal components each time. Please don't forget to scale and transform your features with each iteration, and remember to store the resulting x values in x_train_embed and x_test_embed. I used StandardScaler here, as well as the PCA's transform method, to transform the scaled data:

```
from sklearn.neighbors import NearestCentroid

scores = []
for n_components in range(1, 33, 1):

    # Scale and transform the features as before
    clf = NearestCentroid(shrink_threshold=0.01)
    clf.fit(x_train_embed, y_train)
    y_test_pred = clf.predict(x_test_embed)

    scores.append([n_components, accuracy_score(y_test, y_test_pred)])
```

Plotting the scores gives us the following graph:

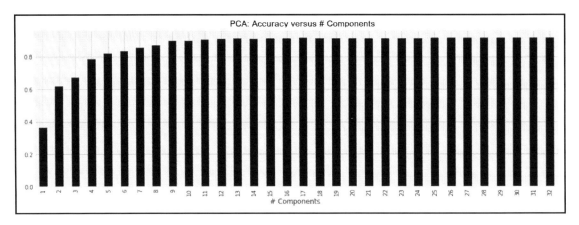

When we use the centroid algorithm with this dataset, we can roughly see that anything above 15 components doesn't add much value. With the help of cross-validation, we can pick the exact number of components that gives best results.

Restoring the original image from its components

Once an image is reduced to its principal components, it can also be restored back, as follows.

1. First, you have to scale your data before using PCA:

```
from sklearn.preprocessing import StandardScaler
scaler = StandardScaler(with_std=False)
x_train_scaled = scaler.fit_transform(x_train)
x_test_scaled = scaler.transform(x_test)
```

Once scaled, you can transform your data using 32 principal components, as follows.

2. Then, you can restore the original data after transformation by using the `inverse_transform` method:

```
from sklearn.decomposition import PCA
embedder = PCA(n_components=32)
embedder.fit(x_train, y_train)

x_train_embed = embedder.transform(x_train_scaled)
x_test_embed = embedder.transform(x_test_scaled)

x_train_restored = embedder.inverse_transform(x_train_embed)
x_test_restored = embedder.inverse_transform(x_test_embed)
```

3. To keep the original images and the restored ones on the same scale, we can use `MinMaxScaler`, as follows:

```
iscaler = MinMaxScaler((x_train.min(), x_train.max()))
x_train_restored = iscaler.fit_transform(x_train_restored)
x_test_restored = iscaler.fit_transform(x_test_restored)
```

Here, you can see a comparison between some digits and themselves, with the less important components removed. These restored versions of the original data can be useful to the classifier, either by using them in place of the training and test sets, or by adding them as additional samples to the training set:

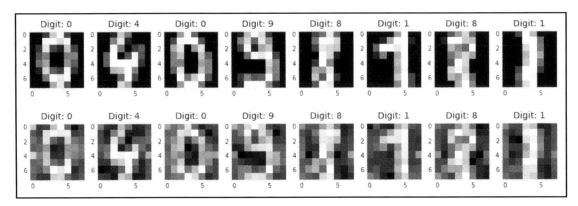

4. Finally, I used `x_train_embed` and `x_test_embed` in place of the original features in our nearest neighbors classifier. I tried a different number of PCA components each time. The darker bars in the following graph show the number of PCA components that resulted in the highest accuracy scores:

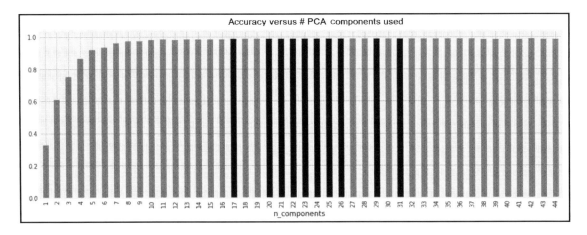

Not only did PCA help us reduce the number of features and the prediction time consequently, but it also helped us achieve a score of 98.9%.

Finding the most informative pixels

Since almost all of the digits are centered in the images, we can intuitively deduce that the pixels on the right and left edges of the images do not carry valuable information. To validate our intuition, we will let the feature selection algorithms from Chapter 4, *Preparing Your Data*, decide for us which pixels are most important. Here, we can use the mutual information algorithm to return a list of pixels and their corresponding importance:

```
from sklearn.feature_selection import mutual_info_classif
mi = mutual_info_classif(x_train, y_train)
```

We then use the preceding information to remove 75% of the pixels:

```
percent_to_remove = 75
mi_threshold = np.quantile(mi, 0.01 * percent_to_remove)
informative_pixels = (mi >= mi_threshold).reshape((8, 8))

plt.imshow(informative_pixels, cmap='Greys')
plt.title(f'Pixels kept when {percent_to_remove}% removed')
```

In the following diagram, the pixels marked in black are the most informative ones, and the rest are the 75% of the pixels that are deemed less important by the mutual information algorithm:

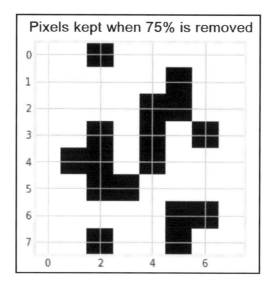

As expected, the pixels on the edges are less informative. Now that we have identified the less informative pixels, we can reduce the number of features in our data by removing the less informative pixels, as follows:

```
from sklearn.feature_selection import SelectPercentile
percent_to_keep = 100 - percent_to_remove
selector = SelectPercentile(mutual_info_classif,
percentile=percent_to_keep)

x_train_mi = selector.fit_transform(x_train, y_train)
x_test_mi = selector.transform(x_test)
```

Training a classifier on the reduced features gives us an accuracy score of 94%. Knowing that the complexity of the nearest neighbors algorithm and its prediction time grows with the number of features, we can understand the value of a slightly less accurate algorithm that only uses **25%** of the data.

Summary

Images are in abundance in our day-to-day life. Robots need computer vision to understand their surroundings. The majority of the posts on social media include pictures. Handwritten documents require image processing to make them consumable by machines. These and many more uses cases are the reason why image processing is an essential competency for machine learning practitioners to master. In this chapter, we learned how to load images and make sense of their pixels. We also learned how to classify images and reduce their dimensions for better visualization and further manipulation.

We used the nearest neighbor algorithm for image classification and regression. This algorithm allowed us to plug our own metrics when needed. We also learned about other algorithms, such as radius neighbors and nearest centroid. The concepts behind these algorithms and their differences are omnipresent in the field of machine learning. Later on, we will see how the clustering and anomaly detection algorithms borrow ideas from the concepts discussed here. In addition to the main algorithms discussed here, concepts such as distance metrics and dimensionality reduction are also ubiquitous.

Due to the importance of image processing, we will not stop here, as we are going to build on the knowledge acquired here in Chapter 7, *Neural Networks – Here Comes the Deep Learning*, where we will use artificial neural networks for image classification.

6

Classifying Text Using Naive Bayes

"Language is a process of free creation; its laws and principles are fixed, but the manner in which the principles of generation are used is free and infinitely varied. Even the interpretation and use of words involves a process of free creation."

– Noam Chomsky

Not all information exists in tables. From Wikipedia to social media, there are billions of written words that we would like our computers to process and extract bits of information from. The sub-field of machine learning that deals with textual data goes by names such as **Text Mining** and **Natural Language Processing** (**NLP**). These different names reflect the fact that the field inherits from multiple disciplines. On the one hand, we have computer science and statistics, and on the other hand, we have linguistics. I'd argue that the influence of linguistics was stronger when the field was at its infancy, but in later stages, practitioners came to favor mathematical and statistical tools, as they require less human intervention and can get away without humans manually codifying linguistic rules into the algorithms:

"Every time I fire a linguist, the performance of our speech recognition system goes up."

– Fred Jelinek

Having said that, it is essential to have a basic understanding of how things have progressed over time and not jump to the bleeding-edge solutions right away. This enables us to pick our tools wisely while being aware of the tradeoffs we are making. Thus, we will start this chapter by processing textual data and presenting it to our algorithms in formats they understand. This preprocessing stage has an important effect on the performance of the downstream algorithms. Therefore, I will make sure to shed light on the pros and cons of each method explained here. Once the data is ready, we will use a **Naive Bayes** classifier to detect the sentiment of different Twitter users based on the messages they send to multiple airway services.

In this chapter, the following topics will be covered:

- Splitting sentences into tokens
- Token normalization
- Using bag of words to represent tokens
- Using n-grams to represent tokens
- Using Word2Vec to represent tokens
- Text classification with a Naive Bayes classifier

Splitting sentences into tokens

"A word after a word after a word is power."

– Margaret Atwood

So far, the data we have dealt with has either been table data with columns as features or image data with pixels as features. In the case of text, things are less obvious. Shall we use sentences, words, or characters as our features? Sentences are very specific. For example, it is very unlikely to have the exact same sentence appearing in two or more Wikipedia articles. Therefore, if we use sentences as features, we will end up with tons of features that do not generalize well.

Characters, on the other hand, are limited. For example, there are only 26 letters in the English language. This small variety is likely to limit the ability of the separate characters to carry enough information for the downstream algorithms to extract. As a result, words are typically used as features for most tasks.

Later in this chapter, we will see that fairly specific tokens are still possible, but let's stick to words as features for now. Finally, we do not want to limit ourselves to dictionary words; Twitter hashtags, numbers, and URLs can also be extracted from text and treated as features. That's why we prefer to use the term *token* instead *word*, since it is more generic. The process where a stream of text is split into tokens is called tokenization, and we are going to learn about that in the next section.

Tokenizing with string split

Different tokenization methods lead to different results. To demonstrate these differences, let's take the following three lines of text and see how can we tokenize them.

Here I write the lines of text as strings and put them into a list:

```
lines = [
    'How to tokenize?\nLike a boss.',
    'Google is accessible via http://www.google.com',
    '1000 new followers! #TwitterFamous',
]
```

One obvious way to do this is to use Python's built-in `split()` method as follows:

```
for line in lines:
    print(line.split())
```

When no parameters are given, `split()` uses white spaces to split strings based on. Thus, we get the following output:

```
['How', 'to', 'tokenize?', 'Like', 'a', 'boss.']
['Google', 'is', 'accessible', 'via', 'http://www.google.com']
['1000', 'new', 'followers!', '#TwitterFamous']
```

You may notice that the punctuation was kept as part of the tokens. The question mark was left at the end of `tokenize`, and the period remained attached to `boss`. The hashtag is made of two words, but since there are no spaces between them, it was kept as a single token along with its leading hash sign.

Tokenizing using regular expressions

We may also use regular expressions to treat sequences of letters and numbers as tokens, and split our sentences accordingly. The pattern used here, "\w+", refers to any sequence of one or more alphanumeric characters or underscores. Compiling our patterns gives us a regular expression object that we can use for matching. Finally, we loop over each line and use the regular expression object to split it into tokens:

```
import re
_token_pattern = r"\w+"
token_pattern = re.compile(_token_pattern)

for line in lines:
    print(token_pattern.findall(line))
```

This gives us the following output:

```
['How', 'to', 'tokenize', 'Like', 'a', 'boss']
['Google', 'is', 'accessible', 'via', 'http', 'www', 'google', 'com']
['1000', 'new', 'followers', 'TwitterFamous']
```

Now, the punctuation has been removed, but the URL has been split into four tokens.

> Scikit-learn uses regular expressions for tokenization by default. However, the following pattern, r"(?u)\b\w\w+\b", is used instead of r"\w+". This pattern ignores all punctuation and words shorter than two letters. So, the "a" token would be omitted. You can still overwrite the default pattern by providing your custom one.

Using placeholders before tokenizing

To deal with the previous problem, we may decide to replace the numbers, URLs, and hashtags with placeholders before tokenizing our sentences. This is useful if we don't really care to differentiate between their content. A URL may be just a URL to me, regardless of where it leads to. The following function converts its input into lower case, then replaces any URL it finds with a _url_ placeholder. Similarly, it converts the hashtags and numbers into their corresponding placeholders. Finally, the input is split based on white spaces, and the resulting tokens are returned:

```
_token_pattern = r"\w+"
token_pattern = re.compile(_token_pattern)

def tokenizer(line):
    line = line.lower()
```

```
        line = re.sub(r'http[s]?://[\w\/\-\.\?]+','_url_', line)
        line = re.sub(r'#\w+', '_hashtag_', line)
        line = re.sub(r'\d+','_num_', line)
        return token_pattern.findall(line)

    for line in lines:
        print(tokenizer(line))
```

This gives us the following output:

```
['how', 'to', 'tokenize', 'like', 'a', 'boss']
['google', 'is', 'accessible', 'via', '_url_']
['_num_', 'new', 'followers', '_hashtag_']
```

As you can see, the new placeholder tells us that a URL existed in the second sentence, but it doesn't really care where the URL links to. If we have another sentence with a different URL, it will just get the same placeholder as well. The same goes for the numbers and hashtags.

Depending on your use case, this may not be ideal if your hashtags carry information that you would not like to lose. Again, this is a tradeoff you have to make based on your use case. Usually, you can intuitively tell which technique is more suitable for the problem at hand, but sometimes evaluating a model after multiple tokenization techniques can be the only way to tell which one is more suitable. Finally, in practice, you may use libraries such as **NLTK** and **spaCy** to tokenize your text. They already have the necessary regular expressions under the hood. We will be using spaCy later on in this chapter.

Note how I converted the sentence into lower case before processing it. This is called normalization. Without normalization, a capitalized word and a lowercase version of it will be seen as two different tokens. This is not ideal, since *Boy* and *boy* are conceptually the same, hence normalization is usually required. Scikit-learn converts input text to lower case by default.

Vectorizing text into matrices

In text mining, a dataset is usually called a **corpus**. Each data sample in it is usually called a **document**. Documents are made of **tokens**, and a set of distinct tokens is called a **vocabulary**. Putting this information into a matrix is called **vectorization**. In the following sections, we are going to see the different kinds of vectorizations that we can get.

Vector space model

We still miss our beloved feature matrices, where we expect each token to have its own column and each document to be represented by a separate row. This kind of representation for textual data is known as the **vector space model**. From a linear-algebraic point of view, the documents in this representation are seen as vectors (rows), and the different terms are the dimensions of this space (columns), hence the name vector space model. In the next section, we will learn how to vectorize our documents.

Bag of words

We need to convert the documents into tokens and put them into the vector space model. CountVectorizer can be used here to tokenize the documents and put them into the desired matrix. Here, we are going to use it with the help of the tokenizer we created in the previous section. As usual, we import and initialize CountVectorizer, and then we use its fit_transform method to convert our documents. We also specified that we want to use the tokenizer we built in the previous section:

```
from sklearn.feature_extraction.text import CountVectorizer
vec = CountVectorizer(lowercase=True, tokenizer=tokenizer)
x = vec.fit_transform(lines)
```

Most of the cells in the returned matrix are zeros. To save space, it is saved as a sparse matrix; however, we can turn it into a dense matrix using its todense() method. The vectorizer holds the set of encountered vocabulary, which can be retrieved using get_feature_names(). Using this information, we can convert x into a DataFrame as follows:

```
pd.DataFrame(
    x.todense(),
    columns=vec.get_feature_names()
)
```

This gives us the following matrix:

doc-id	_hashtag_	_num_	_url_	a	accessible	boss	followers	google	how	is	like	new	to	tokenize	via
0	0	0	0	1	0	1	0	0	1	0	1	0	1	1	0
1	0	0	1	0	1	0	0	1	0	1	0	0	0	0	1
2	1	1	0	0	0	0	1	0	0	0	0	1	0	0	0

Each cell contains the number of times each token appears in each document. However, the vocabulary does not follow any order; therefore, it is not possible to tell the order of the tokens in each document from this matrix.

Different sentences, same representation

Take these two sentences with opposite meanings:

```
flight_delayed_lines = [
    'Flight was delayed, I am not happy',
    'Flight was not delayed, I am happy'
]
```

If we use the count vectorizer to represent them, we will end up with the following matrix:

doc-id	am	delayed	flight	happy	not	was
0	1	1	1	1	1	1
1	1	1	1	1	1	1

As you can see, the order of the tokens in the sentences is lost. That is why this method is known as **bag of words** – the result is like a bag that words are just put into without any order. Obviously, this makes it impossible to tell which of the two people is happy and which is not. To fix this problem, we may need to use **n-grams**, as we will do in the following section.

N-grams

Rather than treating each term as a token, we can treat the combinations of each two consecutive terms as a single token. All we have to do is to set ngram_range in CountVectorizer to (2,2), as follows:

```
from sklearn.feature_extraction.text import CountVectorizer
vec = CountVectorizer(ngram_range=(2,2))
x = vec.fit_transform(flight_delayed_lines)
```

Using similar code to that used in the previous section, we can put the resulting x into a DataFrame and get the following matrix:

doc-id	am happy	am not	delayed am	flight was	not delayed	not happy	was delayed	was not
0	0	1	1	1	0	1	1	0
1	1	0	1	1	1	0	0	1

Now we can tell who is happy and who is not. When using word pairs, this is known as **bigrams**. We can also do 3-grams (with three consecutive words), 4-grams, or any other number of grams. Setting ngram_range to (1,1) takes us back to the original representation where each separate word is a token, which is **unigrams**. We can also mix unigrams with bigrams by setting ngram_range to (1,2). In brief, this range tells the tokenizer the minimum and maximum values for *n* to use in our n-grams.

If you set *n* to a high value – say, 8 – this means that sequences of eight words are treated as tokens. Now, how likely do you think it is that a sequence of eight words will appear more than once in your dataset? Most likely, you will see it once in your training set and never again into the test set. That's why *n* is usually set to something between 2 and 3, with some unigrams also being used to capture rare words.

Using characters instead of words

Up until now, words have been the atoms of our textual universe. However, some situations may require us to tokenize our documents based on characters instead. In situations where word boundaries are not clear, such as in hashtags and URLs, the use of characters as tokens may help. Natural languages tend to have different frequencies for their characters. The letter **e** is the most commonly used character in the English language, and character combinations such as **th**, **er**, and **on** are also very common. Other languages, such as French and Dutch, have different character frequencies. If our aim is to classify documents based on their languages, the use of characters instead of words can come in handy.

The very same `CountVectorizer` can help us tokenize our documents into characters. We can also combine this with the `n-grams` setting to get subsequences within words, as follows:

```
from sklearn.feature_extraction.text import CountVectorizer
vec = CountVectorizer(analyzer='char', ngram_range=(4,4))
x = vec.fit_transform(flight_delayed_lines)
```

We can put the resulting `x` into a DataFrame, as we did earlier, to get the following matrix:

doc-id	am	del	hap	i a	not	was	,i	am h	am n	appy	...	not	ot d	ot h	s de	s no	t de	t ha	t wa	was	yed,
0	1	1	1	1	1	1	1	0	1	1	...	1	0	1	1	0	0	1	1	1	1
1	1	1	1	1	1	1	1	1	0	1	...	1	1	0	0	1	1	0	1	1	1

All our tokens are made of four characters now. Whitespaces are also treated as characters, as you can see. With characters, it is more common to go for higher values of *n*.

Capturing important words with TF-IDF

Another discipline that we borrow lots of ideas from here is the **information retrieval** field. It's the field responsible for the algorithms that run search engines such as Google, Bing, and DuckDuckGo.

Now, take the following quotation:

> *"From a linguistic point of view, you can't really take much objection to the notion that a show is a show is a show."*

> – *Walter Becker*

The word **linguistic** and the word **that** both appeared exactly once in the previous quotation. Nevertheless, we would only worry about the word **linguistic**, not the word **that**, if we were searching for this quotation on the internet. We know that it is more significant, although it appeared only once, just as many times as **that**. The word **show** appeared three times. From a count vectorizer's point of view, it should carry three times more information than the word **linguistic**. I assume you also disagree with the vectorizer about that. Those issues are fundamentally the raison d'être of **Term Frequency-Inverse Document Frequency** (**TF-IDF**). The IDF part not only involves weighting the value of the words based on how frequently they appear in a certain document, but also discounting weights from them if they happen to be very common in other documents. The word **that** is so common across other documents that it shouldn't be given as much value as **linguistic**. Furthermore, IDF uses a logarithmic scale to better represent the information a word carries based on its frequency in a document.

Let's use the following three documents to demonstrate how TF-IDF works:

```
lines_fruits = [
    'I like apples',
    'I like oranges',
    'I like pears',
]
```

`TfidfVectorizer` has an almost identical interface to that of `CountVectorizer`:

```
from sklearn.feature_extraction.text import TfidfVectorizer
vec = TfidfVectorizer(token_pattern=r'\w+')
x = vec.fit_transform(lines_fruits)
```

Here is a comparison for the outputs of the two vectorizers side by side:

CountVectorizer	apples	i	like	oranges	pears	TfidfVectorizer	apples	i	like	oranges	pears
0	1.0	1.0	1.0	0.0	0.0	0	0.77	0.45	0.45	0.00	0.00
1	0.0	1.0	1.0	1.0	0.0	1	0.00	0.45	0.45	0.77	0.00
2	0.0	1.0	1.0	0.0	1.0	2	0.00	0.45	0.45	0.00	0.77

As you can see, unlike in `CountVectorizer`, not all words were treated equally by `TfidfVectorizer`. More emphasis was given to the fruit names compared to the other, less informative words that happened to appear in all three sentences.

Both CountVectorizer and TfidfVectorizer have a parameter called stop_words. It can be used to specify tokens to be ignored. You can provide your own list of less informative words, such as **a**, **an**, and **the**. You can also provide the english keyword to specify the common stop words in the English language. Having said that, it is important to note that some words can be informative for one task but not for another. Furthermore, IDF usually does what you need it to do automatically and gives low weights to non-informative words. That is why I usually prefer not to manually remove stop words, instead trying things such as TfidfVectorizer, feature selection, and regularization first.

Besides its original use case, TfidfVectorizer is commonly used as a preprocessing step for text classification. Nevertheless, it usually gives good results when longer documents are to be classified. For short documents, it may produce noisy transformation, and it is advised to give CountVectorizer a try in such cases.

In a basic search engine, when someone types a query, it gets converted into the same vector space where all the documents to be searched exist, using TF-IDF. Once the search query and the documents exist as vectors in the same space, a simple distance measure such as cosine distance can be used to find the closest documents to the query. Modern search engines vary from this basic idea, but it is a good base to build your understanding of information retrieval on.

Representing meanings with word embedding

As documents are collections of tokens, their vector representations are basically the sum of the vectors of the tokens they contain. As we have seen earlier, the **I like apples** document was represented by CountVectorizer using the vector [1,1,1,0,0]:

	apples	i	like	oranges	pears
CountVectorizer					
0	1.0	1.0	1.0	0.0	0.0
1	0.0	1.0	1.0	1.0	0.0

From this representation, we can also deduce that the terms **I**, **like**, **apples**, and **oranges** are represented by the following four five-dimensional vectors, [0,1,0,0,0], [0,0,1,0,0], [1,0,0,0,0], and [0,0,0,1,0]. We have a five-dimensional space, given our vocabulary of five terms. Each term has a magnitude of 1 in one dimension and 0 in the other four dimensions. From a linear algebraic point of view, all five terms are orthogonal (perpendicular) to each other. Nevertheless, **apples**, **pears**, and **oranges** are all fruits, and conceptually they have some similarity that was not captured by this model. Therefore, we would ideally like to represent them with vectors that are closer to each other, unlike these orthogonal vectors. The same issue here applied to `TfidfVectorizer`, by the way. This was the driver for researchers to come up with better representations, and word embedding is the coolest kid on the natural language processing block nowadays, as it tries to capture meaning better than traditional vectorizers. In the next section, we will get to know one popular embedding technique, Word2Vec.

Word2Vec

Without getting into the details too much, Word2Vec uses neural networks to predict words from their context, that is, from their surrounding words. By doing so, it learns better representations for the different words, and these representations incorporate the meanings of the words they represent. Unlike the previously mentioned vectorizers, the dimensionality of the word representation is not directly linked to the size of our vocabulary. We get to choose the length of our embedding vectors. Once each word is represented by a vector, the document's representation is usually the summation of all the vectors of its words. Averaging is also an option instead of summation.

Since the size of our vectors is independent of the size of the vocabulary of the documents we are dealing with, researchers can reuse a pre-trained Word2Vec model that wasn't made specifically for their particular problem. This ability to re-use pre-trained models is known as transfer learning. Some researchers can train an embedding on a huge amount of documents using expensive machines and release the resulting vectors for the entire world to use. Then, the next time we deal with a specific natural language processing task, all we need to do is to get these vectors and use them to represent our new documents. spaCy (`https://spacy.io/`) is an open source software library that comes with word vectors for different languages.

In the following few lines of code, we will install spaCy, download its language model data, and use it to convert words into vectors:

1. To use spaCy, we can install the library and download its pre-trained models for the English language by running the following commands in our terminal:

```
pip install spacy
python -m spacy download en_core_web_lg
```

2. Then, we can assign the downloaded vectors to our five words as follows:

```
import spacy
nlp = spacy.load('en_core_web_lg')

terms = ['I', 'like', 'apples', 'oranges', 'pears']
vectors = [
    nlp(term).vector.tolist() for term in terms
]
```

3. Here is the representation for **apples**:

```
# pd.Series(vectors[terms.index('apples')]).rename('apples')

0       -0.633400
1        0.189810
2       -0.535440
3       -0.526580
          ...
296     -0.238810
297     -1.178400
298      0.255040
299      0.611710
Name: apples, Length: 300, dtype: float64
```

I promised you that the representations for **apples**, **oranges**, and **pears** would not be orthogonal as in the case with `CountVectorizer`. However, with 300 dimensions, it is hard for me to visually prove that. Luckily, we have already learned how to calculate the cosine of the angle between two vectors. Orthogonal vectors should have 90° angles between them, whose cosines are equal to 0. The cosine for the zero angle between two vectors going in the exact same direction is 1.

Here, we calculate the cosine between all the five vectors we got from spaCy. I used some pandas and seaborn styling to make the numbers clearer:

```
import seaborn as sns
from sklearn.metrics.pairwise import cosine_similarity
```

```
cm = sns.light_palette("Gray", as_cmap=True)

pd.DataFrame(
    cosine_similarity(vectors),
    index=terms, columns=terms,
).round(3).style.background_gradient(cmap=cm)
```

Then, I showed the results in the following DataFrame:

	I	like	apples	oranges	pears
I	1	0.555	0.204	0.188	0.204
like	0.555	1	0.33	0.277	0.33
apples	0.204	0.33	1	0.778	1
oranges	0.188	0.277	0.778	1	0.778
pears	0.204	0.33	1	0.778	1

Clearly, the new representation understands that fruit names are more similar to each other than they are to words such as **I** and **like**. It also considered **apples** and **pears** to be very similar to each other, as opposed to **oranges**.

You may have noticed that Word2Vec suffers from the same problem as unigrams; words are encoded without much attention being paid to their context. The representation for the word "book" in "I will read a book" is the same as its representation in "I will book a flight." That's why newer techniques, such as **Embeddings from Language Models (ELMo)**, **Bidirectional Encoder Representations from Transformers (BERT)** and OpenAI's recent **GPT-3** are gaining more popularity nowadays as they respect the words' context. I expect them to be included in more libraries soon for anyone to easily use them.

The embedding concept is recycled and reused by machine learning practitioners everywhere nowadays. Apart from its use in natural language processing, it is used for feature reduction and in recommendation systems. For instance, every time a customer adds an item to their online shopping cart, if we treat the cart as a sentence and the items as words, we end up with item embeddings (**Item2Vec**). These new representations for the items can easily be plugged into a downstream classifier or a recommender system.

Before moving to text classification, we need to stop and spend some time first to learn about the classifier we are going to use – the **Naive Bayes classifier**.

Understanding Naive Bayes

The Naive Bayes classifier is commonly used in classifying textual data. In the following sections, we are going to see its different flavors and learn how to configure their parameters. But first, to understand the Naive Bayes classifier, we need to first go through Thomas Bayes' theorem, which he published in the 18th century.

The Bayes rule

When talking about classifiers, we can describe the probability of a certain sample belonging to a certain class using conditional probability, $P(y|x)$. This is the probability of a sample belonging to class y given its features, x. The pipe sign (|) is what we use to refer to conditional probability, that is, y given x. The Bayes rule is capable of expressing this conditional probability in terms of $P(x|y)$, $P(x)$, and $P(y)$, using the following formula:

$$P(y|x) = \frac{P(x|y) \times P(y)}{P(x)}$$

Usually, we ignore the denominator part of the equation and convert it into a proportion as follows:

$$P(y|x) \propto P(x|y) \times P(y)$$

The probability of a class, $P(y)$, is known as the prior probability. It's basically the number of samples that belong to a certain class out of all training samples. The conditional probability, $P(x|y)$, is known as the likelihood. It's what we calculate from the training samples. Once the two probabilities are known at training time, we can use them to predict the chance of a new sample belonging to a certain class at prediction time, $P(y|x)$, also known as the posterior probability. Calculating the likelihood part of the equation is not as simple as we expect. So, in the next section, we are going to discuss the assumption we can make to ease this calculation.

Calculating the likelihood naively

A data sample is made of multiple features, which means that in reality, the x part of $P(x|y)$ is made of $x_1, x_2, x_3, ... x_k$, where k is the number of features. Thus, the conditional probability can be expressed as $P(x_1, x_2, x_3, ... x_k|y)$. In practice, this means that we need to calculate this conditional probability for all possible combinations of x. The main drawback of this is the lack of generalization of our models.

Let's use the following toy example to make things clearer:

Text	Does the text suggest that the writer likes fruit?
I like apples	Yes
I like oranges	Yes
I hate pears	No

If the previous table is our training data, the likelihood probability, $P(x|y)$, for the first sample is the probability of seeing the three words **I**, **like**, and **apples** together, given the target, **Yes**. Similarly, for the second sample, it is the probability of seeing the three words **I**, **like**, and **oranges** together, given the target, **Yes**. The same goes for the third sample, where the target is **No** instead of **Yes**. Now, say we are given a new sample, **I hate apples**. The problem is that we have never seen these three words together before. You might say, "But we've seen each individual word of the sentence before, just separately!" That's correct, but our formula only cares about combinations of words. It cannot learn anything from each separate feature on its own.

You may recall from `Chapter 4`, *Preparing Your Data*, that $P(x_1, x_2, x_3, ... x_k|y)$ can only be expressed as $P(x_1|y)* P(x_2|y)x_3* .. * P(x_k|y)$ if $x_1, x_2, x_3, ... x_k$ are independent. Their independence is not something we can be sure of, yet we still make this naive assumption in order to make the model more generalizable. As a result of this assumption and dealing with separate words, we can now learn something about the phrase **I hate apples**, despite not seeing it before. This naive yet useful assumption of independence is what gave the classifier's name its "naive" prefix.

Naive Bayes implementations

In scikit-learn, there are various Naive Bayes implementations.

- The **multinomial Naive Bayes** classifier is the most commonly used implementation for text classification. Its implementation is most similar to what we saw in the previous section.

- The **Bernoulli Naive Bayes** classifier assumes the features to be binary. Rather than counting how many times a term appears in each document, in the Bernoulli version, we only care whether a term exists or not. The way the likelihood is calculated explicitly penalizes the non-occurrence of the terms in the documents, and it might perform better on some datasets, especially those with shorter documents.
- **Gaussian Naive Bayes** is used with continuous features. It assumes the features to be normally distributed and calculates the likelihood probabilities using maximum likelihood estimation. This implementation is useful for other cases aside from text analysis.

Furthermore, you can also read about two other implementations, **complement Naive Bayes** and **categorical Naive Bayes**, in the scikit-learn user guide (`https://scikit-learn.org/stable/modules/naive_bayes.html`).

Additive smoothing

When a term not seen during training appears during prediction, we set its probability to 0. This sounds logical, yet it is a problematic decision to make given our naive assumption. Since $P(x_1, x_2, x_3, ... x_k | y)$ is equal to $P(x_1|y)* P(x_2|y)* P(x_3|y) * .. * P(x_k|y)$, setting the conditional probability for any term to zero will set the entire $P(x_1, x_2, x_3, ... x_k | y)$ to zero as a result. To avoid this problem, we pretend that a new document that contains the whole vocabulary was added to each class. Conceptually, this new hypothetical document takes a portion of the probability mass assigned to the terms we have seen and reassigns it to the unseen terms. The `alpha` parameter controls how much of the probability mass we want to reassign to the unseen terms. Setting `alpha` to 1 is called **Laplace smoothing**, while setting it to values between 0 and 1 is called **Lidstone smoothing**.

I find myself using Laplace smoothing a lot when calculating ratios. In addition to preventing us from dividing by zero, it also helps to deal with uncertainties. Let me explain further using the following two examples:

- **Example 1**: 10,000 people saw a link, and 9,000 of them clicked on it. We can obviously estimate the click-through rate to be 90%.
- **Example 2**: If our data has only one person, and that person saw the link and clicked on it, would we be confident enough to say that the click-through rate was 100%?

In the previous examples, if we pretended that there were two additional users, where only one of them clicked on the link, the click-through rate in the first example would become 9,001 out of 10,002, which is still almost 90%. In the second example, though, we would be dividing 2 by 3, which would leave 60%, instead of the 100% calculated earlier. Laplace smoothing and Lidstone smoothing can be linked to the Bayesian way of thinking. Those two users, where 50% of them clicked on the link, are our prior belief. Initially, we do not know much, so we assume a 50% click-through rate. Now, in the first example, we have enough data to overrule this prior belief, while in the second case, the fewer data points were only able to move the prior so much.

That's enough theory for now – let's use everything we have learned so far to tell whether some reviewers are happy about their movie-watching experience or not.

Classifying text using a Naive Bayes classifier

In this section, we are going to get a list of sentences and classify them based on the user's sentiment. We want to tell whether the sentence carries a positive or a negative sentiment. *Dimitrios Kotzias et al* created this dataset for their research paper, *From Group to Individual Labels using Deep Features*. They collected a list of random sentences from three different websites, where each sentence is labeled with either 1 (positive sentiment) or 0 (negative sentiment).

In total, there are 2,745 sentences in the data set. In the following sections, we are going to download the dataset, preprocess it, and classify the sentences in it.

Downloading the data

You can just open the browser, download the CSV files into a local folder, and use pandas to load the files into DataFrames. However, I prefer to use Python to download the files, rather than the browser. I don't do this out of geekiness, but to ensure the reproducibility of my entire process by putting it into code. Anyone can just run my Python code and get the same results, without having to read a lousy documentation file, find a link to the compressed file, and follow the instructions to get the data.

Here are the steps to download the data we need:

1. First, let's create a folder to store the downloaded data into it. The following code checks whether the required folder exists or not. If it is not there, it creates it into the current working directory:

```
import os

data_dir = f'{os.getcwd()}/data'

if not os.path.exists(data_dir):
    os.mkdir(data_dir)
```

2. Then we need to install the `requests` library using `pip`, as we will use it to download the data:

```
pip install requests
```

3. Then, we download the compressed data as follows:

```
import requests

url =
'https://archive.ics.uci.edu/ml/machine-learning-databases/00331/se
ntiment%20labelled%20sentences.zip'

response = requests.get(url)
```

4. Now, we can uncompress the data and store it into the data folder we have just created. We will be using the `zipfile` module to uncompress our data. The `ZipFile` method expects to read a file object. Thus, we use `BytesIO` to convert the content of the response into a file-like object. Then we extract the content of the zip file into our folder as follows:

```
import zipfile

from io import BytesIO

with zipfile.ZipFile(file=BytesIO(response.content), mode='r') as
compressed_file:
    compressed_file.extractall(data_dir)
```

5. Now that our data is written into 3 separate files in our data folder, we can load each one of the 3 files into a separate data frame. Then, we can combine the 3 data frames into a single data frame as follows:

```
df_list = []

for csv_file in ['imdb_labelled.txt', 'yelp_labelled.txt',
'amazon_cells_labelled.txt']:

    csv_file_with_path = f'{data_dir}/sentiment labelled
sentences/{csv_file}'
    temp_df = pd.read_csv(
        csv_file_with_path,
        sep="\t", header=0,
        names=['text', 'sentiment']
    )
    df_list.append(temp_df)
df = pd.concat(df_list)
```

6. We can display the distribution of the sentiment labels using the following code:

```
explode = [0.05, 0.05]
colors = ['#777777', '#111111']
df['sentiment'].value_counts().plot(
    kind='pie', colors=colors, explode=explode
)
```

As we can see, the two classes are more or less equal. It is a good practice to check the distribution of your classes before running any classification task:

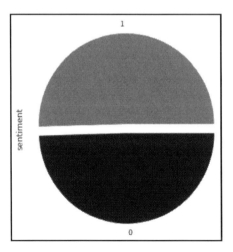

7. We can also display a few sample sentences using the following code, after tweaking pandas' settings to display more characters per cell:

```
pd.options.display.max_colwidth = 90
df[['text', 'sentiment']].sample(5, random_state=42)
```

I set the `random_state` to an arbitrary value to make sure we both get the same samples as below:

	text	sentiment
471	This is a stunning movie.	1
278	I had the mac salad and it was pretty bland so I will not be getting that again.	0
20	The food, amazing.	1
150	Audio Quality is poor, very poor.	0
430	His acting alongside Olivia De Havilland was brilliant and the ending was fantastic!	1

Preparing the data

Now we need to prepare the data for our classifier to use it:

1. As we usually do, we start by splitting the DataFrame into training and testing sets. I kept 40% of the data set for testing, and also set `random_state` to an arbitrary value to make sure we both get the same random split:

```
from sklearn.model_selection import train_test_split
df_train, df_test = train_test_split(df, test_size=0.4,
random_state=42)
```

2. Then we get our labels from the sentiment column as follows:

```
y_train = df_train['sentiment']
y_test = df_test['sentiment']
```

3. As for the textual features, let's convert them using `CountVectorizer`. We will include unigrams as well as bigrams and trigrams. We can also ignore rare words by setting `min_df` to `3` to exclude words appearing in fewer than three documents. This is a useful practice for removing spelling mistakes and noisy tokens. Finally, we can strip accents from letters and convert them to `ASCII`:

```
from sklearn.feature_extraction.text import CountVectorizer

vec = CountVectorizer(ngram_range=(1,3), min_df=3,
strip_accents='ascii')
x_train = vec.fit_transform(df_train['text'])
x_test = vec.transform(df_test['text'])
```

4. In the end, we can use the Naive Bayes classifier to classify our data. We set `fit_prior=True` for the model to use the distribution of the class labels in the training data as its prior:

```
from sklearn.naive_bayes import MultinomialNB
clf = MultinomialNB(fit_prior=True)
clf.fit(x_train, y_train)
y_test_pred = clf.predict(x_test)
```

This time, our old good accuracy score may not be informative enough. We want to know how accurate we are per class. Furthermore, depending on our use case, we may need to tell whether the model was able to identify all the negative tweets, even if it did that at the expense of misclassifying some positive tweets. To be able to get this information, we need to use the `precision` and `recall` scores.

Precision, recall, and F1 score

Out of the samples that were assigned to the positive class, the percentage of them that were actually positive is the **precision** of this class. For the positive tweets, the percentage of them that the classifier correctly predicted to be positive is the **recall** for this class. As you can see, the precision and recall are calculated per class. Here is how we formally express the **precision score** in terms of true positives and false positives:

$$Precision = \frac{TruePositive}{TruePositive + FalsePositive}$$

The **recall score** is expressed in terms of true positives and false negatives:

$$Recall = \frac{TruePositive}{TruePositive + FalseNegative}$$

To summarize the two previous scores into one number, the F_1 *score* can be used. It combines the precision and recall scores using the following formula:

$$F_1\,Score = \frac{2 \times (precision \times recall)}{precision + recall}$$

Here we calculate the three aforementioned metrics for our classifier:

```
p, r, f, s = precision_recall_fscore_support(y_test, y_test_pred)
```

To make it clear, I put the resulting metrics into the following table. Keep in mind that the support is just the number of samples in each class:

	Precision	Recall	F	Support
0	0.81	0.78	0.79	565
1	0.77	0.80	0.79	533

We have equivalent scores given that the sizes of the two classes are almost equal. In cases where the classes are imbalanced, it is more common to see one class achieving a higher precision or a higher recall compared to the other.

Since these metrics are calculated per class label, we can also get their macro averages. For this example here, the macro average precision score will be the average of **0.81**, and **0.77**, which is **0.79**. A micro average, on the other hand, calculates these scores globally based on the overall number of true positive, false positive, and false negative samples.

Pipelines

In the previous chapters, we used a grid search to find the optimal hyperparameters for our estimators. Now, we have multiple things to optimize at once. One the one hand, we want to optimize the Naive Bayes hyperparameters, but on the other hand, we also want to optimize the parameters of the vectorizer used at the preprocessing step. Since a grid search expects one object only, scikit-learn provides a `pipeline` wrapper where we can combine multiple transformers and estimators into one.

As the name suggests, the pipeline is made of a set of sequential steps. Here we start with `CountVectorizer` and have `MultinomialNB` as the second and final step:

```
from sklearn.pipeline import Pipeline
from sklearn.feature_extraction.text import CountVectorizer
from sklearn.naive_bayes import MultinomialNB

pipe = Pipeline(steps=[
    ('CountVectorizer', CountVectorizer()),
    ('MultinomialNB', MultinomialNB())]
)
```

All objects but the one in the last step are expected to be `transformers`; that is, they should have the `fit`, `transform`, and `fit_transform` methods. The object in the last step is expected to be `estimator`, meaning it should have the `fit` and `predict` methods. You can also build your custom transformers and estimators and use them in the pipeline as long as they have the expected methods.

Now that we have our pipeline ready, we can plug it into `GridSearchCV` to find the optimal hyperparameters.

Optimizing for different scores

"What gets measured gets managed."

– Peter Drucker

When we used `GridSearchCV` before, we did not specify which metric we want to optimize our hyperparameters for. The classifier's accuracy was used by default. Alternatively, you can also choose to optimize your hyperparameters for the precision score or the recall score. We will set our grid search here to optimize for the macro precision score.

We start by setting the different hyperparameters that we want to search within. Since we are using a pipeline here, we prefix each hyperparameter with the name of the step it is designated for, in order for the pipeline to assign the parameter to the correct step:

```
param_grid = {
    'CountVectorizer__ngram_range': [(1,1), (1,2), (1,3)],
    'MultinomialNB__alpha': [0.1, 1],
    'MultinomialNB__fit_prior': [True, False],
}
```

By default, the priors, `P(y)`, in the Bayes rule are set based on the number of samples in each class. However, we can set them to be constant for all classes by setting `fit_prior=False`.

Here, we run `GridSearchCV` while letting it know that we care about precision the most:

```
from sklearn.model_selection import GridSearchCV
search = GridSearchCV(pipe, param_grid, scoring='precision_macro',
n_jobs=-1)
search.fit(df_train['text'], y_train)
print(search.best_params_)
```

This gives us the following hyperparameters:

- `ngram_range`: (1, 3)
- `alpha`: 1
- `fit_prior`: False

We get a macro precision of 80.5% and macro recall of 80.5%.

Due to the balanced class distributions, it was expected for the prior not to add much value. We also get similar precision and recall scores. Thus, it doesn't make sense now to re-run the grid search again for an optimized recall. We will most likely get identical results anyway. Nevertheless, things will likely be different when you deal with highly imbalanced classes, and you want to maximize the recall of one class at the expense of the others.

In the next section, we are going to use word embeddings to represent our tokens. Let's see if this form of transfer learning will help our classifier perform better.

Creating a custom transformer

Before ending this chapter, we can also create a custom transformer based on the `Word2Vec` embedding and use it in our classification pipeline instead of `CountVectorizer`. In order to be able to use our custom transformer in the pipeline, we need to make sure it has `fit`, `transform`, and `fit_transform` methods.

Here is our new transformer, which we will call `WordEmbeddingVectorizer`:

```
import spacy

class WordEmbeddingVectorizer:

    def __init__(self, language_model='en_core_web_md'):
        self.nlp = spacy.load(language_model)

    def fit(self):
        pass

    def transform(self, x, y=None):
        return pd.Series(x).apply(
            lambda doc: self.nlp(doc).vector.tolist()
        ).values.tolist()

    def fit_transform(self, x, y=None):
        return self.transform(x)
```

The `fit` method here is impotent—it does not do anything since we are using a pre-trained model from spaCy. We can use the newly created transformer as follows:

```
vec = WordEmbeddingVectorizer()
x_train_w2v = vec.transform(df_train['text'])
```

Instead of the Naive Bayes classifier, we can also use this transformer with other classifiers, such as `LogisticRegression` or `Multi-layer Perceptron`.

> The `apply` function in pandas can be slow, especially when dealing with high volumes of data. I like to use a library called `tqdm`, which allows me to replace the `apply()` method with `progress_apply()`, which then displays a progress bar while running. All you have to do after importing the library is run `tqdm.pandas()`; this adds the `progress_apply()` method to the pandas Series and DataFrame objects. Fun fact: the word `tqdm` means *progress* in Arabic.

Summary

Personally, I find the field of natural language processing very exciting. The vast majority of our knowledge as humans is contained in books, documents, and web pages. Knowing how to automatically extract this information and organize it with the help of machine learning is essential to our scientific progress and endeavors in automation. This is why multiple scientific fields, such as information retrieval, statistics, and linguistics, borrow ideas from each other and try to solve the same problem from different angles. In this chapter, we also borrowed ideas from all these fields and learned how to represent textual data in formats suitable to machine learning algorithms. We also learned about the utilities that scikit-learn provides to aid in building and optimizing end-to-end solutions. We also encountered concepts such as transfer learning, and we were able to seamlessly incorporate spaCy's language models into scikit-learn.

From the next chapter, we are going to deal with slightly advanced topics. In the next chapter, we will learn about artificial neural networks (multi-layer perceptron). This is a very hot topic nowadays, and understanding its main concepts helps anyone who wants to get deeper into deep learning. Since neural networks are commonly used in image processing, we will seize the opportunity to build on what we learned in Chapter 5, Image Processing with Nearest Neighbors and expand our image processing knowledge even further.

2
Section 2: Advanced Supervised Learning

This section comprises information regarding how to deal with imbalanced data and optimizing your algorithm for a practical bias/variance trade-off. It also goes deeper into more advanced algorithms, such as artificial neural networks and the ensemble methods.

This section comprises the following chapters:

- Chapter 7, *Neural Networks – Here Comes Deep Learning*
- Chapter 8, *Ensembles – When One Model Is Not Enough*
- Chapter 9, *The Y is as Important as the X*
- Chapter 10, *Imbalanced Learning – Not Even 1% Win the Lottery*

Neural Networks – Here Comes Deep Learning

7

It is not uncommon to read news articles or encounter people who misuse the term *deep learning* in place of *machine learning*. This is due to the fact that this particular sub-field of machine learning has become very successful at solving plenty of previously unsolvable image processing and natural language processing problems. This success has caused many to confuse the child field with its parent.

The term *deep learning* refers to deep **Artificial Neural Networks** (**ANNs**). The latter concept comes in different forms and shapes. In this chapter, we are going to cover one subset of **feedforward neural networks** known as the **Multilayer Perceptron** (**MLP**). It is one of the most commonly used types and is implemented by scikit-learn. As its name suggests, it is composed of multiple layers, and it is a feedforward network as there are no cyclic connections between its layers. The more layers there are, the deeper the network is. These deep networks can exist in multiple forms, such as **MLP**, **Convolutional Neural Networks** (**CNNs**), or **Long Short-Term Memory** (**LSTM**). The latter two are not implemented by scikit-learn, yet this will not stop us from discussing the main concepts behind CNNs and manually mimicking them using the tools from the scientific Python ecosystem.

In this chapter, we are going to cover the following topics:

- Getting to know MLP
- Classifying items of clothing
- Untangling convolutions
- MLP regressors

Getting to know MLP

When learning a new algorithm, you can get discouraged by the number of hyperparameters and find it hard to decide where to start. Therefore, I suggest we start by answering the following two questions:

- How has the algorithm been architected?
- How does the algorithm train?

In the following sections, we are going to answer both of these questions and learn about the corresponding hyperparameters one by one.

Understanding the algorithm's architecture

Luckily, the knowledge we gained about linear models in Chapter 3, *Making Decisions with Linear Equations*, will give us a good headstart here. In brief, linear models can be outlined in the following diagram:

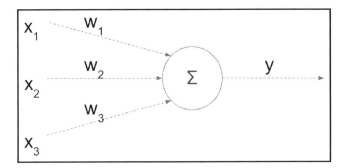

Each of the input features (x_i) is multiplied by a weight (w_i), and the sum of these products is the output of the model (y). Additionally, we sometimes add an extra bias (threshold), along with its weight. Nevertheless, one main problem with linear models is that they are in fact linear (duh!). Furthermore, each feature gets its own weight, regardless of its neighbors. This simple architecture prevents the model from capturing any interactions between its features. So, you can stack more layers next to each other, as follows:

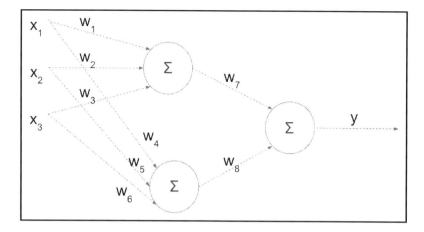

This sounds like a potential solution; however, based on simple mathematical derivations, these combinations of multiplications and summations can still be reduced into a single linear equation. It is as if all these layers have no effect at all. Therefore, to get to the desired effect, we want to apply non-linear transformations after each summation. These non-linear transformations are known as activation functions, and they turn the model to a non-linear one. Let's see where they fit into the model, then I will explain further:

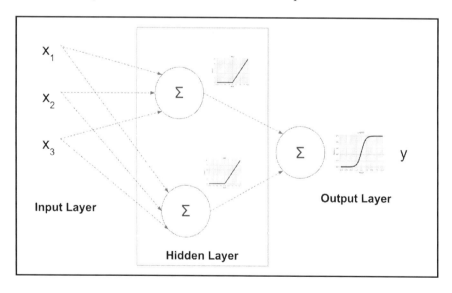

This model has a single hidden layer with two hidden nodes, which are shown inside the box. In practice, you may have multiple hidden layers with a number of nodes. The aforementioned activation functions are applied at the outputs of the hidden nodes. Here, we used a **Rectified Linear Unit (ReLU)**, it is an activation function; for the negative values, it returns `0`, and it keeps the positive values unchanged. In addition to the `relu` function, `identity`, `logistic`, and `tanh` activation functions are also supported for the hidden layers, and they are set using the `activation` hyperparameter. Here is how each of these four activation functions look:

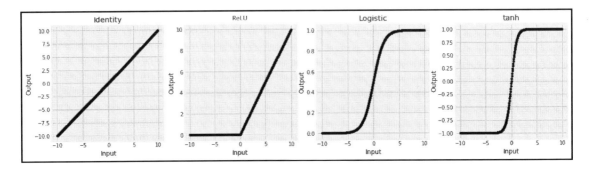

As mentioned earlier, since the `identity` function keeps its inputs untouched without any non-linear transformations, it is seldom used as it will end up reducing the model into a simple linear one. It is also cursed by having a constant gradient, which is not very helpful for the gradient descent algorithm used for training. Therefore, the `relu` function is usually a good non-linear alternative. It is the current default setting and is a good first choice; the `logistic` or the `tanh` activation functions are the next alternative options.

The output layer also has its own activation function, but it serves a different purpose. If you recall from Chapter 3, *Making Decisions with Linear Equations*, we used the `logistic` function to turn a linear regression into a classifier—that is, logistic regression. The output's activation function serves the exact same purpose here as well. This list has the possible output activation functions and their corresponding use cases:

- **Identity function**: Set when doing regression using `MLPRegressor`
- **Logistic function**: Set when performing a binary classification using `MLPClassifier`
- **Softmax function**: Set when using `MLPClassifier` to differentiate between three or more classes

We do not set the output activation functions by hand; they are automatically chosen based on whether `MLPRegressor` or `MLPClassifier` is used and on the number of classes available for the latter to classify.

If we look at the network architecture, it is clear that another important hyperparameter to set is the number of hidden layers and the number of nodes in each layer. This is set using the `hidden_layer_sizes` hyperparameter, which accepts tuples. To achieve the architecture in the previous figure—that is, one hidden layer with two nodes—we will set `hidden_layer_sizes` to 2. Setting it to (10, 10, 5) gives us three hidden layers; the first two have 10 nodes each, while the third one has 5 nodes.

Training the neural network

"Psychologists tell us that in order to learn from experience, two ingredients are necessary: frequent practice and immediate feedback."

– Richard Thaler

A big chunk of researchers' time is spent on improving how their neural networks train. This is also reflected in the number of hyperparameters related to the training algorithms used. To better understand these hyperparameters, we need to examine the following training workflow:

1. Get a subset of the training samples.
2. Run them through the network and make predictions.
3. Calculate the training loss by comparing the actual values and predictions.
4. Use the calculated loss to update the network weights.
5. Return to *step 1* to get more samples, and if all the samples are already used, go through the training data over and over until the training process converges.

Going through these steps one by one, you can see the need to set the size of the training subset at the first stage. This is what the `batch_size` parameter sets. As we will see in a bit, you can go from using one sample at a time to using the entire training set all at once to anything in between. The first and second steps are straightforward, but the third step dictates that we should know which loss function to use. As for the available loss functions, we do not have much choice when working with scikit-learn. A **log loss function** is selected for us when performing classifications and **mean squared error** is what is available for regression. The fourth step is the trickiest part with the most of hyperparameters to set. We calculate the gradient of the loss function with respect to the network weights.

This gradient tells us the direction to move toward to decrease the loss function. In other words, we use the gradient to update the weights in the hope that we can iteratively decrease the loss function to its minimum. The logic responsible for this operation is known as the solver. Solvers deserve their own separate section, though, which will come in a bit. Finally, the number of times we go through the training data over and over is called epochs and is set using the `max_iter` hyperparameter. We also may decide to stop earlier (`early_stopping`) if the model is not learning any more. The `validation_fraction`, `n_iter_no_change`, and `tol` hyperparameters help us decide when to stop. More on how they work in the next section.

Configuring the solvers

After calculating the loss function (also known as the cost or objective function), we need to find the optimum network weights that minimize the loss function. In the linear models from `Chapter 3`, *Making Decisions with Linear Equations*, the loss functions were chosen to be convex. A convex function, as seen in the following figure, has one minimum, which is both its global minimum as well as its local one. This simplifies the solvers' job when trying to optimize this function. In the case of non-linear neural networks, the loss function is typically non-convex, which requires extra care during training, hence more attention is given to the solvers here:

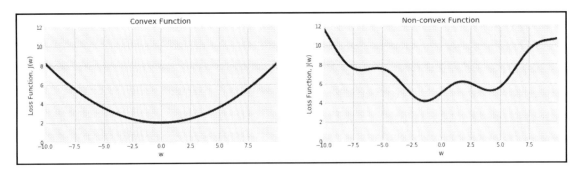

The supported solvers for MLP can be grouped into **Limited Memory Broyden–Fletcher–Goldfarb–Shanno (LBFGS)** and **gradient descent (Stochastic Gradient Descent (SGD)** and Adam). In both variants, we want to pick a random point on the loss function, calculate its slope (gradient), and use it to figure out in which direction we should move next. Remember that in reality, we are dealing with way higher dimensions than the two-dimensional graphs shown here. Furthermore, we cannot usually see the entire graph as we can now:

- The **LBFGS** algorithm uses both the slope (first derivative) and the rate of change of the slope (second derivative), which helps in providing better coverage; however, it doesn't scale well with the size of the training data. It can be very slow to train, and so this algorithm is recommended for smaller datasets, unless more powerful concurrent machines come to the rescue.
- The **gradient descent** algorithm relies on the first derivative only. So, more effort is needed to help it move effectively. The calculated gradient is combined with `learning_rate`. This controls how much it moves each time after calculating the gradient. Moving too quickly may result in overshooting and missing the local minimum, while moving too slowly may cause the algorithm not to converge soon enough. We start our quest with a rate defined by `learning_rate_init`. If we set `learning_rate='constant'`, the initial rate is kept unchanged throughout the training process. Otherwise, we can set the rate to decrease with each step (in scaling) or to only decrease whenever the model is not able to learn enough anymore (adaptive).
- **Gradient descent** can use the entire training data to calculate the gradient, use a single sample at a time (`sgd`), or consume the data in small subsets (mini-batch gradient descent). These choices are controlled by `batch_size`. Having a dataset that cannot fit into memory may prevent us from using the entire dataset at once, while using small batches may cause the loss function to fluctuate. We will see this effect in practice in the next section.

- The problem with the learning rate is that it doesn't adapt to the shape of the curve, especially as we are only using the first derivative here. We want to control the learning speed, depending on how steep the curve at our feet is. One notable adjustment to make the learning process smarter is the concept of `momentum`. This adapts the learning process based on current and previous updates. The `momentum` is enabled for the `sgd` solver by default, and its magnitude can be set using the `momentum` hyperparameter. The `adam` solver incorporates this concept and combines it with the ability to compute separate learning rates for each one of the network weights. It is parameterized by `beta_1` and `beta_2`. They are usually kept at their default values of `0.9` and `0.999`, respectively. The `adam` solver is the default solver since it requires fewer tuning efforts compared to the `sgd` solver. Nevertheless, the `sgd` solver can converge to better solutions if tuned correctly.

- Finally, deciding when to stop the training process is another essential decision to make. We loop over the data more than once, bounded by the `max_iter` setting. Yet, we can stop before `max_iter` is reached if we feel that we aren't learning enough. We define how much learning is enough using `tol`, then we can stop the training process right away or give it a few more chances (`n_iter_no_change`) before we decide to stop it. Furthermore, we can set a separate fraction of the training set aside (`validation_fraction`) and use it to evaluate our learning process better. Then, if we set `early_stopping =True`, the training process will stop once the improvement for the validation set does not meet the `tol` threshold for `n_iter_no_change` epochs.

Now that we have a good high-level picture of how things work, I feel the best way forward is to put all these hyperparameters into practice and see their effect on real data. In the next section, we will load an image dataset and use it to learn more about the aforementioned hyperparameters.

Classifying items of clothing

In this section, we are going to classify clothing items based on their images. We are going to use a dataset release by Zalando. Zalando is an e-commerce website based in Berlin. They released a dataset of 70,000 pictures of clothing items, along with their labels. Each item belongs to one of the following 10 labels:

```
{ 0: 'T-shirt/top ', 1: 'Trouser ', 2: 'Pullover ', 3: 'Dress ', 4:
'Coat ', 5: 'Sandal ', 6: 'Shirt ', 7: 'Sneaker ', 8: 'Bag ', 9:
'Ankle boot' }
```

The data is published on the OpenML platform, so we can easily download it using the built-in downloader in scikit-learn.

Downloading the Fashion-MNIST dataset

Each dataset on the OpenML platform has a specific ID. We can give this ID to `fetch_openml()` to download the required dataset, as follows:

```
from sklearn.datasets import fetch_openml
fashion_mnist = fetch_openml(data_id=40996)
```

The class labels are given as numbers. To extract their names, we can parse the following line from the description, as follows:

```
labels_s = '0 T-shirt/top \n1 Trouser \n2 Pullover \n3 Dress \n4 Coat \n5
Sandal \n6 Shirt \n7 Sneaker \n8 Bag \n9 Ankle boot'

fashion_label_translation = {
    int(k): v for k, v in [
        item.split(maxsplit=1) for item in labels_s.split('\n')
    ]
}

def translate_label(y, translation=fashion_label_translation):
    return pd.Series(y).apply(lambda y: translation[int(y)]).values
```

We can also create a function similar to the one we created in Chapter 5, *Image Processing with Nearest Neighbors*, to display the images in the dataset:

```
def display_fashion(img, target, ax):
    if len(img.shape):
        w = int(np.sqrt(img.shape[0]))
        img = img.reshape((w, w))
    ax.imshow(img, cmap='Greys')
    ax.set_title(f'{target}')
    ax.grid(False)
```

The previous function expects an image and a target label in addition to the `matplotlib` axis to display the image on. We are going to see how to use it in the upcoming sections.

Preparing the data for classification

When developing a model and optimizing its hyperparameters, you will need to run it over and over multiple times. Therefore, it is advised that you start working with a smaller dataset to minimize the training time. Once you reach an acceptable model, you can then add more data and do your final hyperparameter-tuning. Later on, we will see how to tell whether the data at hand is enough and whether more samples are needed; but for now, let's stick to a subset of 10,000 images.

I deliberately avoided setting any random states when sampling from the original dataset and when splitting the sampled data into a training and a test set. By not setting a random state, you should expect the final results to vary from one run to the other. I made this choice since my main objective here is to focus on the underlying concepts, and I did not want you to obsess over the final results. In the end, the data you will deal with in real-life scenarios will vary from one problem to the other, and we have already learned in previous chapters how to better understand the boundaries of our model's performance via cross-validation. So, in this chapter, as in many other chapters in this book, don't worry too much if the mentioned model's accuracy numbers, coefficients, or learning behavior vary slightly from yours.

We will use the `train_test_split()` function twice. Initially, we will use it for sampling. Afterward, we will reuse it for its designated purpose of splitting the data into training and test sets:

```
from sklearn.model_selection import train_test_split

fashion_mnist_sample = {}

fashion_mnist_sample['data'], _, fashion_mnist_sample['target'], _ =
train_test_split(
    fashion_mnist['data'], fashion_mnist['target'], train_size=10000
)

x, y = fashion_mnist_sample['data'], fashion_mnist_sample['target']
x_train, x_test, y_train, y_test = train_test_split(x, y, test_size=0.2)
```

The pixels here take values between 0 and 255. Usually, this is fine; however, the solvers we will use converge better when the data is put into tighter ranges. MinMaxScaler is going to help us achieve this, as can be seen in the following code, whereas StandardScaler is also an option:

```
from sklearn.preprocessing import MinMaxScaler

scaler = MinMaxScaler()

x_train = scaler.fit_transform(x_train)
x_test = scaler.transform(x_test)
```

We can now translate the numerical labels into names using the function we created in the previous section:

```
translation = fashion_label_translation
y_train_translated = translate_label(y_train, translation=translation)
y_test_translated = translate_label(y_test, translation=translation)
```

If your original labels came in as strings, you can use LabelEncoder to convert them into numerical values:

```
from sklearn.preprocessing import LabelEncoder

le = LabelEncoder()
y_train_encoded = le.fit_transform(y_train_translated)
y_test_encoded = le.transform(y_test_translated)
```

Finally, let's use the following code to see how the images look:

```
import random

fig, axs = plt.subplots(1, 10, figsize=(16, 12))

for i in range(10):
    rand = random.choice(range(x_train.shape[0]))
    display_fashion(x_train[rand], y_train_translated[rand], axs[i])

fig.show()
```

Here, we see 10 random images alongside their labels. We loop over 10 random images and use the display function we created earlier to display them next to each other:

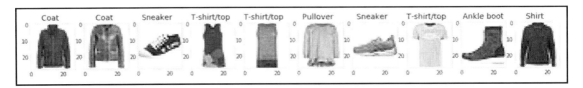

Now that the data is ready, it is time to see the effect of the hyperparameters in practice.

Experiencing the effects of the hyperparameters

After the neural network is trained, you can check its weights (coefs_), intercepts (intercepts_), and the final value of the loss function (loss_). One additional piece of information is the computed loss after each epoch (loss_curve_). This trace of calculated losses is very useful for the learning process.

Here, we train a neural network with two hidden layers of 100 nodes each, and we set the maximum number of epoch to 500. We leave all the other hyperparameters to their default values for now:

```
from sklearn.neural_network import MLPClassifier
clf = MLPClassifier(hidden_layer_sizes=(100, 100), max_iter=500)
clf.fit(x_train, y_train_encoded)
y_test_pred = clf.predict(x_test)
```

After the network is trained, we can plot the loss curve using the following line of code:

```
pd.Series(clf.loss_curve_).plot(
    title=f'Loss Curve; stopped after {clf.n_iter_} epochs'
)
```

This gives us the following graph:

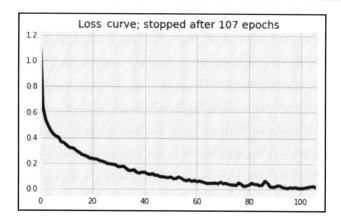

Despite the fact that the algorithm was told to continue learning for up to 500 epochs, it stopped after the 107ᵗʰ epoch. The default value for n_iter_no_change is 10 epochs. This means that the learning rate was not improving enough since the 97ᵗʰ epoch, and so the network came to a halt 10 epochs later. Keep in mind that early_stopping is set to False by default, which means that this decision was made regardless of the 10% validation set that was set aside by default. If we want to use the validation set for the early stopping decision, we should set early_stopping=True.

Learning not too quickly and not too slowly

As mentioned earlier, the gradient of the loss function (*J*) with respect to the weights (*w*) is used to update the network's weights. The updates are done according to the following equation, where *lr* is the learning rate:

$$w_{new} = w_{old} - lr\frac{\partial J(w)}{\partial w}$$

You might wonder about the need for a learning rate; why don't we just use the gradient as it is by setting *lr* = 1? In this section, we are going to answer this question by witnessing the effect of the learning rate on the training process.

Another hidden gem in the MLP estimator is validation_scores_. Like loss_curve_, this one is also not documented, and its interface may change with future releases. In the case of MLPClassifier, validation_scores_ keeps track of the classifier's accuracy on the validation set, whereas for MLPRegressor, it keeps track of the regressor's R² score instead.

We are going to use the validation score (`validation_scores_`) to see the effect of the different learning rates. Since these scores are stored only when `early_stopping` is set to `True` and we do not want to stop early, we will also set `n_iter_no_change` to be the same value as `max_iter` to cancel the early stopping effect.

The default learning rate is `0.001`, and it stays constant during the training process by default. Here, we are going to take an even smaller subset of the training data—1,000 samples—and try different learning rates from `0.0001` to `1`:

```
from sklearn.neural_network import MLPClassifier

learning_rate_init_options = [1, 0.1, 0.01, 0.001, 0.0001]

fig, axs = plt.subplots(1, len(learning_rate_init_options), figsize=(15,
5), sharex=True, sharey=True)

for i, learning_rate_init in enumerate(learning_rate_init_options):
    print(f'{learning_rate_init} ', end='')
    clf = MLPClassifier(
        hidden_layer_sizes=(500, ),
        learning_rate='constant',
        learning_rate_init=learning_rate_init,
        validation_fraction=0.2,
        early_stopping=True,
        n_iter_no_change=120,
        max_iter=120,
        solver='sgd',
        batch_size=25,
        verbose=0,
    )
    clf.fit(x_train[:1000,:], y_train_encoded[:1000])
    pd.Series(clf.validation_scores_).plot(
        title=f'learning_rate={learning_rate_init}',
        kind='line',
        color='k',
        ax=axs[i]
    )
fig.show()
```

The following graphs compare the progress of the validation scores for the different learning rates. The code used for formatting the axes was omitted for brevity:

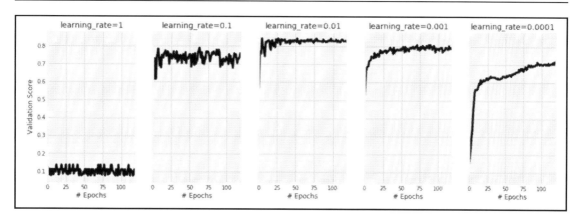

As we can see, when setting the learning rate to 1, the network wasn't able to learn and the accuracy score was stuck around 10%. This is because the bigger steps taken to update the weights caused the gradient descent to overshoot and miss the local minima. Ideally, we want the gradient descent to move wisely over the curve; it shouldn't rush and miss the optimum solutions. On the other hand, we can see that a very slow learning rate, 0.0001, caused the network to take forever to train. It's clear that 120 epochs wasn't enough, then, and more epochs were needed. For this example, a learning rate of 0.01 looks like a good balance.

 The concept of learning rate is commonly used in iterative methods to prevent overshooting. It might have different names and different justifications, but in essence, it serves the same purpose. For example, in the **reinforcement learning** field, the **discount factor** in the **Bellman equation** might resemble the learning rate here.

Picking a suitable batch size

When dealing with massive training data, you don't want to use it all at once when calculating the gradient, especially when it is not possible to fit this data in memory. Using the data in small subsets is something we can configure. Here, we are going to try different batch sizes while keeping everything else constant. Keep in mind that with batch_size set to 1, the model is going to be very slow as it updates its weights after each training instance:

```
from sklearn.neural_network import MLPClassifier

batch_sizes = [1, 10, 100, 1500]

fig, axs = plt.subplots(1, len(batch_sizes), figsize=(15, 5), sharex=True,
```

```
        sharey=True)

for i, batch_size in enumerate(batch_sizes):
    print(f'{batch_size} ', end='')
    clf = MLPClassifier(
        hidden_layer_sizes=(500, ),
        learning_rate='constant',
        learning_rate_init=0.001,
        momentum=0,
        max_iter=250,
        early_stopping=True,
        n_iter_no_change=250,
        solver='sgd',
        batch_size=batch_size,
        verbose=0,
    )
    clf.fit(x_train[:1500,:], y_train_encoded[:1500])
    pd.Series(clf.validation_scores_).plot(
        title=f'batch_size={batch_size}',
        color='k',
        kind='line',
        ax=axs[i]
    )
fig.show()
```

This figure gives us a visual comparison between the four batch size settings and their effects. Parts of the formatting code were omitted for brevity:

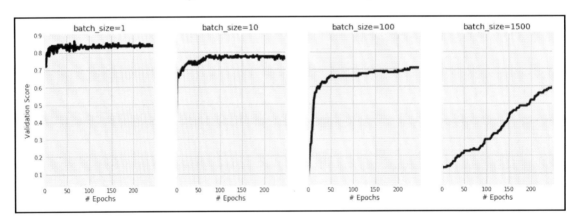

You can see why the use of mini-batch gradient descent is becoming the norm among practitioners, not only because of the memory constraints but also because smaller batches helped our model here learn better. This final outcome was achieved despite the higher fluctuations in the validation scores for the smaller batch sizes. On the other hand, setting `batch_size` to 1 slows down the learning process.

So far, we have tweaked multiple hyperparameters and witnessed their effects on the training process. In addition to these hyperparameters, two additional questions are still waiting for answers:

- How many training samples are enough?
- How many epochs are enough?

Checking whether more training samples are needed

We want to compare when the entire training sample (100%) is used when 75%, 50%, 25%, 10%, and 5% of it is used. The `learning_curve` function is useful for this comparison. It uses cross-validation to calculate the average training and test scores for the different sample sizes. Here, we are going to define the different sampling ratios and specify that three-fold cross-validation is needed:

```
from sklearn.model_selection import learning_curve

train_sizes = [1, 0.75, 0.5, 0.25, 0.1, 0.05]

train_sizes, train_scores, test_scores = learning_curve(
    MLPClassifier(
        hidden_layer_sizes=(100, 100),
        solver='adam',
        early_stopping=False
    ),
    x_train, y_train_encoded,
    train_sizes=train_sizes,
    scoring="precision_macro",
    cv=3,
    verbose=2,
    n_jobs=-1
)
```

When done, we can use the following code to plot the progress of the training and test scores with an increase in the sample size:

```
df_learning_curve = pd.DataFrame(
    {
        'train_sizes': train_sizes,
```

```
          'train_scores': train_scores.mean(axis=1),
          'test_scores': test_scores.mean(axis=1)
    }
).set_index('train_sizes')

df_learning_curve['train_scores'].plot(
    title='Learning Curves', ls=':',
)

df_learning_curve['test_scores'].plot(
    title='Learning Curves', ls='-',
)
```

The resulting graphs show the increase in the classifier's accuracy with more training data. Notice how the training score is constant, while the test score is what we really care about, and it seems to saturate after a certain amount of data:

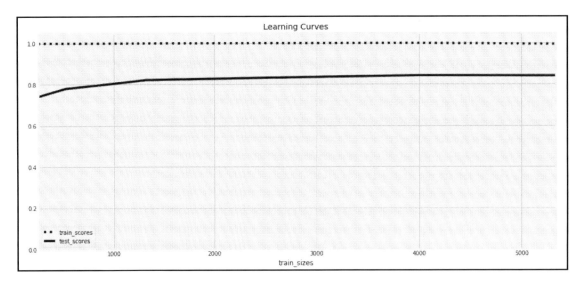

Earlier in this chapter, we took a sample of 10,000 images out of the original 70,000 images. We then split it into 8,000 for training and 2,000 for testing. From the learning curve graph, we can see that it is possible to settle for an even smaller training set. Somewhere after 2,000 the additional samples don't add much value.

Usually, we want to use as many data samples as we have to train our models. Nevertheless, when tuning the model's hyperparameters, you need to compromise and use a smaller sample to speed up the development process. Once that's done, it is then advised to train the final model on the entire dataset.

Checking whether more epochs are needed

This time, we are going to use the `validation_curve` function. It works in a similar fashion to the `learning_curve` function, but rather than comparing the different training sample sizes, it compares the different hyperparameter settings. Here, we will see the effect of using different values for `max_iter`:

```
from sklearn.model_selection import validation_curve

max_iter_range = [5, 10, 25, 50, 75, 100, 150]

train_scores, test_scores = validation_curve(
    MLPClassifier(
        hidden_layer_sizes=(100, 100),
        solver='adam',
        early_stopping=False
    ),
    x_train, y_train_encoded,
    param_name="max_iter", param_range=max_iter_range,
    scoring="precision_macro",
    cv=3,
    verbose=2,
    n_jobs=-1
)
```

With the training and test scores, we can plot them as we did in the previous section to get the following graph:

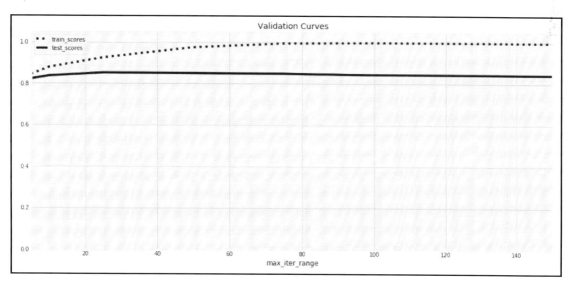

In this example, we can see that the test score stopped improving roughly after 25 epochs. The training score continued to improve beyond that until it reached 100%, which is a symptom of overfitting. In practice, we may not need this graph as we use the `early_stopping`, `tol`, and `n_iter_no_change` hyperparameters to stop the training process once we have learned enough and before we overfit.

Choosing the optimum architecture and hyperparameters

So far, we haven't talked about the network architecture. How many layers should we have and how many nodes should we put in each layer? We also haven't compared the different activation functions. As you can see, there are plenty of hyperparameters to choose from. Previously in this book, we mentioned tools such as `GridSearchCV` and `RandomizedSearchCV` that help you pick the best hyperparameters. These are still good tools to use, but they can be too slow if we decide to use them to tune every possible value for every parameter we have. They can also become too slow when used with too many training samples or for too many epochs.

The tools we have seen in the previous sections should help us find our needle in a slightly smaller haystack by ruling out some hyperparameter ranges. They will also allow us to stick to smaller datasets and for shorter training times. Then, we can effectively use `GridSearchCV` and `RandomizedSearchCV` to fine-tune our neural network.

Parallelism is also advised where possible. `GridSearchCV` and `RandomizedSearchCV` allow us to use the different processors on our machines to train multiple models at the same time. We can achieve that via the `n_jobs` setting. This means that you can significantly speed up the hyperparameter-tuning process by using machines with a high number of processors. As for the data size, since we are going to perform k-fold cross-validation and the training data will be split further down, we should add more data than the amount estimated in the previous section. Now, without further ado, let's use `GridSearchCV` to tune our network:

```
from sklearn.model_selection import GridSearchCV

param_grid = {
    'hidden_layer_sizes': [(50,), (50, 50), (100, 50), (100, 100), (500,
100), (500, 100, 100)],
    'activation': ['logistic', 'tanh', 'relu'],
    'learning_rate_init': [0.01, 0.001],
    'solver': ['sgd', 'adam'],
}
```

```
gs = GridSearchCV(
    estimator=MLPClassifier(
        max_iter=50,
        batch_size=50,
        early_stopping=True,
    ),
    param_grid=param_grid,
    cv=4,
    verbose=2,
    n_jobs=-1
)

gs.fit(x_train[:2500,:], y_train_encoded[:2500])
```

It ran for 14 minutes on four CPUs, and the following hyperparameters were picked:

- **Activation**: `relu`
- **Hidden layer sizes**: `(500, 100)`
- **Initial learning rate**: `0.01`
- **Solver**: `adam`

The selected model achieved a **micro F-score** of **85.6%** on the test set. By using the `precision_recall_fscore_support` function, you can see in more detail which classes were easier to predict than others:

	Precision	Recall	F	Support
Ankle boot	0.93	0.93	0.93	199
Bag	0.98	0.93	0.95	200
Coat	0.84	0.8	0.82	214
Dress	0.88	0.87	0.87	209
Pullover	0.75	0.75	0.75	185
Sandal	0.89	0.93	0.91	202
Shirt	0.64	0.71	0.67	201
Sneaker	0.91	0.91	0.91	210
T-shirt/top	0.79	0.78	0.79	187
Trouser	0.97	0.94	0.96	193

Ideally, we should retrain again using the entire training set, but I've left this for now. In the end, developing an optimum neural network is usually seen as a mixture of art and science. Nevertheless, knowing your hyperparameters and how to measure their effects should make it a straightforward endeavor. Then, tools such as `GridSearchCV` and `RandomizedSearchCV` are at your disposal for automating parts of the process. Automation trumps dexterity many times.

Before moving on to the next topic, I'd like to digress a bit and show you how to build your own activation function.

Adding your own activation function

One common problem with many activation functions is the vanishing gradient problem. If you look at the curves for the `logistic` and `tanh` activation functions, you can see that for high positive and negative values, the curve is almost horizontal. This means that the gradient of the curve is almost constant for these high values. This hinders the learning process. The `relu` activation function tried to solve this problem for one part but failed to deal with it for the negative values. This drove the researchers to keep proposing different activations functions. Here, we are going to compare the **ReLU** activation to a modified version of it, **Leaky ReLU**:

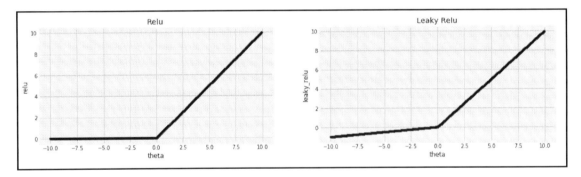

As you can see in the **Leaky ReLU** example, the line is not constant for the negative values anymore, but rather, decreasing at a small rate. To add **Leaky ReLU**, I had to look for how the `relu` function is built in scikit-learn and shamelessly modify the code for my needs. There are basically two methods to build. The methods are used in the forward path and just apply the activation function on its inputs, while the second method applies the derivative of the activation function to the calculated error. Here are the two existing methods for `relu`, after I slightly modified the code for brevity:

```
def relu(X):
    return np.clip(X, 0, np.finfo(X.dtype).max)

def inplace_relu_derivative(Z, delta):
    delta[Z == 0] = 0
```

In the first method, NumPy's `clip()` method is used to set the negative values to 0. Since the `clip` method requires both the lower- and upper-bounds, the cryptic part of the code just gets the maximum values of this data type to set it as the upper-bound. The second method takes the output of the activation function (`Z`), as well as the calculated error (`delta`). It is supposed to multiply the error by the gradient of the activation's output. Nevertheless, for this particular activation function, the gradient is 1 for positive values and 0 for the negative values. So, the error was set to 0 for the negative values—that is, it was set to 0 whenever `relu` returned 0.

`leaky_relu` keeps the positive values unchanged and multiplies the negative values by a small value, `0.01`. Now, all we need to do is to build out new methods using this information:

```
leaky_relu_slope = 0.01

def leaky_relu(X):
    X_min = leaky_relu_slope * np.array(X)
    return np.clip(X, X_min, np.finfo(X.dtype).max)

def inplace_leaky_relu_derivative(Z, delta):
    delta[Z < 0] = leaky_relu_slope * delta[Z < 0]
```

Recall that the slope for `leaky_relu` is 1 for the positive values and is equal to the `leaky_relu_slope` constant for the negative values. That's why we multiplied the deltas where Z is negative by `leaky_relu_slope`. Now, before using our new methods, we have to inject them into the scikit-learn's code base, as follows:

```
from sklearn.neural_network._base import ACTIVATIONS, DERIVATIVES

ACTIVATIONS['leaky_relu'] = leaky_relu
DERIVATIVES['leaky_relu'] = inplace_leaky_relu_derivative
```

Then, you can just use `MLPClassifier` as if it were there from the beginning:

```
clf = MLPClassifier(activation='leaky_relu')
```

Hacking libraries like these forces us to read its source code and understand it better. It also shows the value of open source, where you are not bounded by what is already there. In the next section, we are going to continue hacking and build our own convolutional layers.

Untangling the convolutions

"Look deep into nature, and then you will understand everything better"

– Albert Einstein

No chapter about the use of neural networks to classify images is allowed to end without touching on CNNs. Despite the fact that scikit-learn does not implement convolutional layers, we can still understand the concept and see how it works.

Let's start with the following 5 x 5 image and see how to apply a convolutional layer to it:

```
x_example = array(
    [[0, 0, 0, 0, 0],
     [0, 0, 0, 0, 0],
     [0, 0, 1, 1, 0],
     [0, 0, 1, 1, 0],
     [0, 0, 0, 0, 0]]
)
```

In natural language processing, words usually serve as a middle ground between characters and entire sentences when it comes to feature extraction. In this image, maybe smaller patches serve as better units of information than a separate pixel. The objective of this section is to find ways to represent these small *2 x 2, 3 x 3,* or *N x N* patches in an image. We can start with averages as summaries. We can basically take the average of each *3 x 3* patch by multiplying each pixel in it by 1, and then dividing the total by 9; there are 9 pixels in the patch. For the pixels on the edges, as they don't have neighbors in all directions, we can pretend that there is an extra 1-pixel border around the image where all pixels are set to 0. By doing so, we get another *5 x 5* array.

This kind of operation is known as **convolutions**, and **SciPy** provides a way of doing it. The *3 x 3* all-ones matrix used and is also known as the kernel or weights. Here, we specify the all-ones kernel and divide by 9 later. We also specify the need for an all-zeros border by setting `mode` to `constant` and `cval` to 0, as you can see in the following code:

```
from scipy import ndimage

kernel = [[1,1,1],[1,1,1],[1,1,1]]
x_example_convolve = ndimage.convolve(x_example, kernel, mode='constant',
cval=0)
x_example_convolve = x_example_convolve / 9
```

Here is a comparison between the original image and the output of the convolution:

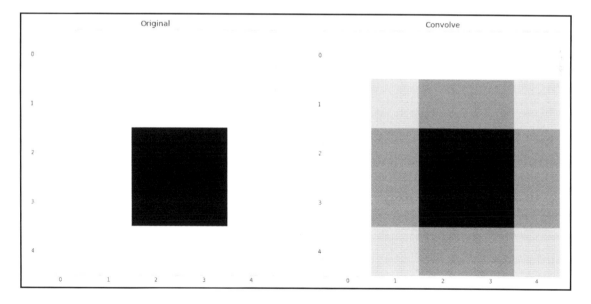

Calculating the mean gave us a blurred version of the original image, so next time you need to blur an image, you know what to do. Multiplying each pixel by a certain weight and calculating the sum of these products sounds like a linear model. Furthermore, we can think of averages as linear models where all weights are set to $\frac{1}{N}$. So, you may say that we are building mini-linear models for each patch of the image. Keep this analogy in mind, but for now, we have to set the model's weights by hand.

While each patch gets the exact same linear model as the others, there is nothing stopping the pixels within each patch from being multiplied by different weights. In fact, different kernels with different weights give different effects. In the next section, we are going to witness the effect of the different kernels on our **Fashion-MNIST** dataset.

Extracting features by convolving

Rather than dealing with the images one by one, we can tweak the code to convolve over multiple images at once. The images in our Fashion-MNIST dataset are flattened, so we need to reshape them into *28 x 28* pixels each. Then, we convolve using the given kernel, and finally, make sure that all pixel values are between 0 and 1 using our favorite MinMaxScaler parameter:

```
from scipy import ndimage
from sklearn.preprocessing import MinMaxScaler

def convolve(x, kernel=[[1,1,1],[1,1,1],[1,1,1]]):
    w = int(np.sqrt(x.shape[1]))
    x = ndimage.convolve(
        x.reshape((x.shape[0], w, w)), [kernel],
        mode='constant', cval=0.0
    )
    x = x.reshape(x.shape[0], x.shape[1]*x.shape[2])
    return MinMaxScaler().fit_transform(x)
```

Next, we can use it as our training and test data, as follows:

```
sharpen_kernel = [[0,-1,0], [-1,5,-1], [0,-1,0]]
x_train_conv = convolve(x_train, sharpen_kernel)
x_test_conv = convolve(x_test, sharpen_kernel)
```

Here are few kernels: the first one is used to sharpen an image, then comes a kernel to emphasize vertical edges, while the last one emphasizes the horizontal ones:

- **Sharpen**: `[[0,-1,0], [-1,5,-1], [0,-1,0]]`
- **V-edge**: `[[-1,0,1], [-2,0,2], [-1,0,1]]`
- **H-edge**: `[[-1,-2,-1], [0,0,0], [1,2,1]]`

Giving those kernels to the convolve function we have just created will give us the following effects:

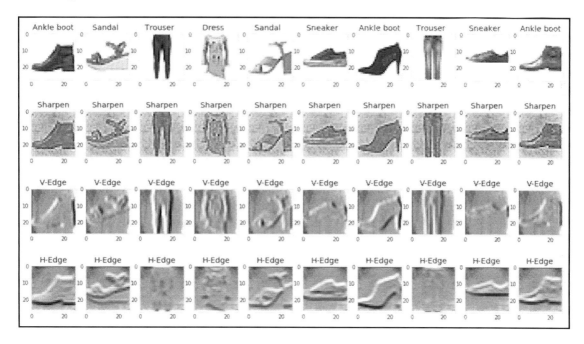

You can find more kernels on the internet, or you can try your own and see the effects they make. The kernels are also intuitive; the sharpening kernel clearly gives more weight to the central pixels versus its surroundings.

Each of the different convolutional transformations captures certain information from our images. We can thus see them as a feature engineering layer, where we extract features to feed to our classifier. Nevertheless, the size of our data will grow with each additional convolutional transformation we append to our data. In the next section, we will see how to deal with this issue.

Reducing the dimensionality of the data via max pooling

Ideally, we would like to feed the outputs from more than one of the previous convolutional transformations into our neural network. Nevertheless, if our images are made of 784 pixels, then concatenating the outputs of just three convolutional functions will result in 2,352 features, *784 x 3*. This will slow down our training process, and as we have learned earlier in this book, the more features are not always the merrier.

To shrink an image to one-quarter of its size—that is, half its width and half its height—you can divide it into multiple *2 x 2* patches, then take the maximum value in each of these patches to represent the entire patch. This is exactly what **max pooling** does. To implement it, we need to install another library called scikit-image using pip in your computer terminal:

```
pip install scikit-image
```

Then, we can create our max pooling function, as follows:

```
from skimage.measure import block_reduce
from sklearn.preprocessing import MinMaxScaler

def maxpool(x, size=(2,2)):
    w = int(np.sqrt(x.shape[1]))
    x = np.array([block_reduce(img.reshape((w, w)), block_size=(size[0],
size[1]), func=np.max) for img in x])
    x = x.reshape(x.shape[0], x.shape[1]*x.shape[2])
    return MinMaxScaler().fit_transform(x)
```

We can then apply it to the outputs of one of the convolutions, as follows:

```
x_train_maxpool = maxpool(x_train_conv, size=(5,5))
x_test_maxpool = maxpool(x_test_conv, size=(5,5))
```

Applying max pooling on *5 x 5* patches will reduce the size of our data from *28 x 28* to *6 x 6*, which is less than 5% of its original size.

Putting it all together

The `FeatureUnion` pipeline in scikit-learn can combine the output of multiple transformers. In other words, if scikit-learn had transformers that could convolve over images and max pool the output of these convolutions, you would have been able to combine the outputs of more than one of these transformers, each with its specific kernel. Luckily, we can build this transformer ourselves and combine their outputs via `FeatureUnion`. We just need them to provide the fit, transform, and fit_transform methods, as follows:

```
class ConvolutionTransformer:
    def __init__(self, kernel=[], max_pool=False, max_pool_size=(2,2)):
        self.kernel = kernel
        self.max_pool = max_pool
        self.max_pool_size = max_pool_size
    def fit(self, x):
        return x
    def transform(self, x, y=None):
        x = convolve(x, self.kernel)
        if self.max_pool:
            x = maxpool(x, self.max_pool_size)
        return x
    def fit_transform(self, x, y=None):
        x = self.fit(x)
        return self.transform(x)
```

You can specify the kernel to use at the initialization step. You can also skip the max pooling part by setting `max_pool` to `False`. Here, we define our three kernels and combine their outputs while pooling each *4 x 4* patch in our images:

```
kernels = [
    ('Sharpen', [[0,-1,0], [-1,5,-1], [0,-1,0]]),
    ('V-Edge', [[-1,0,1], [-2,0,2], [-1,0,1]]),
    ('H-Edge', [[-1,-2,-1], [0,0,0], [1,2,1]]),
]

from sklearn.pipeline import FeatureUnion

funion = FeatureUnion(
    [
        (kernel[0], ConvolutionTransformer(kernel=kernel[1], max_pool=True,
max_pool_size=(4,4)))
        for kernel in kernels
    ]
)
```

```
x_train_convs = funion.fit_transform(x_train)
x_test_convs = funion.fit_transform(x_test)
```

Then, we can use the output of the `FeatureUnion` pipeline into our neural network, as follows:

```
from sklearn.neural_network import MLPClassifier

mlp = MLPClassifier(
    hidden_layer_sizes=(500, 300),
    activation='relu',
    learning_rate_init=0.01,
    solver='adam',
    max_iter=80,
    batch_size=50,
    early_stopping=True,
)

mlp.fit(x_train_convs, y_train)
y_test_predict = mlp.predict(x_test_convs)
```

This network achieved a **micro F-score** of **79%**. You may try adding more kernel and tune the network's hyperparameters and see whether we can achieve a better score than the one we got without the convolutions.

 We had to set the kernel weights of the convolutions by hand. We then displayed their outputs to see whether they make intuitive sense and hope they will improve our model's performance when used. This doesn't sound like a real data-driven approach. You would ideally want the weights to be learned from the data. That's exactly what the real CNNs do. I would suggest you look into TensorFlow and PyTorch for their CNN implementations. It would be nice if you could compare their accuracy to the model we have built here.

MLP regressors

As well as `MLPClassifier`, there is its regressor sibling, `MLPRegressor`. The two share an almost identical interface. The main difference between the two is the loss functions used by each of them and the activation functions of the output layer. The regressor optimizes a squared loss, and the last layer is activated by an identity function. All other hyperparameters are the same, including the four activation options for the hidden layers.

Both estimators have a `partial_fit()` method. You can use it to update the model once you get a hold of additional training data after the estimator has already been fitted. `score()` in `MLPRegressor` calculates the regressor's R^2, as opposed to the classifier's accuracy, which is calculated by `MLPClassifier`.

Summary

We have now developed a good understanding of ANNs and their underlying technologies. I'd recommend libraries such as TensorFlow and PyTorch for more complex architecture and for scaling up the training process on GPUs. However, you have a good headstart already. Most of the concepts discussed here are transferable to any other library. You will be using more or less the same activation functions and the same solvers, as well as most of the other hyperparameters discussed here. scikit-learn's implementation is still good for prototyping and for cases where we want to move beyond linear models without the need for too many hidden layers.

Furthermore, the solvers discussed here, such as gradient descent, are so ubiquitous in the field of machine learning, and so understanding their concepts is also helpful for understanding other algorithms that aren't neural networks. We saw earlier how gradient descent is used in training linear and logistic regressors as well as support vector machines. We are also going to use them with the gradient boosting algorithms we will look at in the next chapter.

Concepts such as the learning rate and how to estimate the amount of training data needed are good to have at your disposal, regardless of what algorithm you are using. These concepts were easily applied here, thanks to the helpful tools provided by scikit-learn. I sometimes find myself using scikit-learn's tools even when I'm not building a machine learning solution.

If ANNs and deep learning are the opium of the media, then ensemble algorithms are the bread and butter for most practitioners when solving any business problem or when competing for a $10,000 prize on Kaggle.

In the next chapter, we are going to learn about the different ensemble methods and their theoretical background, and then get our hands dirty fine-tuning their hyperparameters.

Ensembles – When One Model Is Not Enough

8

In the previous three chapters, we saw how **neural networks** help directly and indirectly in solving natural language understanding and image processing problems. This is because neural networks are proven to work well with **homogeneous data**; that is, if all the input features are of the same breed—pixels, words, characters, and so on. On the other hand, when it comes to **heterogeneous data**, it is the **ensemble methods** that are known to shine. They are well suited to deal with heterogeneous data—for example, where one column contains users' ages, the other has their incomes, and a third has their city of residence.

You can view ensemble estimators as meta-estimators; they are made up of multiple instances of other estimators. The way they combine their underlying estimators is what differentiates between the different ensemble methods—for example, the **bagging** versus the **boosting** methods. In this chapter, we are going to look at these methods in detail and understand their underlying theory. We will also learn how to diagnose our own models and understand why they make certain decisions.

As always, I would also like to seize the opportunity to shed light on general machine learning concepts while dissecting each individual algorithm. In this chapter, we will see how to handle the estimators' uncertainties using the classifiers' probabilities and the regression ranges.

The following topics will be discussed in this chapter:

- The motivation behind ensembles
- Averaging/bagging ensembles
- Boosting ensembles
- Regression ranges

- The ROC curve
- Area under the curve
- Voting and stacking ensembles

Answering the question why ensembles?

The main idea behind ensembles is to combine multiple estimators so that they make better predictions than a single estimator. However, you should not expect the mere combination of multiple estimators to just lead to better results. The combined predictions of multiple estimators who make the exact same mistakes will be as wrong as each individual estimator in the group. Therefore, it is helpful to think of the possible ways to mitigate the mistakes that individual estimators make. To do so, we have to revisit our old friend the bias and variance dichotomy. We will meet few machine learning teachers better than this pair.

If you recall from `Chapter 2`, *Making Decisions with Trees*, when we allowed our decision trees to grow as much as they can, they tended to fit the training data like a glove but failed to generalize to newer data points. We referred to this as overfitting, and we have seen the same behavior with unregularized linear models and with a small number of nearest neighbors. Conversely, aggressively restricting the growth of trees, limiting the number of the features in linear models, and asking too many neighbors to vote caused the models to become biased and underfit the data at hand. So, we had to tread a thin line between trying to find the optimum balance between the bias-variance and the underfitting-overfitting dichotomies.

In the following sections, we are going to follow a different approach. We will deal with the bias-variance dichotomy as a continuous scale, starting from one side of this scale and using the concept of *ensemble* to move toward the other side. In the next section, we are going to start by looking at high-variance estimators and averaging their results to reduce their variance. Later on, we will start from the other side and use the concept of boosting to reduce the estimators' biases.

Combining multiple estimators via averaging

"To derive the most useful information from multiple sources of evidence, you should always try to make these sources independent of each other."

– Daniel Kahneman

If a single fully grown decision tree overfits, and if having many voters in the nearest neighbors algorithm has an opposite effect, then why not combine the two concepts? Rather than having a single tree, let's have a forest that combines the predictions of each tree in it. Nevertheless, we do not want all the trees in our forest to be identical; we would love them to be as diverse as possible. The **bagging** and random forest meta-estimators are the most common examples here. To achieve diversity, they make sure that each one of the individual estimators they use is trained on a random subset of the training data—hence the *random* prefix in random forest. Each time a random sample is drawn, it can be done with replacement (**bootstrapping**) or without replacement (**pasting**). The term bagging stands for **bootstrap aggregation** as the estimators draw their samples with replacement. Furthermore, for even more diversity, the ensembles can assure that each tree sees a random subset of the training features.

Both ensembles use decision tree estimators by default, but the **bagging** ensemble can be reconfigured to use any other estimator. Ideally, we would like to use high-variance estimators. The decisions made by the individual estimators are combined via voting or averaging.

Boosting multiple biased estimators

"If I have seen further than others, it is by standing upon the shoulders of giants."

–Isaac Newton

In contrast to fully grown trees, a shallow tree tends to be biased. Boosting a biased estimator is commonly performed via **AdaBoost** or **gradient boosting**. The AdaBoost meta-estimator starts with a weak or biased estimator, then each consequent estimator learns from the mistakes made by its predecessors. We saw in Chapter 2, *Making Decisions with Trees*, that we can give each individual training sample a different weight so that the estimators can give more emphasis to some samples versus others. In **AdaBoost**, erroneous predictions made by the preceding estimators are given more weight for their successors to pay more attention to.

The **gradient boosting** meta-estimator follows a slightly different approach. It starts with a biased estimator, computes its loss function, then builds each consequent estimator to minimize the loss function of its predecessors. As we saw earlier, gradient descent always comes in handy when iteratively minimizing loss functions, hence the *gradient* prefix in the name of the gradient boosting algorithm.

Due to the iterative nature of the two ensembles, they both have a learning rate to control their learning speed and to make sure they don't miss the local minima when converging. Like the **bagging** algorithm, **AdaBoost** is not limited to decision trees as its base estimator.

Now that we have a good idea about the different ensemble methods, we can use real-life data to demonstrate how they work in practice. Each of the ensemble methods described here can be used for classification and regression. The classifier and regressor hyperparameters are almost identical for each ensemble. Therefore, I will pick a regression problem to demonstrate each algorithm and briefly show the classification capabilities of the random forest and gradient boosting algorithms since they are the most commonly used ensembles.

In the next section, we are going to download a dataset prepared by the **University of California, Irvine** (**UCI**). It contains 201 samples for different cars, along with their prices. We will be using this dataset in a later section to predict the car prices via regression.

Downloading the UCI Automobile dataset

The Automobile dataset was created by Jeffrey C. Schlimmer and published in UCI's machine learning repository. It contains information about 201 automobiles, along with their prices. The names of the features are missing. Nevertheless, I could get them from the dataset's description (`http://archive.ics.uci.edu/ml/machine-learning-databases/autos/imports-85.names`). So, we can start by seeing the URL and the feature names, as follows:

```
url =
'http://archive.ics.uci.edu/ml/machine-learning-databases/autos/imports-85.data'

header = [
    'symboling',
    'normalized-losses',
    'make',
    # ... some list items are omitted for brevity
    'highway-mpg',
    'price',

]
```

Then, we use the following code to download our data.

```
df = pd.read_csv(url, names=header, na_values='?')
```

It is mentioned in the dataset's description that missing values are replaced with a question mark. To make things more Pythonic, we set `na_values` to `'?'` to replace these question marks with NumPy's **Not a Number** (**NaN**).

Next, we can perform our **Exploratory Data Analysis** (**EDA**), check the percentages of the missing values, and see how to deal with them.

Dealing with missing values

Now, we can check which columns have the most missing values:

```
cols_with_missing = df.isnull().sum()
cols_with_missing[
    cols_with_missing > 0
]
```

This gives us the following list:

```
normalized-losses    41
num-of-doors          2
bore                  4
stroke                4
horsepower            2
peak-rpm              2
price                 4
```

Since the price is our target value, we can just ignore the four records where the prices are unknown:

```
df = df[~df['price'].isnull()]
```

As for the remaining features, I'd say let's drop the `normalized-losses` column since 41 of its values are missing. Later on, we will use the data imputation techniques to deal with the other columns with fewer missing values. You can drop the `normalized-losses` column using the following code:

```
df.drop(labels=['normalized-losses'], axis=1, inplace=True)
```

At this point, we have a data frame with all the required features and their names. Next, we want to split the data into training and test sets, and then prepare our features. The different feature types require different preparations. You may need to separately scale the numerical features and encode the categorical ones. So, it is good practice to be able to differentiate between the numerical and the categorical features.

Differentiating between numerical features and categorical ones

Here, we are going to create a dictionary to separately list the numerical and categorical features. We will also make a combined list of the two, and provide the name of the target column, as in the following code:

```
features = {
    'categorical': [
        'make', 'fuel-type', 'aspiration', 'num-of-doors',
        'body-style', 'drive-wheels', 'engine-location',
        'engine-type', 'num-of-cylinders', 'fuel-system',
    ],
    'numerical': [
        'symboling', 'wheel-base', 'length', 'width', 'height',
        'curb-weight', 'engine-size', 'bore', 'stroke',
        'compression-ratio', 'horsepower', 'peak-rpm',
        'city-mpg', 'highway-mpg',
    ],
}

features['all'] = features['categorical'] + features['numerical']

target = 'price'
```

By doing so, you can deal with the columns differently. Furthermore, just for my own sanity and to not print too many zeros in the future, I rescaled the prices to be in thousands, as follows:

```
df[target] = df[target].astype(np.float64) / 1000
```

You can also display certain features separately. Here, we print a random sample, where just the categorical features are shown:

```
df[features['categorical']].sample(n=3, random_state=42)
```

Here are the resulting rows. I set `random_state` to 42 to make sure we all get the same random rows:

	make	fuel-type	aspiration	num-of-doors	body-style	drive-wheels	engine-location	engine-type	num-of-cylinders	fuel-system
169	toyota	gas	std	two	hatchback	rwd	front	ohc	four	mpfi
175	toyota	gas	std	four	hatchback	fwd	front	ohc	four	mpfi
46	isuzu	gas	std	two	hatchback	rwd	front	ohc	four	spfi

All other transformations, such as scaling, imputing, and encoding, should be done after splitting the data into training and test sets. That way, we can ensure that no information is leaked from the test set into the training samples.

Splitting the data into training and test sets

Here, we keep 25% of the data for testing and use the rest for training:

```
from sklearn.model_selection import train_test_split
df_train, df_test = train_test_split(df, test_size=0.25, random_state=22)
```

Then, we can use the information from the previous section to create our x and y values:

```
x_train = df_train[features['all']]
x_test = df_test[features['all']]

y_train = df_train[target]
y_test = df_test[target]
```

As usual, with regression tasks, it is handy to understand the distribution of the target values:

```
y_train.plot(
    title="Distribution of Car Prices (in 1000's)",
    kind='hist',
)
```

A histogram is usually a good choice for understanding distributions, as seen in the following graph:

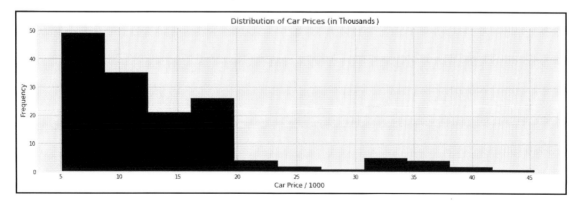

We may come back to this distribution later to put our regressor's mean error in perspective. Additionally, you can use this range for sanity checks. For example, if you know that all the prices you have seen fall in the range of 5,000 to 45,000, you may decide when to put your model in production to fire an alert any time it returns prices far from this range.

Imputing the missing values and encoding the categorical features

Before bringing our ensembles to action, we need to make sure we do not have null values in our data. We will replace the missing values with the most frequent value in each column using the `SimpleImputer` function from Chapter 4, *Preparing Your Data*:

```
from sklearn.impute import SimpleImputer
imp = SimpleImputer(missing_values=np.nan, strategy='most_frequent')

x_train = imp.fit_transform(x_train)
x_test = imp.transform(x_test)
```

You may have already seen me complain many times about the scikit-learn transformers, which do not respect the column names and insist on converting the input data frames into NumPy arrays. To stop myself from complaining again, let me solve my itch by using the following `ColumnNamesKeeper` class. Whenever I wrap it around a transformer, it will make sure all the data frames are kept unharmed:

```
class ColumnNamesKeeper:
    def __init__(self, transformer):
        self._columns = None
        self.transformer = transformer
    def fit(self, x, y=None):
        self._columns = x.columns
        self.transformer.fit(x)
    def transform(self, x, y=None):
        x = self.transformer.transform(x)
        return pd.DataFrame(x, columns=self._columns)
    def fit_transform(self, x, y=None):
        self.fit(x, y)
        return self.transform(x)
```

As you can see, it mainly saves the column name when the `fit` method is called. Then, we can use the saved names to recreate the data frames after the transformation steps.

> The code for `ColumnNamesKeeper` can be simplified further by inheriting from `sklearn.base.BaseEstimator` and `sklearn.base.TransformerMixin`. You can check the source code of any of the library's built-in transformers if you are willing to write more scikit-learn-friendly transformers.

Now, I can call `SimpleImputer` again while preserving `x_train` and `x_test` as data frames:

```
from sklearn.impute import SimpleImputer

imp = ColumnNamesKeeper(
    SimpleImputer(missing_values=np.nan, strategy='most_frequent')
)

x_train = imp.fit_transform(x_train)
x_test = imp.transform(x_test)
```

We learned in Chapter 4, *Preparing Your Data*, that `OrdinalEncoder` is recommended for tree-based algorithms, in addition to any other non-linear algorithms.
The `category_encoders` library doesn't mess with the column names, and so we can use `OrdinalEncoder` without the need for `ColumnNamesKeeper` this time. In the following code snippet, we also specify which columns to encode (the categorical columns) and which to keep unchanged (the remaining ones):

```
from category_encoders.ordinal import OrdinalEncoder
enc = OrdinalEncoder(
    cols=features['categorical'],
    handle_unknown='value'
)
x_train = enc.fit_transform(x_train)
x_test = enc.transform(x_test)
```

In addition to `OrdinalEncoder`, you can also test the encoders mentioned in the target encoding in Chapter 4, *Preparing Your Data*. They, too, are meant to be used with the algorithms explained in this chapter. In the next section, we are going to use the random forest algorithm with the data we have just prepared.

Using random forest for regression

The random forest algorithm is going to be the first ensemble to deal with here. It's an easy-to-grasp algorithm with straightforward hyperparameters. Nevertheless, as we usually do, we will start by training the algorithm using its default values, as follows, then explain its hyperparameters after that:

```
from sklearn.ensemble import RandomForestRegressor
rgr = RandomForestRegressor(n_jobs=-1)
rgr.fit(x_train, y_train)
y_test_pred = rgr.predict(x_test)
```

Since each tree is independent of the others, I set n_jobs to −1 to use my multiple processors to train the trees in parallel. Once they are trained and the predictions are obtained, we can print the following accuracy metrics:

```
from sklearn.metrics import (
    mean_squared_error, mean_absolute_error, median_absolute_error,
r2_score
)

print(
    'R2: {:.2f}, MSE: {:.2f}, RMSE: {:.2f}, MAE {:.2f}'.format(
        r2_score(y_test, y_test_pred),
        mean_squared_error(y_test, y_test_pred),
        np.sqrt(mean_squared_error(y_test, y_test_pred)),
        mean_absolute_error(y_test, y_test_pred),
    )
)
```

This will print the following scores:

```
# R2: 0.90, MSE: 4.54, RMSE: 2.13, MAE 1.35
```

The average car price is 13,400. So, a **Mean Absolute Error (MAE)** of 1.35 seems reasonable. As for the **Mean Squared Error (MSE)**, it makes sense to use its square root to keep it in the same units as the MAE. In brief, given the high R^2 score and the low errors, the algorithm seems to perform well with its default values. Furthermore, you can plot the errors to get a better understanding of the model's performance:

```
df_pred = pd.DataFrame(
    {
        'actuals': y_test,
        'predictions': y_test_pred,
    }
)
```

```
df_pred['error'] = np.abs(y_test - y_test_pred)

fig, axs = plt.subplots(1, 2, figsize=(16, 5), sharey=False)

df_pred.plot(
    title='Actuals vs Predictions',
    kind='scatter',
    x='actuals',
    y='predictions',
    ax=axs[0],
)

df_pred['error'].plot(
    title='Distribution of Error',
    kind='hist',
    ax=axs[1],
)

fig.show()
```

I've excluded some of the formatting lines to keep the code concise. In the end, we get the following graphs:

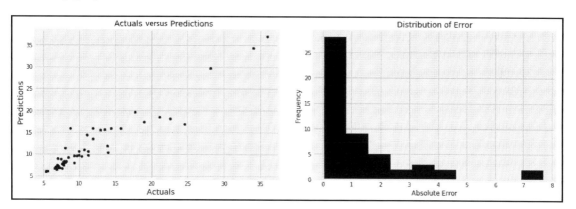

By plotting the predictions versus the actuals, we can make sure that the models don't systematically overestimate or underestimate. This is shown via the 45° slope of the scattered points on the left. A lower slope for the scattered points would have systematically reflected an underestimation. Having the scattered points aligned on a straight line assures us that there aren't non-linearities that the model couldn't capture. The histogram to the right shows that most of the errors are below 2,000. It is good to understand what mean and maximum errors you can expect to get in the future.

Checking the effect of the number of trees

By default, each tree is trained on a random sample from the training data. This is achieved by setting the bootstrap hyperparameter to True. In bootstrap sampling, a sample may be used during training more than once, while another sample may not be used at all.

When max_samples is kept as None, each tree is trained on a random sample of a size that is equal to the entire training data size. You can set max_samples to a fraction that is less than 1, then each tree is trained on a smaller random sub-sample. Similarly, we can set max_features to a fraction that is less than 1 to make sure each tree uses a random subset of the available features. These parameters help each tree to have its own personality and to ensure the diversity of the forest. To put it more formally, these parameters increase the variance of each individual tree. So, it is advised to have as many trees as possible to reduce the variance we have just introduced.

Here, we compare three forests, with a different number of trees in each:

```
mae = []
n_estimators_options = [5, 500, 5000]

for n_estimators in n_estimators_options:

    rgr = RandomForestRegressor(
        n_estimators=n_estimators,
        bootstrap=True,
        max_features=0.75,
        max_samples=0.75,
        n_jobs=-1,
    )

    rgr.fit(x_train, y_train)
    y_test_pred = rgr.predict(x_test)
    mae.append(mean_absolute_error(y_test, y_test_pred))
```

Then, we can plot the MAE for each forest to see the merits of having more trees:

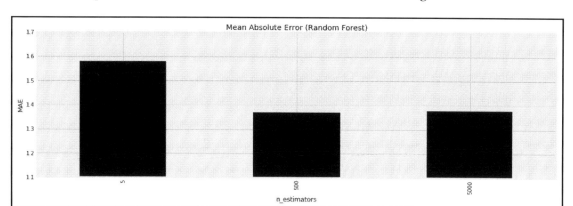

Clearly, we have just encountered a new set of hyperparameters to tune `bootstrap`, `max_features`, and `max_samples`. So, it makes sense to apply cross-validation for hyperparameter tuning.

Understanding the effect of each training feature

Once a random forest is trained, we can list the training features, along with their importance. As usual, we put the outcome in a data frame by using the column names and the `feature_importances_` attribute, as shown:

```
df_feature_importances = pd.DataFrame(
    {
        'Feature': x_train.columns,
        'Importance': rgr.feature_importances_,
    }
).sort_values(
    'Importance', ascending=False
)
```

Here is the resulting data frame:

	Feature	Importance
16	engine-size	0.508621
15	curb-weight	0.223342
20	horsepower	0.064801
23	highway-mpg	0.059187
...	...	...
10	symboling	0.001612
7	engine-type	0.001577
1	fuel-type	0.000707
6	engine-location	0.000643

Unlike with linear models, all the values here are positive. This is because these values only show the importance of each feature, regardless of whether it is positively or negatively correlated with the target. This is common for decision trees, as well as for tree-based ensembles. Thus, we can use **Partial Dependence Plots (PDPs)** to show the relationship between the target and the different features. Here, we only plot it for the top six features according to their importance:

```
from sklearn.inspection import import plot_partial_dependence

fig, ax = plt.subplots(1, 1, figsize=(15, 7), sharey=False)

top_features = df_feature_importances['Feature'].head(6)

plot_partial_dependence(
    rgr, x_train,
    features=top_features,
    n_cols=3,
    n_jobs=-1,
    line_kw={'color': 'k'},
    ax=ax
)

ax.set_title('Partial Dependence')

fig.show()
```

The resulting graphs are easier to read, especially when the relationship between the target and the features is non-linear:

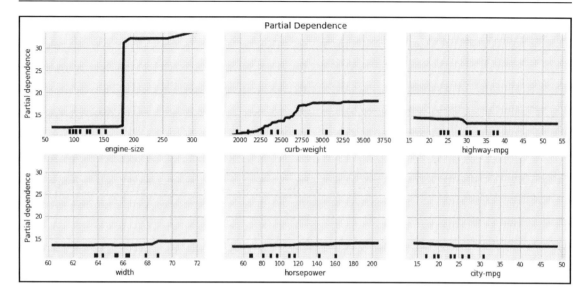

We can now tell that cars with bigger engines, more horsepower, and less mileage per gallon tend to be more expensive.

PDPs are not just useful for ensemble methods, but also for any other complex non-linear model. Despite the fact the neural networks have coefficients for each layer, the PDP is essential in understanding the network as a whole. Furthermore, you can also understand the interaction between the different feature pairs by passing the list of features as a list tuples, with a pair of features in each tuple.

Using random forest for classification

To demonstrate the random forest classifier, we are going to use a synthetic dataset. We first create the dataset using the built-in `make_hastie_10_2` class:

```
from sklearn.datasets import make_hastie_10 2
x, y = make_hastie_10_2(n_samples=6000, random_state=42)
```

This previous code snippet creates a random dataset. I set `random_state` to a fixed number to make sure we both get the same random data. Now, we can split the resulting data into training and test sets:

```
from sklearn.model_selection import train_test_split
x_train, x_test, y_train, y_test = train_test_split(x, y, test_size=0.25,
random_state=42)
```

Then, to evaluate the classifier, we are going to introduce a new concept called the **Receiver Operating Characteristic (ROC)** curve in the next section.

The ROC curve

"Probability is expectation founded upon partial knowledge. A perfect acquaintance with all the circumstances affecting the occurrence of an event would change expectation into certainty, and leave neither room nor demand for a theory of probabilities."

– George Boole (Boolean data types are named after him)

In a classification problem, the classifier assigns probabilities to each sample to reflect how likely it is that each sample belongs to a certain class. We get these probabilities via the classifier's `predict_proba()` method. The `predict()` method is typically a wrapper on top of the `predict_proba()` method. In a binary-classification problem, it assigns each sample to a specific class if the probability of it belonging to the class is above 50%. In practice, we may not always want to stick to this 50% threshold, especially as different thresholds usually change the **True Positive Rates (TPRs)** and **False Positive Rates (FPRs)** for each class. So, you can choose a different threshold to optimize for a desired TPR.

The best way to decide which threshold suits your needs is to use a ROC curve. This helps us see the TPR and FPR for each threshold. To create this curve, we will train our random forest classifier on the synthetic dataset we have just created, but get the classifier's probabilities this time:

```
from sklearn.ensemble import RandomForestClassifier

clf = RandomForestClassifier(
    n_estimators=100,
    oob_score=True,
    n_jobs=-1,
)

clf.fit(x_train, y_train)
y_pred_proba = clf.predict_proba(x_test)[:,1]
```

Then, we can calculate the TPR and FPR for each threshold, as follows:

```
from sklearn.metrics import roc_curve
fpr, tpr, thr = roc_curve(y_test, y_pred_proba)
```

Let's stop for a moment to explain what TPR and FPR mean:

- The **TPR**, also known as **recall** or **sensitivity**, is calculated as the number of **True Positive** (TP) cases divided by all the positive cases; that is, $TPR = \frac{TP}{(TP+FN)}$, where FN is the positive cases falsely classified as negative (false negatives).
- The **True Negative Rates** (TNR), also known as **specificity**, is calculated as the number of **True Negative** (TN) cases divided by all the negative cases; that is, $TNR = \frac{TN}{TN+FP}$, where FP is the negative cases falsely classified as positive (false positives).
- The **FPR** is defined as 1 minus TNR; that is, $FPR = 1 - TNR$.
- The **False Negative Rate (FNR)** is defined as 1 minus TPR; that is, $FNR = 1 - TPR$.

Now, we can put the calculated TPR and FPR for our dataset into the following table:

Threshold	True Positive Rate	False Positive Rate
0.710364	0.001305	0.000000
0.549833	0.259791	0.000000
0.549220	0.262402	0.000000
0.547614	0.274151	0.000000
0.547542	0.274151	0.001362
...	...	...
0.428332	0.994778	0.671662
0.426702	0.994778	0.685286
0.425484	0.994778	0.688011
0.425381	0.994778	0.693460
0.422533	1.000000	1.000000

Even better than a table, we can plot them into a graph using the following code:

```
pd.DataFrame(
    {'FPR': fpr, 'TPR': tpr}
).set_index('FPR')['TPR'].plot(
    title=f'Receiver Operating Characteristic (ROC)',
    label='Random Forest Classifier',
    kind='line',
)
```

I've omitted the graph's styling code for the sake of brevity. I also added a 45° line and the **Area Under the Curve (AUC)**, which I will explain in a bit:

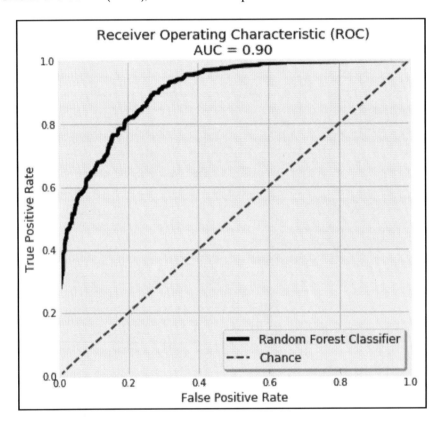

A classifier that randomly assigns each sample to a certain class will have a ROC curve that looks like the dashed 45° line. Any improvement over this will make the curve more convex upward. Obviously, random forest's ROC curve is better than chance. An optimum classifier will touch the upper-left corner of the graph. Therefore, the AUC can be used to reflect how good the classifier is. An area above 0.5 is better than chance, and an area of 1.0 is the best possible value. We typically expect values between 0.5 and 1.0. Here, we got an AUC of 0.94. The AUC can be calculated using the following code:

```
from sklearn.metrics import auc
auc_values = auc(fpr, tpr)
```

We can also use the ROC and AUC to compare two classifiers. Here, I trained the random forest classifier with the bootstrap hyperparameter set to True and compared it to the same classifier when bootstrap was set to False:

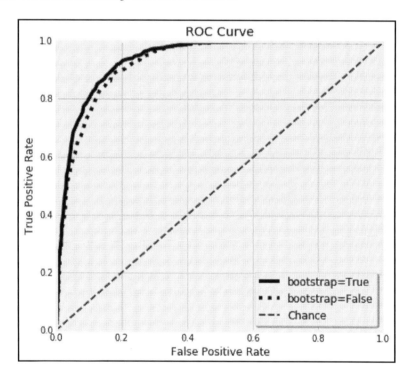

No wonder the bootstrap hyperparameter is set to True by default—it gives better results. Now, you have seen how to use random forest algorithms to solve classification and regression problems. In the next section, we are going to explain a similar ensemble: the bagging ensemble.

Using bagging regressors

We will go back to the Automobile dataset as we are going to use the **bagging regressor** this time. The bagging meta-estimator is very similar to random forest. It is built of multiple estimators, each one trained on a random subset of the data using a bootstrap sampling method. The key difference here is that although decision trees are used as the base estimators by default, any other estimator can be used as well. Out of curiosity, let's use the **K-Nearest Neighbors** (**KNN**) regressor as our base estimator this time. However, we need to prepare the data to suit the new regressor's needs.

Preparing a mixture of numerical and categorical features

It is recommended to put all features on the same scale when using distance-based algorithms such as KNN. Otherwise, the effect of the features with higher magnitudes on the distance metric will overshadow the other features. As we have a mixture of numerical and categorical features here, we need to create two parallel pipelines to prepare each feature set separately.

Here is a top-level view of our pipeline:

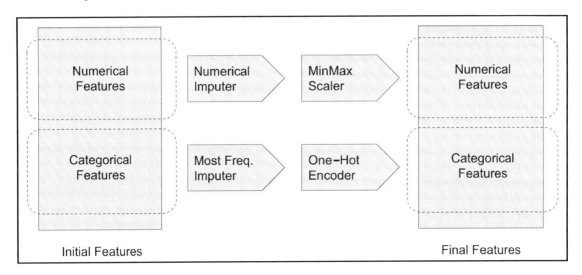

Here, we start by building the four transformers in our pipelines: `Imputer`, `Scaler`, and `OneHotEncoder`. We also wrap them in `ColumnNamesKeeper`, which we created earlier in this chapter:

```
from sklearn.impute import SimpleImputer
from category_encoders.one_hot import OneHotEncoder
from sklearn.preprocessing import MinMaxScaler
from sklearn.pipeline import Pipeline

numerical_mputer = ColumnNamesKeeper(
    SimpleImputer(
        missing_values=np.nan,
        strategy='median'
    )
)

categorical_mputer = ColumnNamesKeeper(
    SimpleImputer(
        missing_values=np.nan,
        strategy='most_frequent'
    )
)

minmax_scaler = ColumnNamesKeeper(
    MinMaxScaler()
)

onehot_encoder = OneHotEncoder(
    cols=features['categorical'],
    handle_unknown='value'
)
```

Then, we put them into two parallel pipelines:

```
numerical_pipeline = Pipeline(
    [
        ('numerical_mputer', numerical_mputer),
        ('minmax_scaler', minmax_scaler)
    ]
)

categorical_pipeline = Pipeline(
    [
        ('categorical_mputer', categorical_mputer),
        ('onehot_encoder', onehot_encoder)
    ]
)
```

Finally, we concatenate the outputs of the pipelines for both the training and the test sets:

```
x_train_knn = pd.concat(
    [
        numerical_pipeline.fit_transform(df_train[features['numerical']]),
categorical_pipeline.fit_transform(df_train[features['categorical']]),
    ],
    axis=1
)

x_test_knn = pd.concat(
    [
        numerical_pipeline.transform(df_test[features['numerical']]),
        categorical_pipeline.transform(df_test[features['categorical']]),
    ],
    axis=1
)
```

At this point, we are ready to build our bagged KNNs.

Combining KNN estimators using a bagging meta-estimator

BaggingRegressor has a base_estimator hyperparameter, where you can set the estimators you want to use. Here, KNeighborsRegressor is used with a single neighbor. Since we are aggregating multiple estimators to reduce their variance, it makes sense to have a high variance estimator in the first place, hence the small number of neighbors here:

```
from sklearn.ensemble import BaggingRegressor
from sklearn.neighbors import KNeighborsRegressor

rgr = BaggingRegressor(
    base_estimator=KNeighborsRegressor(
        n_neighbors=1
    ),
    n_estimators=400,
)

rgr.fit(x_train_knn, df_train[target])
y_test_pred = rgr.predict(x_test_knn)
```

This new setup gives us an MAE of 1.8. We can stop here, or we may decide to improve the ensemble's performance by tuning its big array of hyperparameters.

First of all, we can try different estimators other than KNN, each with its own hyperparameters. Then, the bagging ensemble also has its own hyperparameters. We can change the number of estimators via `n_estimators`. Then, we can decide whether to use the entire training set or a random subset of it for each estimator via `max_samples`. Similarly, we can also pick a random subset of the columns to use for each estimator to use via `max_features`. The choice of whether to use bootstrapping for the rows and the columns can be made via the `bootstrap` and `bootstrap_features` hyperparameters, respectively.

Finally, since each estimator is trained separately, we can use a machine with a high number of CPUs and parallelize the training process by setting `n_jobs` to −1.

Now that we have experienced two versions of the averaging ensembles, it is time to check their boosting counterparts. We will start with the gradient boosting ensemble, then move to the AdaBoost ensemble.

Using gradient boosting to predict automobile prices

If I were ever stranded on a desert island and had to pick one algorithm to take with me, I'd definitely chose the gradient boosting ensemble! It has proven to work very well on many classification and regression problems. We are going to use it with the same automobile data from the previous sections. The classifier and the regressor versions of this ensemble share the exact same hyperparameters, except for the loss functions they use. This means that everything we are going to learn here will be useful to us whenever we decide to use gradient boosting ensembles for classification.

Unlike the averaging ensembles we have seen so far, the boosting ensembles build their estimators iteratively. The knowledge learned from the initial ensemble is used to build its successors. This is the main downside of boosting ensembles, where parallelism is unfeasible. Putting parallelism aside, this iterative nature of the ensemble calls for a learning rate to be set. This helps the gradient descent algorithm reach the loss function's minima easily. Here, we use 500 trees, each with a maximum of 3 nodes, and a learning rate of 0.01. Furthermore, the **Least Squares (LS)** loss is used here; think MSE. More on the available loss functions in a moment:

```
from sklearn.ensemble import GradientBoostingRegressor

rgr = GradientBoostingRegressor(
    n_estimators=1000, learning_rate=0.01, max_depth=3, loss='ls'
```

```
)

rgr.fit(x_train, y_train)
y_test_pred = rgr.predict(x_test)
```

This new algorithm gives us the following performance on the test set:

```
# R2: 0.92, MSE: 3.93, RMSE: 1.98, MAE: 1.42
```

As you can see, this setting gave a lower MSE compared to random forest, while random forest had a better MAE. Another loss function that the gradient boosting regressor can use is **Least Absolute Deviation** (**LAD**); think MAE, this time. LAD may help when dealing with outliers, and it can sometimes reduce the model's MAE performance on the test set. Nevertheless, it did not improve the MAE for the dataset at hand. We also have a percentile (quantile) loss, but before going deeper into the supported loss functions, we need to learn how to diagnose the learning process.

The main hyperparameters to set here are the number of trees, the depth of the trees, the learning rate, and the loss function. As a rule of thumb, you should aim for a higher number of trees and a low learning rate. As we will see in a bit, these two hyperparameters are inversely proportional to each other. Controlling the depth of your trees is purely dependent on your data. In general, we need to have shallow trees and let boosting empower them. Nevertheless, the depth of the tree controls the number of feature interactions we want to capture. In a stub (a tree with a single split), only one feature can be learned at a time. A deeper tree resembles a nested `if` condition where a few more features are at play each time. I usually start with `max_depth` set to around 3 and 5 and tune it along the way.

Plotting the learning deviance

With each additional estimator, we expect the algorithm to learn more and the loss to decrease. Yet, at some point, the additional estimators will keep overfitting on the training data while not offering much improvement for the test data.

To have a clear picture, we need to plot the calculated loss with each additional estimator for both the training and test sets. As for the training loss, it is saved by the gradient boosting meta-estimator into its `loss_` attribute. For the test loss, we can use the meta-estimator's `staged_predict()` methods. This method can be used for a given dataset to make predictions for each intermediate iteration.

Since we have multiple loss functions to choose from, gradient boosting also provides a `loss_()` method, which calculates the loss for us based on the loss function used. Here, we create a new function to calculate the training and test errors for each iteration and put them into a data frame:

```
def calculate_deviance(estimator, x_test, y_test):

    train_errors = estimator.train_score_
    test_errors = [
        estimator.loss_(y_test, y_pred_staged)
        for y_pred_staged in estimator.staged_predict(x_test)
    ]

    return pd.DataFrame(
        {
            'n_estimators': range(1, estimator.estimators_.shape[0]+1),
            'train_error': train_errors,
            'test_error': test_errors,
        }
    ).set_index('n_estimators')
```

Since we are going to use an LS loss here, you can simply replace the `estimator.loss_()` method with `mean_squared_error()` and get the exact same results. But let's keep the `estimator.loss_()` function for a more versatile and reusable code.

Next, we train our gradient boosting regressor, as usual:

```
from sklearn.ensemble import GradientBoostingRegressor

rgr = GradientBoostingRegressor(n_estimators=250, learning_rate=0.02,
loss='ls')
rgr.fit(x_train, y_train)
```

Then, we use the trained model, along with the test set, to plot the training and test learning deviance:

```
fig, ax = plt.subplots(1, 1, figsize=(16, 5), sharey=False)

df_deviance = calculate_deviance(rgr, x_test, y_test)

df_deviance['train_error'].plot(
    kind='line', color='k', linestyle=':', ax=ax
)

df_deviance['test_error'].plot(
    kind='line', color='k', linestyle='-', ax=ax
)

fig.show()
```

Running the code gives us the following graph:

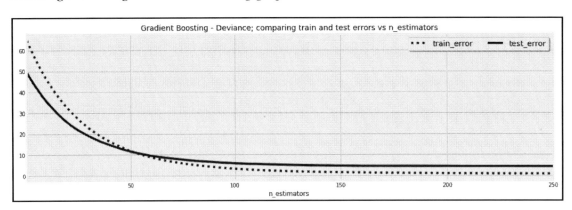

The beauty of this graph is that it tells us that the improvements on the test set stopped after 120 estimators or so, despite the continuous improvement in the training set; that is, it started to overfit. Furthermore, we can use this graph to understand the effect of a chosen learning rate, as we did in Chapter 7, *Neural Networks - Here comes the Deep Learning*.

Comparing the learning rate settings

Rather than training one model, we will train three gradient boosting regressors this time, each with a different learning rate. Then, we will plot the deviance graph for each one side by side, as shown:

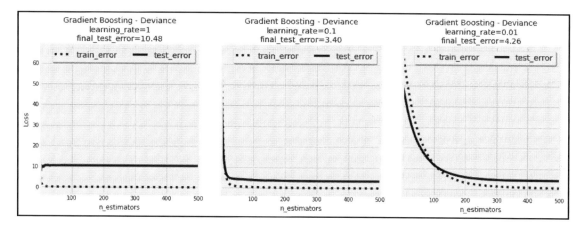

As with other gradient descent-based models, a high learning rate causes the estimator to overshoot and miss the local minima. We can see this in the first graph where no improvements are seen despite the consecutive iterations. The learning rates in the second and third graphs seem reasonable. In comparison, the learning rate in the third graph seems to be too slow for the model to converge in 500 iterations. You may then decide to increase the number of estimators for the third model to allow it to converge.

We have learned from the bagging ensembles that using a random training sample with each estimator may help with overfitting. In the next section, we are going to see whether the same approach can also help the boosting ensembles.

Using different sample sizes

We have been using the entire training set for each iteration. This time, we are going to train three gradient boosting regressors, each with a different subsample size, and plot their deviance graphs as before. We will use a fixed learning rate of 0.01 and the LAD as our loss function, as shown:

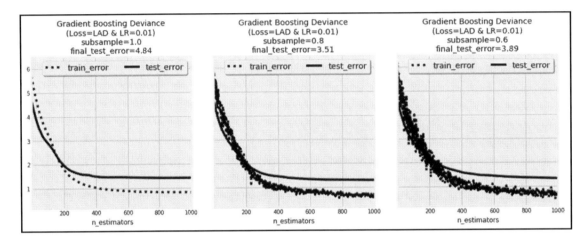

In the first graph, the entire training sample is used for each iteration. So, the training loss did not fluctuate as much as in the other two graphs. Nevertheless, the sampling used in the second model allowed it to reach a better test score, despite its noisy loss graph. This was similarly the case for the third model, but with a slightly larger final error.

Stopping earlier and adapting the learning rate

The n_iter_no_change hyperparameter is used to stop the training process after a certain number of iterations if the validation score is not improving enough. The subset set aside for validation, validation_fraction, is used to calculate the validation score.

The tol hyperparameter is used to decide how much improvement we must consider as being enough.

The `fit` method in the gradient boosting algorithm accepts a callback function that is called after each iteration. It can also be used to set a custom condition to stop the training process based on it. Furthermore, It can be used for monitoring or for any other customizations you need. This callback function is called with three parameters: the order of the current iteration (`n`), an instance of gradient boosting (`estimator`), and its settings (`params`). To demonstrate how this callback function works, let's build a function to change the learning rate to `0.01` for one iteration at every `10` iterations, and keep it at `0.1` for the remaining iterations, as shown:

```
def lr_changer(n, estimator, params):
    if n % 10:
        estimator.learning_rate = 0.01
    else:
        estimator.learning_rate = 0.1
    return False
```

Then, we use our `lr_changer` function, as follows:

```
from sklearn.ensemble import GradientBoostingRegressor
rgr = GradientBoostingRegressor(n_estimators=50, learning_rate=0.01,
loss='ls')
rgr.fit(x_train, y_train, monitor=lr_changer)
```

Now, if we print the deviance as we usually do, we will see how after every 10th iteration, the calculated loss jumps due to the learning rate changes:

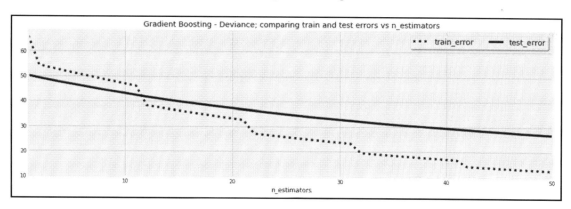

What I've just done is pretty useless, but it demonstrates the possibilities you have at hand. For example, you can borrow ideas such as the adaptive learning rate and the momentum from the solvers used in the neural networks and incorporate them here using this callback function.

Regression ranges

"I try to be a realist and not a pessimist or an optimist."

–Yuval Noah Harari

One last gem that gradient boosting regression offers to us is regression ranges. These are very useful in quantifying the uncertainty of your predictions.

We try our best to make our predictions exactly the same as the actual data. Nevertheless, our data can still be noisy, or the features used may not capture the whole truth. Take the following example:

x_1	x_2	y
0	0	10
1	1	50
0	0	20
0	0	22

Consider a new sample with $x_1 = 0$ and $x_2 = 0$. We already have three training examples with the exact same features, so what would the predicted y value be for this new sample? If a squared loss function is used during the training, then the predicted target will be close to 17.3, which is the mean of the three corresponding targets (10, 20, and 22). Now, if MAE is used, then the predicted target will be closer to 22, which is the median (50th percentile) of the three corresponding targets. Rather than the 50th percentile, we can use any other percentiles when a **quantile** loss function is used. So, to achieve regression ranges, we can use two regressors with two different quantiles as the upper and lower bounds of our range.

Although the regression ranges work regardless of the dimensionality of the data at hand, the format of the page has forced us to come up with a two-dimensional example for more clarity. The following code creates 400 samples to play with:

```
x_sample = np.arange(-10, 10, 0.05)
y_sample = np.random.normal(loc=0, scale=25, size=x_sample.shape[0])
y_sample *= x_sample

pd_random_samples = pd.DataFrame(
    {
        'x': x_sample,
        'y': y_sample
    }
)
```

Here is a scatter plot of the generated *y* versus *x* values:

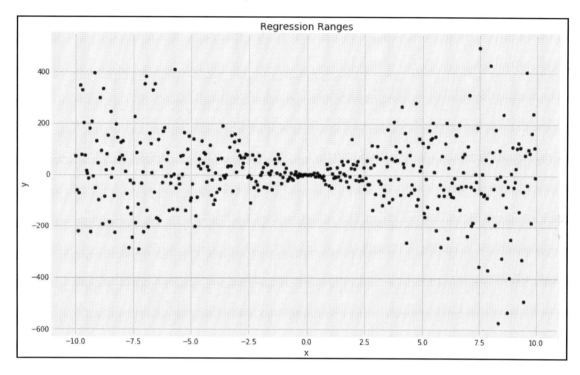

Now, we can train two regressors with the 10th and 90th percentiles as our range boundaries and plot those regression boundaries, along with our scattered data points:

```
from sklearn.ensemble import GradientBoostingRegressor

fig, ax = plt.subplots(1, 1, figsize=(12, 8), sharey=False)

pd_random_samples.plot(
    title='Regression Ranges [10th & 90th Quantiles]',
    kind='scatter', x='x', y='y', color='k', alpha=0.95, ax=ax
)

for quantile in [0.1, 0.9]:
    rgr = GradientBoostingRegressor(n_estimators=10, loss='quantile',
alpha=quantile)
    rgr.fit(pd_random_samples[['x']], pd_random_samples['y'])
    pd_random_samples[f'pred_q{quantile}'] =
rgr.predict(pd_random_samples[['x']])
    pd_random_samples.plot(
        kind='line', x='x', y=f'pred_q{quantile}',
```

```
            linestyle='-', alpha=0.75, color='k', ax=ax
    )
ax.legend(ncol=1, fontsize='x-large', shadow=True)

fig.show()
```

We can see that the majority of the points fall within the range. Ideally, we would expect 80% of the points to fall in the **90-100** range:

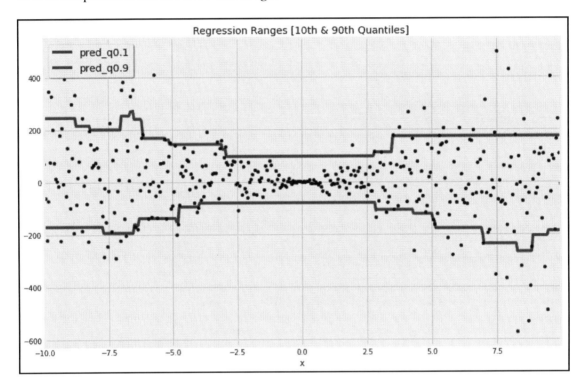

We can now use the same strategy to predict automobile prices:

```
from sklearn.ensemble import GradientBoostingRegressor

rgr_min = GradientBoostingRegressor(n_estimators=50, loss='quantile',
alpha=0.25)
rgr_max = GradientBoostingRegressor(n_estimators=50, loss='quantile',
alpha=0.75)

rgr_min.fit(x_train, y_train, monitor=lr_changer)
rgr_max.fit(x_train, y_train, monitor=lr_changer)

y_test_pred_min = rgr_min.predict(x_test)
```

```
y_test_pred_max = rgr_max.predict(x_test)

df_pred_range = pd.DataFrame(
    {
        'Actuals': y_test,
        'Pred_min': y_test_pred_min,
        'Pred_max': y_test_pred_max,
    }
)
```

Then, we can check what percentage of our test set falls within the regression range:

```
df_pred_range['Actuals in Range?'] = df_pred_range.apply(
    lambda row: 1 if row['Actuals'] >= row['Pred_min'] and row['Actuals']
<= row['Pred_max'] else 0, axis=1
)
```

Calculating the mean of `df_pred_range['Actuals in Range?']` gives us 0.49, which is very close to the 0.5 value we expected. Obviously, we can use wider or narrower ranges, depending on our use case. If your model is going to be used to help car owners sell their cars, you may need to give them reasonable ranges, since telling someone that they can sell their car for any price between \$5 and \$30,000 is pretty accurate yet useless advice. Sometimes, a less accurate yet useful model is better than an accurate and useless one.

Another boosting algorithm that is not used as much nowadays is the AdaBoost algorithm. We will briefly explore it in the next section for the sake of completeness.

Using AdaBoost ensembles

In an AdaBoost ensemble, the mistakes made in each iteration are used to alter the weights of the training samples for the following iterations. As in the boosting meta-estimator, this method can also use any other estimators instead of the decision trees used by default. Here, we have used it with its default estimators on the Automobile dataset:

```
from sklearn.ensemble import AdaBoostRegressor

rgr = AdaBoostRegressor(n_estimators=100)
rgr.fit(x_train, y_train)
y_test_pred = rgr.predict(x_test)
```

The AdaBoost meta-estimator also has a `staged_predict` method, which allows us to plot the improvement in the training or test loss after each iteration. Here is the code for plotting the test error:

```
pd.DataFrame(
    [
        (n, mean_squared_error(y_test, y_pred_staged))
        for n, y_pred_staged in enumerate(rgr.staged_predict(x_test), 1)
    ],
    columns=['n', 'Test Error']
).set_index('n').plot()

fig.show()
```

Here is a plot for the calculated loss after each iteration:

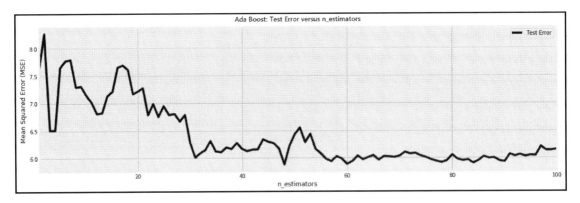

As in the other ensembles, the more estimators we add, the more accurate it becomes. Once we start to overfit, we should be able to stop. That's why having a validation sample is essential in knowing when to stop. I used the test set for demonstration here, but in practice, the test sample should be kept aside and a validation set should be used instead.

Exploring more ensembles

The main ensemble techniques are the ones we have seen so far. The following ones are also good to know about and can be useful for some peculiar cases.

Voting ensembles

Sometimes, we have a number of good estimators, each with its own mistakes. Our objective is not to mitigate their bias or variance, but to combine their predictions in the hope that they don't all make the same mistakes. In these cases, VotingClassifier and VotingRegressor could be used. You can give a higher preference to some estimators versus the others by adjusting the weights hyperparameter. VotingClassifier has different voting strategies, depending on whether the predicted class labels are to be used or whether the predicted probabilities should be used instead.

Stacking ensembles

Rather than voting, you can combine the predictions of multiple estimators by adding an extra one that uses their predictions as input. This strategy is known as **stacking**. The inputs of the final estimator can be limited to the predictions of the previous estimators, or it can be a combination of their predictions and the original training data. To avoid overfitting, the final estimators are usually trained using cross-validation.

Random tree embedding

We have seen how the trees are capable of capturing the non-linearities in the data. So, if we still want to use a simpler algorithm, we can just use the trees to transform the data and leave the prediction for the simple algorithm to do. When building a tree, each data point falls into one of its leaves. Therefore, the IDs of the leaves can be used to represent the different data points. If we build multiple trees, then each data point can be represented by the ID of the leaf it fell on in each tree. These leaves, IDs can be used as our new features and can be fed into a simpler estimator. This kind of embedding is useful for feature compression and allows linear models to capture the non-linearities in the data.

Here, we use an unsupervised RandomTreesEmbedding method to transform our automobile features, and then use the transformed features in a Ridge regression:

```
from sklearn.ensemble import RandomTreesEmbedding
from sklearn.linear_model import Ridge
from sklearn.pipeline import make_pipeline

rgr = make_pipeline(RandomTreesEmbedding(), Ridge())
rgr.fit(x_train, y_train)
y_test_pred = rgr.predict(x_test)

print(f'MSE: {mean_squared_error(y_test, y_test_pred)}')
```

From the preceding block of code, we can observe the following:

- This approach is not limited to `RandomTreesEmbedding`.

- Gradient-boosted trees can also be used to transform the data for a downstream estimator to use.

- Both `GradientBoostingRegressor` and `GradientBoostingClassifier` have an `apply` function, which can be used for feature transformation.

Summary

In this chapter, we saw how algorithms benefit from being assembled in the form of ensembles. We learned how these ensembles can mitigate the bias versus variance trade-off.

When dealing with heterogeneous data, the gradient boosting and random forest algorithms are my first two choices for classification and regression. They do not require any sophisticated data preparation, thanks to their dependence on trees. They are able to deal with non-linear data and capture feature interactions. Above all, the tuning of their hyperparameters is straightforward.

The more estimators in each method, the better, and you should not worry so much about them overfitting. As for gradient boosting, you can pick a lower learning rate if you can afford to have more trees. In addition to these hyperparameters, the depth of the trees in each of the two algorithms should be tuned via trail and error and cross-validation. Since the two algorithms come from different sides of the bias-variance spectrum, you may initially aim for forests with big trees that you can prune later on. Conversely, you can start with shallow trees and rely on your gradient-boosting meta-estimator to boost them.

So far in this book, we have predicted a single target at a time. Here, we predicted the prices of automobiles and that's it. In the next chapter, we will see how to predict multiple targets at a time. Furthermore, when our aim is to use the probabilities given by a classifier, having a calibrated classifier is paramount. We can have a better estimation of our risks if we have probabilities that we trust. Thus, calibrating a classifier is going to be another topic covered in the next chapter.

The Y is as Important as the X

9

A lot of attention is given to the input features, that is, our x's. We have used algorithms to scale them, select from them, and engineer new features to add to them. Nonetheless, we should also give as much attention to the targets, the y's. Sometimes, scaling your targets can help you use a simpler model. Some other times, you may need to predict multiple targets at once. It is, then, essential to know the distribution of your targets and their interdependencies. In this chapter, we are going to focus on the targets and how to deal with them.

In this chapter, we will cover the following topics:

- Scaling your regression targets
- Estimating multiple regression targets
- Dealing with compound classification targets
- Calibrating a classifier's probabilities
- Calculating the precision at K

Scaling your regression targets

In regression problems, sometimes scaling the targets can save time and allow us to use simpler models for the problems at hand. In this section, we are going to see how to make our estimator's life easier by changing the scale of our targets.

In the following example, the relation between the target and the input is non-linear. Therefore, a linear model would not give the best results. We can either use a non-linear algorithm, transform our features, or transform our targets. Out of the three options, transforming the targets can be the easiest sometimes. Notice that we only have one feature here, but when dealing with a number of features, it makes sense to think of transforming your targets first.

The following plot shows the relation between a single feature, x, and a dependent variable, y:

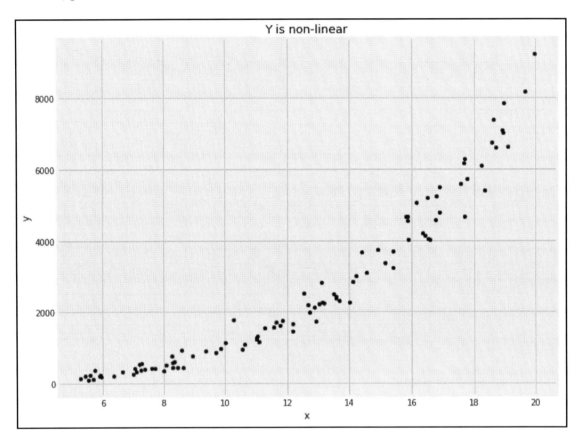

Between you and me, the following code was used to generate data, but for the sake of learning, we can pretend that we do not know the relation between the y's and the x's for now:

```
x = np.random.uniform(low=5, high=20, size=100)
e = np.random.normal(loc=0, scale=0.5, size=100)
y = (x + e) ** 3
```

The one-dimensional input (x) is uniformly distributed between 5 and 20. The relation between *y* and *x* is cubical, with some normally distributed noise added to the *x*'s.

Before splitting out data, we need to transform the *x*'s from a vector into a matrix, as follows:

```
from sklearn.model_selection import train_test_split
x = x.reshape((x.shape[0],1))
x_train, x_test, y_train, y_test = train_test_split(x, y, test_size=0.25)
```

Now, if we split our data into training and test sets, and run a ridge regression, we will get a **Mean Absolute Error (MAE)** of 559. Your mileage may vary due to the randomly generated data. Can we do better than this?

 Please keep in mind that in most of the examples mentioned in this chapter, the final results you will get may differ from mine. I preferred not to use random states when generating and splitting the data as my main goal here is to explain the concepts, regardless of the final results and the accuracy scores we get when running the code.

Let's create a simple transformer to convert the target based on a given `power`. When `power` is set to 1, no transformation is done to the target; otherwise, the target is raised to the given power. Our transformer has a complementary `inverse_transform()` method to retransform the targets back to their original scale:

```
class YTransformer:
    def __init__(self, power=1):
        self.power = power
    def fit(self, x, y):
        pass
    def transform(self, x, y):
        return x, np.power(y, self.power)
    def inverse_transform(self, x, y):
        return x, np.power(y, 1/self.power)
    def fit_transform(self, x, y):
        return self.transform(x, y)
```

Now, we can try different settings for the power and loop over the different transformations until we find the one that gives the best results:

```
from sklearn.linear_model import Ridge
from sklearn.metrics import mean_absolute_error
from sklearn.metrics import r2_score

for power in [1, 1/2, 1/3, 1/4, 1/5]:

    yt = YTransformer(power)
    _, y_train_t = yt.fit_transform(None, y_train)
    _, y_test_t = yt.transform(None, y_test)
```

```
rgs = Ridge()

rgs.fit(x_train, y_train_t)
y_pred_t = rgs.predict(x_test)
_, y_pred = yt.inverse_transform(None, y_pred_t)

print(
    'Transformed y^{:.2f}: MAE={:.0f}, R2={:.2f}'.format(
        power,
        mean_absolute_error(y_test, y_pred),
        r2_score(y_test, y_pred),
    )
)
```

It is essential that we convert the predicted values to their original. Otherwise, the calculated error metrics will not be comparable given the different data scales achieved by the different power settings.

Ergo, the `inverse_transform()` method is used here after the prediction step. Running the code on my randomly generated data gave me the following results:

```
Transformed y^1.00: MAE=559, R2=0.89
Transformed y^0.50: MAE=214, R2=0.98
Transformed y^0.33: MAE=210, R2=0.97
Transformed y^0.25: MAE=243, R2=0.96
Transformed y^0.20: MAE=276, R2=0.95
```

As expected, the lowest error and the highest R^2 are achieved when the right transformation was used, which is when the power is set to $\frac{1}{3}$.

The logarithmic, exponential, and square root transformations are the ones most commonly used by statisticians. It makes sense to use them when performing a prediction task, especially when a linear model is used.

The logarithmic transformation is only useful for positive values. `Log(0)` is undefined, and the logarithm of a negative number gives us imaginary values. Thus, the logarithmic transformation is usually applied when dealing with non-negative targets. One other trick to make sure that we do not encounter `log(0)` is to add 1 to all your target values before transforming them, then subtract 1 after transforming your predictions back. Similarly, for the square root transformation, we have to make sure not to have negative targets in the first place.

Rather than dealing with one target at a time, we may sometimes want to predict multiple targets at once. Combining multiple regression tasks into a single model can simplify your code when they all use the same features. It's also recommended when your targets are interdependent. In the next section, we are going to see how to estimate multiple regression targets at once.

Estimating multiple regression targets

In your online business, you may want to estimate the lifetime value of your users in the next month, the next quarter, and the next year. You could build three different regressors for each one of these three separate estimations. However, when the three estimations use the exact same features, it becomes more practical to build one regressor with three outputs. In the next section, we are going to see how to build a multi-output regressor, then we will learn how to inject interdependencies between those estimations using regression chains.

Building a multi-output regressor

Some regressors allow us to predict multiple targets at once. For example, the ridge regressor allows for a two-dimensional target to be given. In other words, rather than having y as a single-dimensional array, it can be given as a matrix, where each column represents a different target. For the other regressors where only single targets are allowed, we may need to use the multi-output regressor meta-estimator.

To demonstrate this meta-estimator, I am going to use the `make_regression` helper to create a dataset that we can fiddle with:

```
from sklearn.datasets import make_regression

x, y = make_regression(
    n_samples=500, n_features=8, n_informative=8, n_targets=3, noise=30.0
)
```

Here, we create 500 samples, with 8 features and 3 targets; that is, the shapes of the returned x and y are (500, 8) and (500, 3) respectively. We can also give the features and the targets different names, and then split the data into training and test sets as follows:

```
feature_names = [f'Feature # {i}' for i in range(x.shape[1])]
target_names = [f'Target # {i}' for i in range(y.shape[1])]

from sklearn.model_selection import train_test_split
x_train, x_test, y_train, y_test = train_test_split(x, y, test_size=0.25)
```

Since SGDRegressor does not support multiple targets, the following code will throw a value error complaining about the shape of the inputs:

```
from sklearn.linear_model import SGDRegressor

rgr = SGDRegressor()
rgr.fit(x_train, y_train)
```

Therefore, we have to wrap MultiOutputRegressor around SGDRegressor for it to work:

```
from sklearn.multioutput import MultiOutputRegressor
from sklearn.linear_model import SGDRegressor

rgr = MultiOutputRegressor(
    estimator=SGDRegressor(),
    n_jobs=-1
)
rgr.fit(x_train, y_train)
y_pred = rgr.predict(x_test)
```

We can now output predictions into a dataframe:

```
df_pred = pd.DataFrame(y_pred, columns=target_names)
```

Also, check the first few predictions for each one of the three targets. Here is an example of the predictions I got here. Keep in mind that you may get different results:

	Target # 0	Target # 1	Target # 2
0	-467.676944	-211.388640	-337.080270
1	-126.855710	-21.526441	-40.367112
2	-16.770193	49.015083	-169.969358
3	-240.225467	-158.054893	-242.705575

We can also print the model's performance for each target separately:

```
from sklearn.metrics import mean_absolute_error
from sklearn.metrics import r2_score

for t in range(y_train.shape[1]):
    print(
        'Target # {}: MAE={:.2f}, R2={:.2f}'.format(
            t,
            mean_absolute_error(y_test[t], y_pred[t]),
            r2_score(y_test[t], y_pred[t]),
        )
    )
```

In some scenarios, knowing one target may serve as a stepping stone in knowing the others. In the aforementioned lifetime value estimation example, the predictions for the next month are helpful for the quarterly and yearly predictions. To use the predictions for one target as inputs in the consecutive regressors, we need to use the regressor chain meta-estimator.

Chaining multiple regressors

In the dataset from the previous section, we do not know whether the generated targets are interdependent or not. For now, let's assume the second target is dependent on the first one, and the third target is dependent on the first two. We are going to validate these assumptions later. To inject these interdependencies, we are going to use RegressorChain and specify the order of the assumed interdependencies. The order of the IDs in the order list specify that each ID in the list depends on the previous IDs. It makes sense to use a regularized regressor. The regularization is needed to ignore any assumed dependencies that do not exist between the targets.

Here is the code for creating the regressor chain:

```
from sklearn.multioutput import RegressorChain
from sklearn.linear_model import Ridge

rgr = RegressorChain(
    base_estimator=Ridge(
        alpha=1
    ),
    order=[0,1,2],
)
rgr.fit(x_train, y_train)
y_pred = rgr.predict(x_test)
```

The test set performance is almost identical to the one achieved with the `MultiOutputRegressor`. It looks like chaining did not help with the dataset at hand. We can display the coefficients each of the three `Ridge` regressors had after training. The first estimator only uses the input feature, while the later ones assign coefficients to the input features as well as the previous targets. Here is how to display the coefficients for the third estimator in the chain:

```
pd.DataFrame(
    zip(
        rgr.estimators_[-1].coef_,
        feature_names + target_names
    ),
    columns=['Coeff', 'Feature']
)[
    ['Feature', 'Coeff']
].style.bar(
    subset=['Coeff'], align='mid', color='#AAAAAA'
)
```

From the calculated coefficients, we can see that the first two targets were almost ignored by the third estimator in the chain. Since the targets are independent, each estimator in the chain used the input features only. Although the coefficients you will get when running the code may vary, the coefficients given to the first two targets will still be negligible due to the targets' independence:

	Feature	Coeff
0	Feature # 0	70.3604
1	Feature # 1	1.83524
2	Feature # 2	92.8441
3	Feature # 3	89.2213
4	Feature # 4	41.7166
5	Feature # 5	70.8224
6	Feature # 6	27.6219
7	Feature # 7	14.9658
8	Target # 0	0.0901208
9	Target # 1	-0.0268364

In cases where the targets are dependent, we expect to see bigger coefficients assigned to the targets. In practice, we may try different permutations for the `order` hyperparameter until the best performance is found.

As in the regression problems, the classifiers can also deal with multiple targets. Nonetheless, one target can either be binary or have more than two values. This adds more nuance to the classification cases. In the next section, we are going to learn how to build classifiers to meet the needs of compound targets.

Dealing with compound classification targets

As with regressors, classifiers can also have multiple targets. Additionally, due to their discrete targets, a single target can have two or more values. To be able to differentiate between the different cases, machine learning practitioners came up with the following terminologies:

- Multi-class
- Multi-label (and multi-output)

The following matrix summarizes the aforementioned terminologies. I will follow up with an example to clarify more, and will also shed some light on the subtle difference between the multi-label and multi-output terms later in this chapter:

Output Cardinality		
2	Binary Classification	Multi-Label Classification
> 2	Multi-Class Classification	Multi-Output Multi-Class classification
	1	> 1
	Number of Simultaneous Labels	

Imagine a scenario where you are given a picture and you need to classify it based on whether it contains a cat or not. In this case, a binary classifier is needed, that is, where the targets are either zeroes or ones. When the problem involves figuring out whether the picture contains a cat, a dog, or a human being, then the cardinality of our target is beyond two, and the problem is then formulated as a multi-class classification problem.

The pictures can also contain more than one object. One picture can only have a cat in it, while the other has a human being and a cat together. In a multi-label setting, we would build a set of binary classifiers: one to tell whether the picture has a cat or not, another one for dogs, and one for human beings. To inject interdependency between the different targets, you may want to predict all the simultaneous labels at once. In such a scenario, the term multi-output is usually used.

Furthermore, you can solve a multi-class problem using a set of binary-classifiers. Rather than telling whether the picture has a cat, a dog, or a human being, you can have a classifier telling whether it has a cat or not, one for whether a dog exists, and a third for whether there is a human being or not. This can be useful for model interpretability since the coefficients of each of the three classifiers can be mapped to a single class. In the next section, we are going to use the *One-vs-Rest* strategy to convert a multi-class problem into a set of binary ones.

Converting a multi-class problem into a set of binary classifiers

We do not have to stick to the multi-class problems. We can simply convert the multi-class problem at hand into a set of binary classification problems.

Here, we build a dataset with 5,000 samples, 15 features, and 1 label with 4 possible values:

```
from sklearn.datasets import make_classification

x, y = make_classification(
    n_samples=5000, n_features=15, n_informative=8, n_redundant=2,
    n_classes=4, class_sep=0.5,
)
```

After splitting the data as we usually do, and keeping 25% of it for testing, we can apply the *One-vs-Rest* strategy on top of LogisticRegression. As the name suggests, it is a meta-estimator that builds multiple classifiers to tell whether each sample belongs to one class or not, and finally combines all the decisions made:

```
from sklearn.linear_model import LogisticRegression
from sklearn.multiclass import OneVsRestClassifier
from sklearn.metrics import accuracy_score

clf = OneVsRestClassifier(
    estimator=LogisticRegression(solver='saga')
)
clf.fit(x_train, y_train)
y_pred = clf.predict(x_test)
```

I used the saga solver as it converges more quickly for larger datasets. The *One-vs-Rest* strategy gave me an accuracy score of 0.43. We can access the underlying binary classifiers used by the meta-estimator via its estimators method, then we can reveal the coefficients learned for each feature by each one of the underlying binary classifiers.

Another strategy is *One-vs-One*. It builds separate classifiers for each pair of classes, and can be used as follows:

```
from sklearn.linear_model import LogisticRegression
from sklearn.multiclass import OneVsOneClassifier

clf = OneVsOneClassifier(
    estimator=LogisticRegression(solver='saga')
)
clf.fit(x_train, y_train)
y_pred = clf.predict(x_test)

accuracy_score(y_test, y_pred)
```

The *One-vs-One* strategy gave me a comparable accuracy of 0.44. We can see how, when dealing with a large number of classes, the previous two strategies may not scale well. OutputCodeClassifier is a more scalable solution. It can encode the labels into a denser representation by setting its code_size hyperparameter to a value less than one. A lower code_size will increase its computational performance at the expense of its accuracy and interpretability.

In general, *One-vs-Rest* is the most commonly used strategy, and it is a good starting point if your aim is to separate the coefficients for each class.

To make sure the retuned probabilities for all the classes add up to one, the *One-vs-Rest* strategy normalizes the probabilities by dividing them by their total. One other approach to probability normalization is the `Softmax()` function. It instead divides the exponent of each probability by the sum of the exponents of all the probabilities.
The `Softmax()` function is also used in multinomial logistic regression instead of the `Logistic()` function for it to function as a multi-class classifier without the need for the *One-vs-Rest* or *One-vs-One* strategies.

Estimating multiple classification targets

As with `MultiOutputRegressor`, `MultiOutputClassifier` is a meta-estimator that allows the underlying estimators to deal with multiple outputs.

Let's create a new dataset to see how we can use `MultiOutputClassifier`:

```
from sklearn.datasets import make_multilabel_classification

x, y = make_multilabel_classification(
    n_samples=500, n_features=8, n_classes=3, n_labels=2
)
```

The first thing to notice here is that the terms `n_classes` and `n_labels` are misleading in the `make_multilabel_classification` helper. The previous setting creates 500 samples with 3 binary targets. We can confirm this by printing the shapes of the returned x and y, as well as the cardinality of the y's:

```
x.shape, y.shape # ((500, 8), (500, 3))
np.unique(y) # array([0, 1])
```

We then force the third label to be perfectly dependent on the first one. We will make use of this fact in a moment:

```
y[:,-1] = y[:,0]
```

After we split our dataset as we usually do, and dedicate 25% for testing, we will notice that `GradientBoostingClassifier` is not able to deal with the three targets we have. Some classifiers are able to deal with multiple targets without any external help. Nonetheless, the `MultiOutputClassifier` estimator is required for the classifier we decided to use this time:

```
from sklearn.multioutput import MultiOutputClassifier
from sklearn.ensemble import GradientBoostingClassifier

clf = MultiOutputClassifier(
    estimator=GradientBoostingClassifier(
        n_estimators=500,
        learning_rate=0.01,
        subsample=0.8,
    ),
    n_jobs=-1
)
clf.fit(x_train, y_train)
y_pred_multioutput = clf.predict(x_test)
```

We already know that the first and third targets are dependent. Thus, a `ClassifierChain` may be a good alternative to try instead of an `MultiOutputClassifier` estimator. We can then dictate the target's dependencies using its `order` hyperparameter as follows:

```
from sklearn.multioutput import ClassifierChain
from sklearn.ensemble import GradientBoostingClassifier

clf = ClassifierChain(
    base_estimator=GradientBoostingClassifier(
        n_estimators=500,
        learning_rate=0.01,
        subsample=0.8,
    ),
    order=[0,1,2]
)
clf.fit(x_train, y_train)
y_pred_chain = clf.predict(x_test)
```

Now, if we display the coefficients of the third estimator as we did earlier with the `RegressorChain`, we can see that it just copied the predictions it made for the first target and used them as they are. Hence, all the coefficients were set to zero except for the coefficient assigned to the first target, as follows:

	Feature	Coeff
0	Feature # 0	0
1	Feature # 1	0
2	Feature # 2	0
3	Feature # 3	0
4	Feature # 4	0
5	Feature # 5	0
6	Feature # 6	0
7	Feature # 7	0
8	Target # 0	1
9	Target # 1	0

As you can see, we are covered whenever the estimators we want to use do not support multiple targets. We are also able to tell our estimators which targets to use when predicting the next one.

In many real-life scenarios, we care about the classifier's predicted probabilities more than its binary decisions. A well-calibrated classifier produces reliable probabilities, which are paramount in risk calculations and in achieving higher precision.

In the next section, we will see how to calibrate our classifiers if their estimated probabilities are not reliable by default.

Calibrating a classifier's probabilities

"Every business and every product has risks. You can't get around it."

– Lee Iacocca

Say we want to predict whether someone will catch a viral disease. We can then build a classifier to predict whether they will catch the viral infection or not. Nevertheless, when the percentage of those who may catch the infection is too low, the classifier's binary predictions may not be precise enough. Thus, with such uncertainty and limited resources, we may want to only put in quarantine those with more than a 90% chance of catching the infection. The classifier's predicted probability sounds like a good source for such estimation. Nevertheless, we can only call this probability reliable if 9 out of 10 of the samples we predict to be in a certain class with probabilities above 90% are actually in this class. Similarly, 80% of the samples with probabilities above 80% should also end up being in that class. In other words, for a perfectly calibrated model, we should get the following 45° line whenever we plot the % of samples in the target class versus the classifier's predicted probabilities:

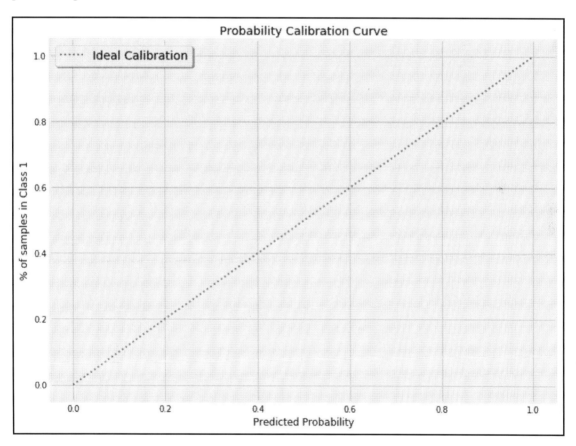

Some models are usually well calibrated, such as the logistic regression classifier. Some other models require us to calibrate their probabilities before using them. To demonstrate this, we are going to create the following binary-classification dataset, with 50,000 samples and 15 features. I used a lower value for `class_sep` to ensure that the two classes aren't easily separable:

```
from sklearn.datasets import make_classification
from sklearn.model_selection import train_test_split

x, y = make_classification(
    n_samples=50000, n_features=15, n_informative=5, n_redundant=10,
    n_classes=2, class_sep=0.001
)

x_train, x_test, y_train, y_test = train_test_split(x, y, test_size=0.25)
```

Then I trained a Gaussian Naive Bayes classifier and stored the predicted probabilities of the positive class. Naive Bayes classifiers tend to return unreliable probabilities due to their naive assumption, as we discussed in Chapter 6, *Classifying Text using Naive Bayes*. The GaussianNB classifier is used here since we are dealing with continuous features:

```
from sklearn.naive_bayes import GaussianNB

clf = GaussianNB()
clf.fit(x_train, y_train)
y_pred_proba = clf.predict_proba(x_test)[:,-1]
```

Scikit-learn has tools for plotting the calibration curves for our classifiers. It splits the estimated probabilities into bins and calculates the fraction of the sample that falls in the positive class for each bin. In the following code snippet, we set the number of bins to 10, and use the calculated probabilities to create a calibration curve:

```
from sklearn.calibration import calibration_curve

fraction_of_positives, mean_predicted_value = calibration_curve(
    y_test, y_pred_proba, n_bins=10
)

fig, ax = plt.subplots(1, 1, figsize=(10, 8))

ax.plot(
    mean_predicted_value, fraction_of_positives, "--",
    label='Uncalibrated GaussianNB', color='k'
)

fig.show()
```

I skipped the parts of the code responsible for the graph's formatting for brevity. Running the code gives me the following curve:

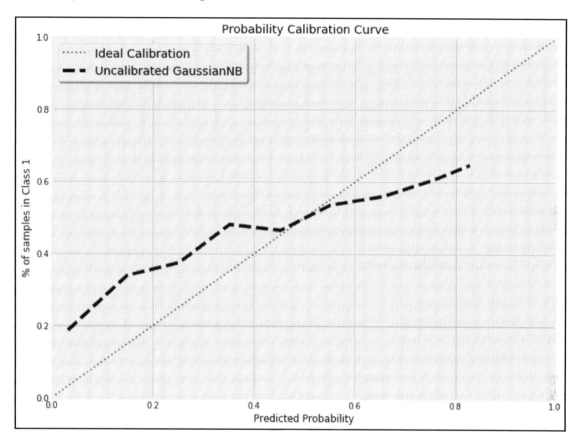

As you can tell, the model is far from being calibrated. Hence, we can use `CalibratedClassifierCV` to adjust its probabilities:

```
from sklearn.calibration import CalibratedClassifierCV
from sklearn.naive_bayes import GaussianNB

clf_calib = CalibratedClassifierCV(GaussianNB(), cv=3, method='isotonic')
clf_calib.fit(x_train, y_train)
y_pred_calib = clf_calib.predict(x_test)
y_pred_proba_calib = clf_calib.predict_proba(x_test)[:,-1]
```

In the next graph, we can see the effect of `CalibratedClassifierCV` on the model, where the new probability estimates are more reliable:

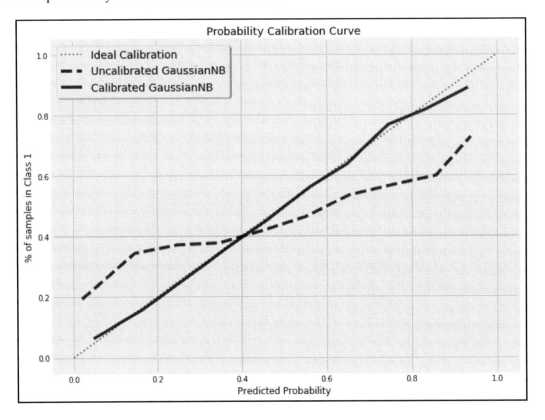

`CalibratedClassifierCV` uses two calibration methods: the `sigmoid()` and `isotonic()` methods. The `sigmoid()` method is recommended for small datasets since the `isotonic()` method tends to overfit. Furthermore, the calibration should be done on separate data from that used for fitting the model. `CalibratedClassifierCV` allows us to cross-validate to separate the data used for fitting the underlying estimator from the data used for calibration. A three-fold cross-validation was used in the previous code.

If linear regression aims to minimize the squared errors while assuming the relation between the targets, y, and the features, x, to be a linear equation expressed by $y = f(x)$, then isotonic regression aims to minimize the squared errors with a different assumption. It assumes $f(x)$ to be a non-linear yet monotonic function. In other words, it either continues to increase or decrease with the increase of x. This monotonicity attribute of isotonic regression makes it suitable for probability calibration.

Besides calibration graphs, the **Brier score** is a good way to check whether a model is calibrated or not. It basically calculates the **Mean Squared Error (MSE)** between the predicted probabilities and the actual targets. Thus, a lower Brier score reflects more reliable probabilities.

In the next section, we are going to learn how to use a classifier to order a list of predictions and then how to evaluate this order.

Calculating the precision at k

In the example of the viral infection from the previous section, your quarantine capacity may be limited to, say, 500 patients. In such a case, you would want as many positive cases to be in the top 500 patients according to their predicted probabilities. In other words, we do not care much about the model's overall precision, since we only care about its precision for the top k samples.

We can calculate the precision for the top k samples using the following code:

```
def precision_at_k_score(y_true, y_pred_proba, k=1000, pos_label=1):
    topk = [
        y_true_ == pos_label
        for y_true_, y_pred_proba_
        in sorted(
            zip(y_true, y_pred_proba),
            key=lambda y: y[1],
            reverse=True
        )[:k]
    ]
    return sum(topk) / len(topk)
```

If you are not a big fan of the functional programming paradigm, then let me explain the code to you in detail. The `zip()` method combines the two lists and returns a list of tuples. The first tuple in the list will contain the first item of `y_true` along with the first item of `y_pred_proba`. The second tuple will hold the second item of each of them, and so on. Then, I sorted the list of tuples in descending order (`reverse=True`) based on the second items of the tuples, that is, `y_pred_proba`. Then, I took the top k items of the sorted list of tuples and compared the `y_true` part of them to the `pos_label` parameter.
The `pos_label` parameter allows me to decide which label to base my precision calculations on. Finally, I calculated the ratio of items in `topk` where an actual member of the class specified by `pos_label` is captured.

Now, we can calculate the precision for the top 500 predictions made by the uncalibrated `GaussianNB` classifier:

```
precision_at_k_score(y_test, y_pred_proba, k=500)
```

This gives us a precision of 82% for the top 500 samples, compared to the overall precision of 62% for all the positively classified samples. Once more, your results may differ from mine.

The precision at the k metric is a very useful tool when dealing with imbalanced data or classes that aren't easy to separate, and you only care about the model's accuracy for the top few predictions. It allows you to tune your model to capture the samples that matter the most. I bet Google cares about the search results you see on the first page way more than the results on the 80th page. And if I only have money to buy 20 stocks in the stock exchange, I would like a model that gets the top 20 stocks right, and I wouldn't care much about its accuracy for the 100th stock.

Summary

When dealing with a classification or a regression problem, we tend to start by thinking about the features we should include in our models. Nonetheless, it is often that the key to the solution lies in the target values. As we have seen in this chapter, rescaling our regression target can help us use a simpler model. Furthermore, calibrating the probabilities given by our classifiers may quickly give a boost to our accuracy scores and help us quantify our uncertainties. We also learned how to deal with multiple targets by writing a single estimator to predict multiple outputs at once. This helps to simplify our code and allows the estimator to use the knowledge it learns from one label to predict the others.

It is common in real-life classification problems that classes are imbalanced. When detecting fraudulent incidents, the majority of your data is usually comprised of non-fraudulent cases. Similarly, for problems such as who would click on your advertisement, and who would subscribe to your newsletter, it is always the minority class that is more interesting for you to detect.

In the next chapter, we are going to see how to make it easier for a classifier to deal with an imbalanced dataset by altering its training data.

Imbalanced Learning – Not Even 1% Win the Lottery
10

Cases where your classes are neatly balanced are more of an exception than the rule. In most of the interesting problems we'll come across, the classes are extremely imbalanced. Luckily, a small fraction of online payments are fraudulent, just like a small fraction of the population catch rare diseases. Conversely, few contestants win the lottery and fewer of your acquaintances become your close friends. That's why we are usually interested in capturing those rare cases.

In this chapter, we will learn how to deal with imbalanced classes. We will start by giving different weights to our training samples to mitigate the class imbalance problem. Afterward, we will learn about other techniques, such as undersampling and oversampling. We will see the effect of these techniques in practice. We will also learn how to combine concepts such as ensemble learning with resampling, and also introduce new scores to validate if our learners are meeting our needs.

The following topics will be covered in this chapter:

- Reweighting the training samples
- Random oversampling
- Random undersampling
- Combing sampling with ensembles
- Equal opportunity score

Let's get started!

Getting the click prediction dataset

Usually, a small percentage of people who see an advertisement click on it. In other words, the percentage of samples in a positive class in such an instance can be just 1% or even less. This makes it hard to predict the **click-through rate** (**CTR**) since the training data is highly imbalanced. In this section, we are going to use a highly imbalanced dataset from the **Knowledge Discovery in Databases** (**KDD**) Cup.

The KDD Cup is an annual competition organized by the ACM Special Interest Group on Knowledge Discovery and Data Mining. In 2012, they released a dataset for the advertisements shown alongside the search results in a search engine. The aim of the competitors was to predict whether a user will click on each ad or not. A modified version of the data has been published on the OpenML platform (`https://www.openml.org/d/1220`). The CTR in the modified dataset is 16.8%. This is our positive class. We can also call it the minority class since the majority of the cases did not lead to an ad being clicked on.

Here, we are going to download the data and put it into a DataFrame, as follows:

```
from sklearn.datasets import fetch_openml
data = fetch_openml(data_id=1220)

df = pd.DataFrame(
    data['data'],
    columns=data['feature_names']
).astype(float)

df['target'] = pd.Series(data['target']).astype(int)
```

We can display 5 random rows of the dataset using the following line of code:

```
df.sample(n=5, random_state=42)
```

We can make sure we get the same random lines if we both set `random_state` to the same value. In *The Hitchhiker's Guide to the Galaxy* by *Douglas Adams*, the number 42 was deemed as the answer to the ultimate question of life, the universe, and everything. So, we will stick to setting `random_state` to 42 throughout this chapter. Here is our five-line sample:

	impression	ad_id	advertiser_id	depth	position	keyword_id	title_id	description_id	user_id	target
12831	1.0	20884487.0	22234.0	1.0	1.0	19303.0	83270.0	74248.0	70.0	0
34147	29.0	10593104.0	1268.0	2.0	1.0	3275.0	2136.0	128.0	0.0	1
7656	1.0	21319021.0	20551.0	2.0	2.0	4766.0	15510.0	15125.0	11569401.0	0
8659	1.0	3831882.0	27486.0	2.0	1.0	1007.0	2869.0	387.0	12581245.0	0
17460	1.0	21442048.0	37039.0	3.0	1.0	35349.0	399482.0	328000.0	0.0	0

There are two things we need to keep in mind about this data:

- The classes are imbalanced, as mentioned earlier. You can check this by running `df['target'].mean()`, which will give you `16.8%`.
- Despite the fact that all the features are numerical, it is clear that all the features ending with the `id` suffix are supposed to be treated as categorical features. For example, the relationship between `ad_id` and the CTR is not expected to be linear, and thus when using a linear model, we may need to encode these features using a *one-hot encoder*. Nevertheless, due to their high cardinality, a one-hot encoding strategy will result in too many features for our classifier to deal with. Therefore, we need to come up with another scalable solution. For now, let's learn how to check the cardinality of each feature:

```
for feature in data['feature_names']:
    print(
        'Cardinality of {}: {:,}'.format(
            feature, df[feature].value_counts().shape[0]
        )
    )
```

This will give us the following results:

```
Cardinality of impression: 99
Cardinality of ad_id: 19,228
Cardinality of advertiser_id: 6,064
Cardinality of depth: 3
Cardinality of position: 3
Cardinality of keyword_id: 19,803
Cardinality of title_id: 25,321
Cardinality of description_id: 22,381
Cardinality of user_id: 30,114
```

Finally, we will convert our data into `x_train`, `x_test`, `y_train`, and `y_test` sets, as follows:

```
from sklearn.model_selection import train_test_split
x, y = df[data['feature_names']], df['target']
x_train, x_test, y_train, y_test = train_test_split(
    x, y, test_size=0.25, random_state=42
)
```

In this section, we downloaded the necessary data and added it to a DataFrame. In the next section, we will install the `imbalanced-learn` library.

Installing the imbalanced-learn library

Due to class imbalance, we will need to resample our training data or apply different techniques to get better classification results. Thus, we are going to rely on the `imbalanced-learn` library here. The project was started in 2014 by *Fernando Nogueira*. It now offers multiple resampling data techniques, as well as metrics for evaluating imbalanced classification problems. The library's interface is compatible with scikit-learn.

You can download the library via `pip` by running the following command in your Terminal:

```
pip install -U imbalanced-learn
```

Now, you can import and use its different modules in your code, as we will see in the following sections. One of the metrics provided by the library is the **geometric mean score**. In Chapter 8, *Ensembles – When One Model is Not Enough*, we learned about the **true positive rate** (TPR), or sensitivity, and the **false positive rate** (FPR), and we used them to draw the area under the curve. We also learned about the **true negative rate** (TNR), or specificity, which is basically 1 minus the FPR. The geometric mean score, for binary classification problems, is the square root of the product of the sensitivity (TPR) and specificity (TNR). By combining these two metrics, we try to maximize the accuracy of each of the classes while taking their imbalances into account. The interface for `geometric_mean_score` is similar to the other scikit-learn metrics. It takes the true and predicted values and returns the calculated score, as follows:

```
from imblearn.metrics import geometric_mean_score
geometric_mean_score(y_true, y_pred)
```

We will be using this metric in addition to the precision and recall scores throughout this chapter.

In the next section, we are going to alter the weights of our training samples and see if this helps us deal with our imbalanced classes.

Predicting the CTR

We have our data and installed the `imbalanced-learn` library. Now, we are ready to build our classifier. As we mentioned earlier, the one-hot encoding techniques we are familiar with will not scale well with the high cardinality of our categorical features. In *Chapter 8*, *Ensembles – When One Model is Not Enough*, we briefly mentioned **random trees embedding** as a technique for transforming our features. It is an ensemble of totally random trees, where each sample of our data will be represented according to the leaves of each tree it ends upon. Here, we are going to build a pipeline where the data will be transformed into a random trees embedding and scaled. Finally, a **logistic regression** classifier will be used to predict whether a click has occurred or not:

```
from sklearn.preprocessing import MaxAbsScaler
from sklearn.linear_model import LogisticRegression
from sklearn.ensemble import RandomTreesEmbedding
from sklearn.pipeline import Pipeline
from sklearn.metrics import precision_score, recall_score
from imblearn.metrics import geometric_mean_score


def predict_and_evalutate(x_train, y_train, x_test, y_test,
sample_weight=None, title='Unweighted'):
    clf = Pipeline(
        [
            ('Embedder', RandomTreesEmbedding(n_estimators=10,
max_leaf_nodes=20, random_state=42)),
            ('Scaler', MaxAbsScaler()),
            ('Classifier', LogisticRegression(solver='saga', max_iter=1000,
random_state=42))
        ]
    )
    clf.fit(x_train, y_train, Classifier__sample_weight=sample_weight)
    y_test_pred = clf.predict(x_test)
    print(
        'Precision: {:.02%}, Recall: {:.02%}; G-mean: {:.02%} @ {}'.format(
            precision_score(y_test, y_test_pred),
            recall_score(y_test, y_test_pred),
            geometric_mean_score(y_test, y_test_pred),
```

```
            title
        )
    )
    return clf
```

We wrapped the whole process into a function so that we can reuse it later in this chapter. The `predict_and_evalutate()` function takes the x's and the y's, as well as the sample weights. We are going to use the sample weights in a moment, but you can ignore them for now. Once you're done predicting, the function will also print the different scores and return an instance of the pipeline that was used.

We can use the function we have just created as follows:

```
clf = predict_and_evalutate(x_train, y_train, x_test, y_test)
```

By default, the precision and recall that are calculated are for the positive class. The previous code gave us a recall of `0.3%`, a precision of `62.5%`, and a geometric mean score of `5.45%`. The recall is less than `1%`, which means that the classifier won't be able to capture the vast majority of the positive/minority class. This is an expected scenario when dealing with imbalanced data. One way to fix this is to give more weights to the samples in the minority class. This is like asking the classifier to give more attention to these samples since we care about capturing them, despite their rareness. In the next section, we are going to see the effect of sample weighting on our classifier.

Weighting the training samples differently

The number of samples in the majority class is about five times those in the minority class. You can double-check this by running the following line of code:

```
(1 - y_train.mean()) / y_train.mean()
```

Thus, it makes sense to give the samples in the minority class five times the weight of the other samples. We can use the same `predict_and_evalutate()` function from the previous section and change the sample weights, as follows:

```
sample_weight = (1 * (y_train == 0)) + (5 * (y_train == 1))
clf = predict_and_evalutate(
    x_train, y_train, x_test, y_test,
    sample_weight=sample_weight
)
```

Now, the recall jumps to `13.4%` at the expense of the precision, which went down to `24.8%`. The geometric mean score went down from `5.5%` to `34%`, thanks to the new weights.

The `predict_and_evalutate()` function returns an instance of the pipeline that was used. We can get the last component of the pipeline, the logistic regression classifier, via `clf[-1]`. Then, we can access the coefficients of the classifier that were assigned to each feature as we intercept it. Due to the embedding step, we may end up with up to 200 features; 10 estimators x up to 20 leaf nodes. The following function prints the last nine features, as well as the intercept, along with their coefficients:

```
def calculate_feature_coeff(clf):
    return pd.DataFrame(
        {
            'Features': [
                f'EmbFeature{e}'
                for e in range(len(clf[-1].coef_[0]))
            ] + ['Intercept'],
            'Coeff': list(
                clf[-1].coef_[0]
            ) + [clf[-1].intercept_[0]]
        }

    ).set_index('Features').tail(10)
```

The output of `calculate_feature_coeff(clf).round(2)` can also be rounded to two decimal points so that it looks as follows:

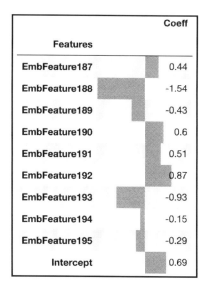

Features	Coeff
EmbFeature187	0.44
EmbFeature188	-1.54
EmbFeature189	-0.43
EmbFeature190	0.6
EmbFeature191	0.51
EmbFeature192	0.87
EmbFeature193	-0.93
EmbFeature194	-0.15
EmbFeature195	-0.29
Intercept	0.69

Now, let's compare three weighting strategies side by side. With a weight of one, both the minority and the majority classes get the same weights. Then, we give the minority class double the weight of the majority class, as well as five times its weight, as follows:

```
df_coef_list = []
weight_options = [1, 2, 5]

for w in weight_options:
    print(f'\nMinority Class (Positive Class) Weight = Weight x {w}')
    sample_weight = (1 * (y_train == 0)) + (w * (y_train == 1))
    clf = predict_and_evalutate(
        x_train, y_train, x_test, y_test,
        sample_weight=sample_weight
    )
    df_coef = calculate_feature_coeff(clf)
    df_coef = df_coef.rename(columns={'Coeff': f'Coeff [w={w}]'})
    df_coef_list.append(df_coef)
```

This gives us the following results:

```
Minority Class (Positive Class) Weight = Weight x 1
Precision: 62.50%, Recall: 0.30%; G-mean: 5.45% @  Unbalanced

Minority Class (Positive Class) Weight = Weight x 2
Precision: 36.36%, Recall: 2.14%; G-mean: 14.57% @  Unbalanced

Minority Class (Positive Class) Weight = Weight x 5
Precision: 24.78%, Recall: 13.38%; G-mean: 35.04% @  Unbalanced
```

It is easy to see how the weighting affects the precision and the recall. It is as if one of them always improves at the expense of the other. This behavior is the result of moving the classifier's boundaries. As we know, the class boundaries are defined by the coefficients of the different features, as well as the intercept. I bet you are tempted to see the coefficients of the three previous models side by side. Luckily, we have saved the coefficients in `df_coef_list` so that we can display them using the following code snippet:

```
pd.concat(df_coef_list, axis=1).round(2).style.bar(
    subset=[f'Coeff [w={w}]' for w in weight_options],
    color='#999',
    align='zero'
)
```

This gives us the following visual comparison between the three classifiers:

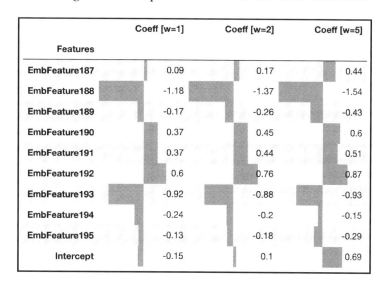

Features	Coeff [w=1]	Coeff [w=2]	Coeff [w=5]
EmbFeature187	0.09	0.17	0.44
EmbFeature188	-1.18	-1.37	-1.54
EmbFeature189	-0.17	-0.26	-0.43
EmbFeature190	0.37	0.45	0.6
EmbFeature191	0.37	0.44	0.51
EmbFeature192	0.6	0.76	0.87
EmbFeature193	-0.92	-0.88	-0.93
EmbFeature194	-0.24	-0.2	-0.15
EmbFeature195	-0.13	-0.18	-0.29
Intercept	-0.15	0.1	0.69

The coefficients of the features did change slightly, but the changes in the intercept are more noticeable. In summary, the weighting affects the intercept the most and moves the class boundaries as a result.

A sample is classified as a member of the positive class if the predicted probability is above 50%. The movement of the intercept, without any changes in the other coefficients, is equivalent to changing the probability threshold so that it's above or below that 50%. If the weighting only affected the intercept, we might suggest that we should try different probability thresholds until we get the desired precision-recall tradeoff. To check whether the weighting offered any additional benefit on top of altering the intercept, we have to check the area under the **Receiver Operating Characteristic (ROC)** curve.

The effect of the weighting on the ROC

Did the weighting improve the area under the ROC curve? To answer this question, let's start by creating a function that will display the ROC curve and print the **area under the curve (AUC)**:

```
from sklearn.metrics import roc_curve, auc

def plot_roc_curve(y, y_proba, ax, label):
    fpr, tpr, thr = roc_curve(y, y_proba)
    auc_value = auc(fpr, tpr)
    pd.DataFrame(
```

```
                {
                    'FPR': fpr,
                    'TPR': tpr
                }
            ).set_index('FPR')['TPR'].plot(
                label=label + f'; AUC = {auc_value:.3f}',
                kind='line',
                xlim=(0,1),
                ylim=(0,1),
                color='k',
                ax=ax
            )
            return (fpr, tpr, auc_value)
```

Now, we can loop over the three weighting options and render their corresponding curves, as follows:

```
from sklearn.metrics import roc_curve, auc

fig, ax = plt.subplots(1, 1, figsize=(15, 8), sharey=False)

ax.plot(
    [0, 1], [0, 1],
    linestyle='--',
    lw=2, color='k',
    label='Chance', alpha=.8
)


for w in weight_options:

    sample_weight = (1 * (y_train == 0)) + (w * (y_train == 1))
    clf = Pipeline(
        [
            ('Embedder', RandomTreesEmbedding(n_estimators=20,
max_leaf_nodes=20, random_state=42)),
            ('Scaler', MaxAbsScaler()),
            ('Classifier', LogisticRegression(solver='lbfgs',
max_iter=2000, random_state=42))
        ]
    )
    clf.fit(x_train, y_train, Classifier__sample_weight=sample_weight)
    y_test_pred_proba = clf.predict_proba(x_test)[:,1]

    plot_roc_curve(
        y_test, y_test_pred_proba,
        label=f'\nMinority Class Weight = Weight x {w}',
        ax=ax
    )
```

```
ax.set_title('Receiver Operating Characteristic (ROC)')
ax.set_xlabel('False Positive Rate')
ax.set_ylabel('True Positive Rate')

ax.legend(ncol=1, fontsize='large', shadow=True)

fig.show()
```

These three curves are displayed here:

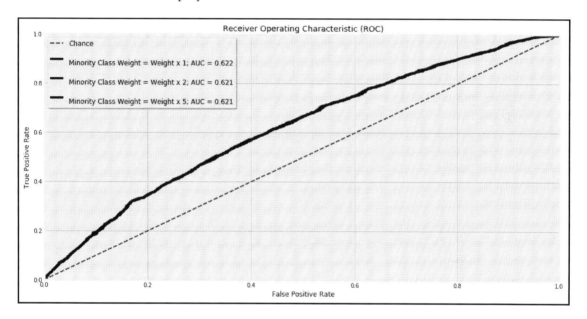

The ROC curve is meant to show the tradeoff between the TPR and the FPR for the different probability thresholds. If the area under the ROC curve is more or less than the same for the three weighting strategies, then the weighting did not offer much value beyond altering the classifier's intercept. Thus, it is up to us if we want to increase the recall at the expense of the precision to either reweight our training samples or to try different probability thresholds for our classification decision.

In addition to the sample weighting, we can resample the training data so that we train on a more balanced set. In the next section, we are going to see the different sampling techniques offered by the `imbalanced-learn` library.

Sampling the training data

"It's not denial. I'm just selective about the reality I accept."

- Bill Watterson

If the machine learning models were humans, they would have believed that the end justifies the means. When 99% of their training data belongs to one class, and their aim is to optimize their objective function, we cannot blame them if they focus on getting that single class right since it contributes to 99% of the solution. In the previous section, we tried to change this behavior by giving more weights to the minority class, or classes. Another strategy might entail removing some samples from the majority class or adding new samples to the minority class until the two classes are balanced.

Undersampling the majority class

"Truth, like gold, is to be obtained not by its growth, but by washing away from it all that is not gold."

- Leo Tolstoy

We can randomly remove samples from the majority class until it becomes the same size as the minority class. When dealing with non-binary classification tasks, we can remove samples from all the classes until they all become the same size as the minority class. This technique is known as **Random Undersampling**. The following code shows how `RandomUnderSampler()` can be used to downsample the majority class:

```
from imblearn.under_sampling import RandomUnderSampler

rus = RandomUnderSampler()
x_train_resampled, y_train_resampled = rus.fit_resample(x_train, y_train)
```

Rather than keeping the classes balanced, you can just reduce their imbalance by setting the `sampling_strategy` hyperparameter. Its value dictates the final ratio of the minority class versus the majority class. In the following example, we kept the final size of the majority class so that it's twice that of the minority class:

```
from imblearn.under_sampling import RandomUnderSampler

rus = RandomUnderSampler(sampling_strategy=0.5)
x_train_resampled, y_train_resampled = rus.fit_resample(x_train, y_train)
```

The downsampling process doesn't have to be random. For example, we can use the nearest neighbors algorithm to remove the samples that do not agree with their neighbors. The `EditedNearestNeighbours` module allows you to set the number of neighbors to check via its `n_neighbors` hyperparameter, as follows:

```
from imblearn.under_sampling import EditedNearestNeighbours

enn = EditedNearestNeighbours(n_neighbors=5)
x_train_resampled, y_train_resampled = enn.fit_resample(x_train, y_train)
```

The previous techniques belong to what is known as **prototype selection**. In this situation, we select samples from already existing ones. In contrast to Prototype Selection, the **prototype generation** approach generates new samples to summarize the existing ones. The *ClusterCentroids* algorithm puts the majority class samples into clusters and uses the cluster centroids instead of the original samples. More on clustering and cluster centroids will be provided in Chapter 11, *Clustering – Making Sense of Unlabeled Data*.

To compare the aforementioned algorithms, let's create a function that takes the x's and y's, in addition to the sampler instance, and then trains them and returns the predicted values for the test set:

```
from sklearn.preprocessing import MaxAbsScaler
from sklearn.linear_model import LogisticRegression
from sklearn.ensemble import RandomTreesEmbedding
from sklearn.pipeline import Pipeline

def sample_and_predict(x_train, y_train, x_test, y_test, sampler=None):
    if sampler:
        x_train, y_train = sampler.fit_resample(x_train, y_train)
    clf = Pipeline(
        [
            ('Embedder', RandomTreesEmbedding(n_estimators=10,
max_leaf_nodes=20, random_state=42)),
            ('Scaler', MaxAbsScaler()),
            ('Classifier', LogisticRegression(solver='saga', max_iter=1000,
random_state=42))
        ]
    )
    clf.fit(x_train, y_train)
    y_test_pred_proba = clf.predict_proba(x_test)[:,1]
    return y_test, y_test_pred_proba
```

Now, we can use the `sample_and_predict()` function we have just created and plot the resulting ROC curve for the following two sampling techniques:

```python
from sklearn.metrics import roc_curve, auc
from imblearn.under_sampling import RandomUnderSampler
from imblearn.under_sampling import EditedNearestNeighbours

fig, ax = plt.subplots(1, 1, figsize=(15, 8), sharey=False)

# Original Data

y_test, y_test_pred_proba = sample_and_predict(x_train, y_train, x_test,
y_test, sampler=None)
plot_roc_curve(
    y_test, y_test_pred_proba,
    label='Original Data',
    ax=ax
)


# RandomUnderSampler

rus = RandomUnderSampler(random_state=42)
y_test, y_test_pred_proba = sample_and_predict(x_train, y_train, x_test,
y_test, sampler=rus)

plot_roc_curve(
    y_test, y_test_pred_proba,
    label='RandomUnderSampler',
    ax=ax
)

# EditedNearestNeighbours

nc = EditedNearestNeighbours(n_neighbors=5)
y_test, y_test_pred_proba = sample_and_predict(x_train, y_train, x_test,
y_test, sampler=nc)

plot_roc_curve(
    y_test, y_test_pred_proba,
    label='EditedNearestNeighbours',
    ax=ax
)

ax.legend(ncol=1, fontsize='large', shadow=True)

fig.show()
```

The resulting ROC curve will look as follows:

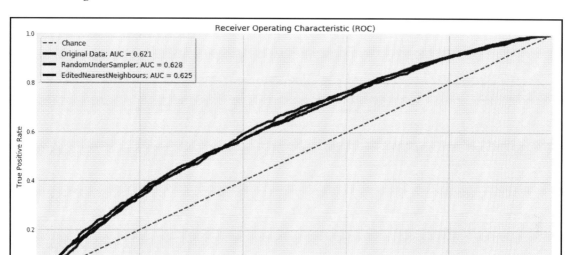

Here, we can see the value of the sampling techniques on the resulting area under the ROC curve in comparison to training on the original unsampled set. The three graphs may be too close for us to tell them apart, as is the case here, so it makes sense to check the resulting AUC number instead.

Oversampling the minority class

Besides undersampling, we can also increase the data points of the minority class. `RandomOverSampler` naively clones random samples of the minority class until it becomes the same size as the majority class. `SMOTE` and `ADASYN`, on the other hand, generate new synthetic samples by interpolation.

Here, we are comparing `RandomOverSampler` to the `SMOTE` oversampling algorithm:

```
from sklearn.metrics import roc_curve, auc
from imblearn.over_sampling import RandomOverSampler
from imblearn.over_sampling import SMOTE

fig, ax = plt.subplots(1, 1, figsize=(15, 8), sharey=False)

# RandomOverSampler
```

```
ros = RandomOverSampler(random_state=42)
y_test, y_test_pred_proba = sample_and_predict(x_train, y_train, x_test,
y_test, sampler=ros)
plot_roc_curve(
    y_test, y_test_pred_proba,
    label='RandomOverSampler',
    ax=ax
)

# SMOTE

smote = SMOTE(random_state=42)
y_test, y_test_pred_proba = sample_and_predict(x_train, y_train, x_test,
y_test, sampler=smote)
plot_roc_curve(
    y_test, y_test_pred_proba,
    label='SMOTE',
    ax=ax
)

ax.legend(ncol=1, fontsize='large', shadow=True)

fig.show()
```

The resulting ROC curve helps us compare the performance of the two techniques being used on the dataset at hand:

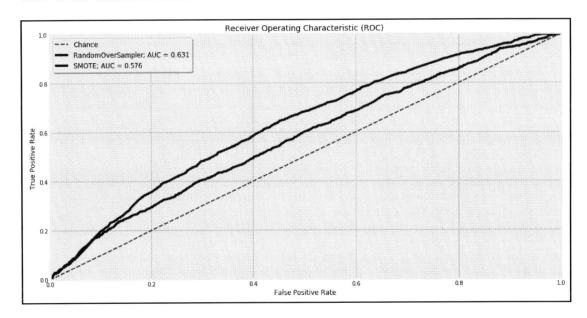

As we can see, the SMOTE algorithm did not perform on our current dataset, while RandomOverSampler pushed the curve upward. So far, the classifiers we've used have been agnostic to the sampling techniques we've applied. We can simply remove the logistic regression classifier and plug in any other classifier here without changing the data sampling code. In contrast to the algorithms we've used, the data sampling process is an integral part of some ensemble algorithms. In the next section, we'll learn how to make use of this fact to get the best of both worlds.

Combining data sampling with ensembles

In Chapter 8, *Ensembles – When One Model is Not Enough,* we learned about bagging algorithms. They basically allow multiple estimators to learn from different subsets of the dataset, in the hope that these diverse training subsets will allow the different estimators to come to a better decision when combined. Now that we've undersampled the majority class to keep our training data balanced, it is natural that we combine the two ideas together; that is, the bagging and the under-sampling techniques.

BalancedBaggingClassifier builds several estimators on different randomly selected subsets of data, where the classes are balanced during the sampling process. Similarly, BalancedRandomForestClassifier builds its trees on balanced samples. In the following code, we're plotting the ROC curves for the two ensembles:

```
from imblearn.ensemble import BalancedRandomForestClassifier
from imblearn.ensemble import BalancedBaggingClassifier

fig, ax = plt.subplots(1, 1, figsize=(15, 8), sharey=False)

# BalancedBaggingClassifier

clf = BalancedBaggingClassifier(n_estimators=500, n_jobs=-1,
random_state=42)
clf.fit(x_train, y_train)
y_test_pred_proba = clf.predict_proba(x_test)[:,1]

plot_roc_curve(
    y_test, y_test_pred_proba,
    label='Balanced Bagging Classifier',
    ax=ax
)

# BalancedRandomForestClassifier
clf = BalancedRandomForestClassifier(n_estimators=500, n_jobs=-1,
random_state=42)
clf.fit(x_train, y_train)
```

```
y_test_pred_proba = clf.predict_proba(x_test)[:,1]

plot_roc_curve(
    y_test, y_test_pred_proba,
    label='Balanced Random Forest Classifier',
    ax=ax
)

fig.show()
```

Some formatting lines have been omitted for brevity. Running the previous code gives us the following graph:

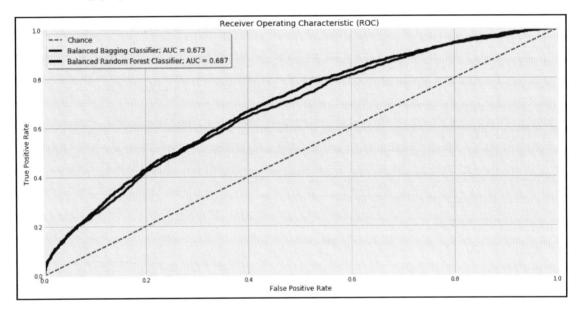

From this, it's clear that the combination of undersampling and ensembles achieved better results than our earlier models.

In addition to the bagging algorithms, RUSBoostClassifier combines the random undersampling technique with the adaBoost classifier.

Equal opportunity score

So far, we've only focused on the imbalances in the class labels. In some situations, the imbalance in a particular feature may also be problematic. Say, historically, that the vast majority of the engineers in your company were men. Now, if you build an algorithm to filter the new applicants based on your existing data, would it discriminate against the female candidates?

The **equal opportunity score** tries to evaluate how dependent a model is of a certain feature. Simply put, a model is considered to give an equal opportunity to the different value of a certain feature if the relationship between the model's predictions and the actual targets is the same, regardless of the value of this feature. Formally, this means that the conditional probability of the predicted target, which is conditional on the actual target, and the applicant's gender should be the same, regardless of gender. These conditional probabilities are shown in the following equation:

$$P(Hired_{predicted}|Hired_{true}, Gender = M) = P(Hired_{predicted}|Hired_{true}, Gender = F)$$

The previous equation only gives a binary outcome. Therefore, we can turn it into a ratio where we have a value between 0 and 1. Since we do not know which gender gets a better opportunity, we take the minimum value of the two possible fractions using the following equation:

$$MIN(\frac{P(Hired_{predicted}|Hired_{true}, Gender = M)}{P(Hired_{predicted}|Hired_{true}, Gender = F)}, \frac{P(Hired_{predicted}|Hired_{true}, Gender = F)}{P(Hired_{predicted}|Hired_{true}, Gender = FM)})$$

To demonstrate this metric, let's assume we have a model trained on the applicant's `IQ` and `Gender`. This following code shows its predictions on the test set, where both the true label and the predictions are listed side by side:

```
df_engineers = pd.DataFrame(
    {
        'IQ': [110, 120, 124, 123, 112, 114],
        'Gender': ['M', 'F', 'M', 'F', 'M', 'F'],
        'Is Hired? (True Label)': [0, 1, 1, 1, 1, 0],
        'Is Hired? (Predicted Label)': [1, 0, 1, 1, 1, 0],
    }
)
```

Now, we can create a function to calculate the equal opportunity score for us, as follows:

```
def equal_opportunity_score(df, true_label, predicted_label, feature_name,
feature_value):
    opportunity_to_value = df[
        (df[true_label] == 1) & (df[feature_name] == feature_value)
    ][predicted_label].mean() / df[
        (df[true_label] == 1) & (df[feature_name] != feature_value)
    ][predicted_label].mean()
    opportunity_to_other_values = 1 / opportunity_to_value
    better_opportunity_to_value = opportunity_to_value >
opportunity_to_other_values
    return {
        'Score': min(opportunity_to_value, opportunity_to_other_values),
        f'Better Opportunity to {feature_value}':
better_opportunity_to_value
    }
```

When called with our `df_engineers` DataFrame, it will give us `0.5`. Having a value that's less than one tells us that the female applicants have less of an opportunity to get hired by our model:

```
equal_opportunity_score(
    df=df_engineers,
    true_label='Is Hired? (True Label)',
    predicted_label='Is Hired? (Predicted Label)',
    feature_name='Gender',
    feature_value='F'
)
```

Obviously, we can exclude the gender feature from this model altogether, yet this score is still useful if there are any remaining features that depend on the applicant's gender. Additionally, we need to alter this score when dealing with a non-binary classifier and/or a non-binary feature. You can read about this score in more detail in the original paper by *Moritz Hardt et al.*

Summary

In this chapter, we learned how to deal with class imbalances. This is a recurrent problem in machine learning, where most of the value lies in the minority class. This phenomenon is common enough that the *black swan* metaphor was coined to explain it. When the machine learning algorithms try to blindly optimize their out-of-the-box objective functions, they usually miss those black swans. Hence, we have to use techniques such as sample weighting, sample removal, and sample generation to force the algorithms to meet our own objectives.

This was the last chapter in this book about supervised learning algorithms. There is a rough estimate that 80% of the machine learning problems in business setups and academia are supervised learning ones, which is why about 80% of this book focused on that paradigm. From the next chapter onward, we will start covering the other machine learning paradigms, which is where about 20% of the real-life value resides. We will start by looking at clustering algorithms, and then move on and look at other problems where the data is also unlabeled.

3
Section 3: Unsupervised Learning and More

If your data is not labeled, then this part will help you find ways to make sense of it. You will learn how to organize a massive dataset, identify outliers in it, and figure out users' preferences based on their past behavior.

This section comprises the following chapters:

- Chapter 11, *Clustering – Making Sense of Unlabeled Data*
- Chapter 12, *Anomaly Detection – Finding Outliers in Data*
- Chapter 13, *Recommender System – Getting to Know Their Taste*

11
Clustering – Making Sense of Unlabeled Data

Clustering is the poster child of unsupervised learning methods. It is usually our first choice when we need to add meaning to unlabeled data. In an e-commerce website, the marketing team may ask you to put your users into a few buckets so that they can tailor the messages they send to each group of them. If no one has labeled those millions of users for you, then clustering is your only way to put these users into buckets. When dealing with a large number of documents, videos, or web pages, and there are no categories assigned to this content, and you are not willing to ask *Marie Kondo* for help, then clustering is your only way to declutter this mess.

Since this is our first chapter about supervised learning algorithms, we will start with some theoretical background about clustering. Then, we will have a look at three commonly used clustering algorithms, in addition to the methods used for evaluating them.

In this chapter, we are going to cover the following topics:

- Understanding clustering
- K-means clustering
- Agglomerative clustering
- DBSCAN

Let's get started!

Understanding clustering

Machine learning algorithms can be seen as optimization problems. They take data samples, and an objective function, and try to optimize this function. In the case of supervised learning, the objective function is based on the labels given to it. We try to minimize the differences between our predictions and the actual labels. In the case of unsupervised learning, things are different due to the lack of labels. Clustering algorithms, in essence, try to put the data samples into clusters so that it minimizes the intracluster distances and maximizes the intercluster distances. In other words, we want samples that are in the same cluster to be as similar as possible, and samples from different clusters to be as different as possible.

Nevertheless, there is one trivial solution to this optimization problem. If we treat each sample as its own cluster, then the intracluster distances are all zeros and the intercluster distances are at their maximum. Obviously, this is not what we want from our clustering algorithm. Thus, to avoid this trivial solution, we usually add a constraint to our optimization function. For example, we may predefine the number of clusters we need to make sure the aforementioned trivial solution is avoided. One other possible constraint involves setting the minimum number of samples per cluster. We will see those constraints in practice when we discuss each of the different clustering algorithms in this chapter.

The lack of labels also dictates the different metrics for evaluating how good the resulting clusters are. That's why I decided to emphasize the objective function of clustering algorithms here, since understanding the objective of an algorithm makes it easier to understand its evaluation metrics. We will come across a couple of evaluation metrics throughout this chapter.

One way to measure the intracluster distances is to calculate the distances between each point in the cluster and the cluster's centroid. The concept of the centroid should be familiar to you by now since we discussed the **nearest centroid** algorithm in `Chapter 5`, *Image Processing with Nearest Neighbors*. The centroid is basically the mean of all the samples in the clusters. Furthermore, the average Euclidean distance between some samples and their mean has another name that we all learned about in primary school – **standard deviation**. The very same distance measure can be used to measure the dissimilarity between the clusters' centroids.

At this point, we are ready to explore our first algorithm, known as **K-means**. However, we need to create some sample data first so that we can use it to demonstrate our algorithms. In the next section, after explaining the algorithm, we are going to create the needed data and use the K-means algorithm to cluster it.

K-means clustering

"We all know we are unique individuals, but we tend to see others as representatives of groups."

- Deborah Tannen

In the previous section, we discussed the constraint we put on our objective function by specifying the number of clusters we need. This is what the *K* stands for: the number of clusters. We also discussed the cluster's centroid, hence the word means. The algorithm works as follows:

1. It starts by picking *K* random points and setting them as the cluster centroids.
2. Then, it assigns each data point to the nearest centroid to it to form *K* clusters.
3. Then, it calculates a new centroid for the newly formed clusters.
4. Since the centroids have been updated, we need to go back to *step 2* to reassign the samples to their new clusters based on the updated centroids. However, if the centroids didn't move much, we know that the algorithm has converged, and we stop.

As you can see, this is an iterative algorithm. It keeps iterating until it converges, but we can limit the number of iterations by setting its `max_iter` hyperparameter. Additionally, we may decide to tolerate bigger centroid movements and stop earlier by setting the `tol` hyperparameter to a larger value. The different choices regarding the initial cluster centroids may lead to different results. Setting the algorithm's `init` hyperparameter to `k-means++` makes sure the initial centroids are distant from each other. This usually leads to better results than random initialization. The choice of *K* is also given using the `n_clusters` hyperparameter. To demonstrate the usage of this algorithm and its hyperparameters, let's start by creating a sample dataset.

Creating a blob-shaped dataset

We usually visualize clusters as rounded blobs of scattered data points. This sort of shape is also known as a convex cluster and is one of the easiest shapes for algorithms to deal with. Later on, we will generate harder-to-cluster datasets, but let's start with the easy blobs for now.

The `make_blobs` function helps us create a blob-shaped dataset. Here, we set the number of samples to `100` and divide them into four clusters. Each data point only has two features. This will make it easier for us to visualize the data later on. The clusters have different standard deviations; that is, some clusters are more dispersed than the others. The function also returns labels. We will keep the labels aside to validate our algorithm later on. Finally, we put the x's and the y's into a DataFrame and call it `df_blobs`:

```
from sklearn.datasets import make_blobs

x, y = make_blobs(n_samples=100, centers=4, n_features=2, cluster_std=[1,
1.5, 2, 2], random_state=7)

df_blobs = pd.DataFrame(
    {
        'x1': x[:,0],
        'x2': x[:,1],
        'y': y
    }
)
```

To make sure you get the exact same data I did, set the `random_state` parameter of the data generating function to a specific random seed. Now that the data is ready, we need to create a function to visualize this data.

Visualizing our sample data

We are going to use the following function throughout this chapter. It takes the 2D x's and y labels and plots them into the given Matplotlib axis, *ax*. In real-life scenarios, no labels are given, but still, we can give this function the labels predicted by the clustering algorithm instead. The resulting plot gets a title, along with the number of clusters that have been deduced from the cardinality of the given y:

```
def plot_2d_clusters(x, y, ax):
    y_uniques = pd.Series(y).unique()
    for y_unique_item in y_uniques:
      x[
            y == y_unique_item
        ].plot(
            title=f'{len(y_uniques)} Clusters',
            kind='scatter',
            x='x1', y='x2',
            marker=f'${y_unique_item}$',
            ax=ax,
        )
```

We can use the new `plot_2d_clusters()` function as follows:

```
fig, ax = plt.subplots(1, 1, figsize=(10, 6))
x, y = df_blobs[['x1', 'x2']], df_blobs['y']
plot_2d_clusters(x, y, ax)
```

This will give us the following diagram:

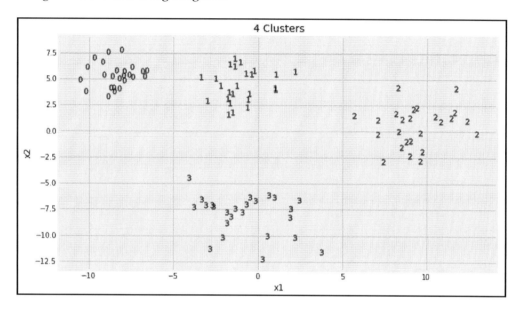

Each data point is marked according to its given label. Now, we will pretend those labels haven't been given to us and see whether the K-means algorithm will be able to predict them or not.

Clustering with K-means

Now that we're pretending that no labels have been given, how can we tell what value to use for *K*, that is, the `n_clusters` hyperparameter? We can't. We will just pick any number for now; later on, we will learn how to find the best value for `n_clusters`. Let's set it to five for now. We will keep all the other hyperparameters at their default values. Once the algorithm is initialized, we can use its `fit_predict` method, as follows:

```
from sklearn.cluster import KMeans
kmeans = KMeans(n_clusters=2, random_state=7)
x, y = df_blobs[['x1', 'x2']], df_blobs['y']
y_pred = kmeans.fit_predict(x)
```

Note that the concept of fitting on a training set and predicting a test date seldom makes sense here. We usually fit and predict on the same dataset. We also don't pass any labels to the `fit` or `fit_predict` methods.

Now that we've predicted the new labels, we can use the `plot_2d_clusters()` function to compare our predictions to the original labels, as follows:

```
fig, axs = plt.subplots(1, 2, figsize=(14, 6))

x, y = df_blobs[['x1', 'x2']], df_blobs['y']
plot_2d_clusters(x, y, axs[0])
plot_2d_clusters(x, y_pred, axs[1])

axs[0].set_title(f'Actuals: {axs[0].get_title()}')
axs[1].set_title(f'KMeans: {axs[1].get_title()}')
```

I prepended the words `Actuals` and `KMeans` to their corresponding figure titles. The resulting clusters are shown in the following screenshot:

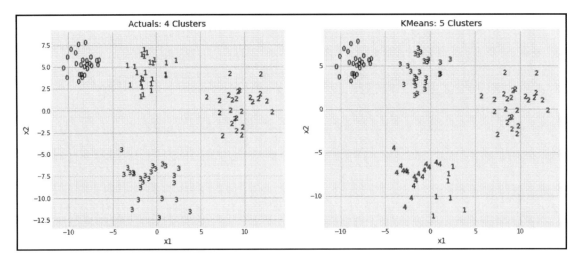

One of the original four clusters has been split into two since we set *K* to five. Other than that, the predictions for the other clusters make sense. The labels that have been given to the clusters are arbitrary. The original cluster with label one was called three by the algorithm. This should not bother us at all, as long as the clusters have the exact same members. This should not bother the clustering evaluation metrics either. They usually take this fact into account and ignore the label names when evaluating a clustering algorithm.

Still, how do we determine the value of *K*? We have no other choice but to run the algorithm multiple times with different numbers of clusters and pick the best one. In the following code snippet, we're looping over three different values for `n_clusters`. We also have access to the final centroids, which are calculated for each cluster after the algorithm converges. Seeing these centroids clarifies how the algorithm assigned each data point to its own cluster. The last line in our code snippet uses a triangular marker to plot the centroids in each of the three graphs:

```
from sklearn.cluster import KMeans

n_clusters_options = [2, 4, 6]

fig, axs = plt.subplots(1, len(n_clusters_options), figsize=(16, 6))

for i, n_clusters in enumerate(n_clusters_options):
    x, y = df_blobs[['x1', 'x2']], df_blobs['y']

    kmeans = KMeans(n_clusters=n_clusters, random_state=7)
    y_pred = kmeans.fit_predict(x)
    plot_2d_clusters(x, y_pred, axs[i])
    axs[i].plot(
        kmeans.cluster_centers_[:,0], kmeans.cluster_centers_[:,1],
        'k^', ms=12, alpha=0.75
    )
```

Here are the results of the three choices, side by side:

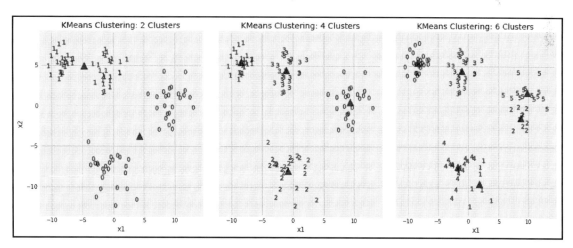

A visual investigation of the three graphs tells us that the choice of four clusters was the right choice. Nevertheless, we have to remember that we are dealing with 2D data points here. The same visual investigation would have been much harder if our data samples contained more than two features. In the next section, we are going to learn about the silhouette score and use it to pick the optimum number of clusters, without the need for visual aid.

The silhouette score

The **silhouette score** is a measure of how similar a sample is to its own cluster compared to the samples in the other clusters. For each sample, we will calculate the average distance between this sample and all the other samples in the same cluster. Let's call this mean distance A. Then, we calculate the average distance between the same sample and all the other samples in the nearest cluster. Let's call this other mean distance B. Now, we can define the silhouette score, as follows:

$$Silhouette = \frac{B - A}{max(A, B)}$$

Now, rather than performing a visual investigation of the clusters, we are going to loop over multiple values for n_clusters and store the silhouette score after each iteration. As you can see, silhouette_score takes two parameters – the data points (x) and the predicted cluster labels (y_pred):

```
from sklearn.cluster import KMeans
from sklearn.metrics import silhouette_score

n_clusters_options = [2, 3, 4, 5, 6, 7, 8]
silhouette_scores = []

for i, n_clusters in enumerate(n_clusters_options):

    x, y = df_blobs[['x1', 'x2']], df_blobs['y']
    kmeans = KMeans(n_clusters=n_clusters, random_state=7)
    y_pred = kmeans.fit_predict(x)

    silhouette_scores.append(silhouette_score(x, y_pred))
```

We can just pick the n_clusters value that gives the best score. Here, we put the calculated scores into a DataFrame and use a bar chart to compare them:

```
fig, ax = plt.subplots(1, 1, figsize=(12, 6), sharey=False)

pd.DataFrame(
    {
        'n_clusters': n_clusters_options,
        'silhouette_score': silhouette_scores,
    }
).set_index('n_clusters').plot(
    title='KMeans: Silhouette Score vs # Clusters chosen',
    kind='bar',
    ax=ax
)
```

The resulting scores confirm our initial decision that four is the best choice for the number of clusters:

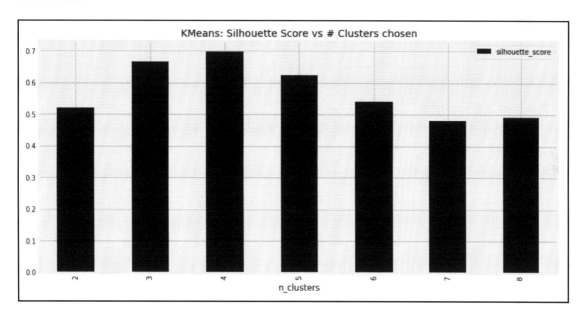

In addition to picking the number of clusters, the choice of the algorithm's initial centroid also affects its accuracy. A bad choice may lead the K-means algorithm to converge at an undesirable local minimum. In the next section, we are going to witness how the initial centroids may affect the algorithm's final decision.

Choosing the initial centroids

By default, the K-means implementation of scikit-learn picks random initial centroids that are further apart from each other. It also tries multiple initial centroids and picks the one that gives the best results. Having said that, we can also set the initial centroids by hand. In the following code snippet, we will compare two initial settings to see their effect on the final results. We will then print the two outcomes side by side:

```
from sklearn.cluster import KMeans

initial_centroid_options = np.array([
    [(-10,5), (0, 5), (10, 0), (-10, 0)],
    [(0,0), (0.1, 0.1), (0, 0), (0.1, 0.1)],
])

fig, axs = plt.subplots(1, 2, figsize=(16, 6))

for i, initial_centroids in enumerate(initial_centroid_options):
    x, y = df_blobs[['x1', 'x2']], df_blobs['y']
    kmeans = KMeans(
        init=initial_centroids, max_iter=500, n_clusters=4, random_state=7
    )
    y_pred = kmeans.fit_predict(x)
    plot_2d_clusters(x, y_pred, axs[i])
    axs[i].plot(
        kmeans.cluster_centers_[:,0], kmeans.cluster_centers_[:,1], 'k^'
    )
```

The following graphs show the resulting clusters after the algorithm converges. Parts of the styling code were omitted for brevity:

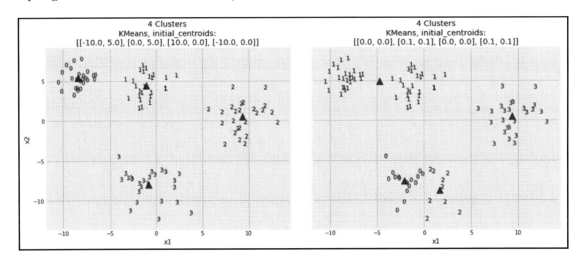

Clearly, the first initial setup helped the algorithm, while the second one led it to bad results. Thus, we have to be aware of the algorithm's initialization since its results are nondeterministic.

In the field of machine learning, the term transfer learning refers to the set of problems where we need to repurpose the knowledge gained while solving one problem and apply it to a slightly different problem. Humans also need transfer learning. The K-means algorithm has a `fit_transform` method. If our data (x) is made of N samples and M features, the method will transform it into N samples and K columns instead. The values in the columns are based on the predicted clusters. Usually, K is much smaller than N. Thus, you can repurpose your K-means clustering algorithm so that it can be used as a dimensionality reduction step, before feeding its transformed output to a simple classifier or regressor. Similarly, in a **multi-class** classification problem, a clustering algorithm can be used to reduce the cardinality of the targets.

In contrast to the K-means algorithm, **agglomerative clustering** is another algorithm whose results are deterministic. It doesn't rely on any initial choices since it approaches the clustering problem from a different angle. Agglomerative clustering is the topic of the next section.

Agglomerative clustering

"The most populous city is but an agglomeration of wildernesses."

- Aldous Huxley

In the K-means clustering algorithm, we had our K cluster from day one. With each iteration, some samples may change their allegiances and some clusters may change their centroids, but in the end, the clusters are defined from the very beginning. Conversely, in agglomerative clustering, no clusters exist at the beginning. Initially, each sample belongs to its own cluster. We have as many clusters in the beginning as there are data samples. Then, we find the two closest samples and aggregate them into one cluster. After that, we keep iterating by combining the next closest two samples, two clusters, or the next closest sample and a cluster. As you can see, with each iteration, the number of clusters decreases by one until all our samples join a single cluster. Putting all the samples into one cluster sounds unintuitive. Thus, we have the option to stop the algorithm at any iteration, depending on the final number of clusters we need.

With that, let's learn how to use the agglomerative clustering algorithm. All you have to do for the algorithm to prematurely abort its agglomeration mission is to let it know the final number of clusters we need via its `n_clusters` hyperparameter. Obviously, since I mentioned that the algorithm combines the closed clusters, we need to dive into how intercluster distances are being calculated, but let's ignore this for now – we will get to it in a bit. Here is how the algorithm is used when the number of clusters has been set to 4:

```
from sklearn.cluster import AgglomerativeClustering

x, y = df_blobs[['x1', 'x2']], df_blobs['y']

agglo = AgglomerativeClustering(n_clusters=4)
y_pred = agglo.fit_predict(x)
```

Since we set the number of clusters to 4, the predicted `y_pred` will have values from zero to three.

In fact, the agglomerative clustering algorithm did not stop when the number of clusters was four. It continued to aggregate the clusters and kept track of which clusters are members of which bigger clusters using an internal tree structure. When we specified that we just needed four clusters, it revisited this internal tree and inferred the clusters' labels accordingly. In the next section, we are going to learn how to access the algorithm's internal hierarchy and trace the tree it builds.

Tracing the agglomerative clustering's children

As we mentioned previously, each sample or cluster becomes a member of another cluster, which, in turn, becomes a member of a bigger cluster, and so forth. This hierarchy is stored in the algorithm's `children_` attribute. This attribute is in the form of a list of lists. The outer list has as many members as the number of data samples, minus one. Each of the member lists is made up of two numbers. We can list the last five members of the `children_` attribute as follows:

```
agglo.children_[-5:]
```

This will give us the following list:

```
array([[182, 193],
       [188, 192],
       [189, 191],
       [194, 195],
       [196, 197]])
```

The very last element of the list is the root of the tree. It has two children, 196 and 197. Those are the IDs of the children of this root node. An ID that is greater than or equal to the number of data samples is a cluster ID, while the smaller IDs refer to individual samples. If you subtract the number of data samples from a cluster ID, it will give you the location in the children list where you can get the members of this cluster. From this information, we can build the following recursive function, which takes a list of children and the number of data samples and returns the nested tree of all the clusters and their members, as follows:

```
def get_children(node, n_samples):
    if node[0] >= n_samples:
        child_cluster_id = node[0] - n_samples
        left = get_children(
            agglo.children_[child_cluster_id],
            n_samples
        )
    else:
        left = node[0]
    if node[1] >= n_samples:
        child_cluster_id = node[1] - n_samples
        right = get_children(
            agglo.children_[child_cluster_id],
            n_samples
        )
    else:
        right = node[1]
    return [left, right]
```

We can call the function we've just created like so:

```
root = agglo.children_[-1]
n_samples = df_blobs.shape[0]
tree = get_children(root, n_samples)
```

At this point, `tree[0]` and `tree[1]` contain the IDs of the samples in the left-hand side and right-hand side of the tree – these are the members of the two biggest clusters. If our aim is to divide our samples into four clusters instead of two, we can use `tree[0][0]`, `trec[0][1]`, `tree[1][0]`, and `tree[1][1]`. Here is what `tree[0][0]` looks like:

```
[[[46, [[25, 73], [21, 66]]], [87, 88]],
 [[[22, 64], [4, [49, 98]]],
  [[19, [55, 72]], [[37, 70], [[[47, 82], [13, [39, 92]]], [2, [8,
35]]]]]]]]
```

This nestedness allows us to set how deep we want our clusters to be and retrieve their members accordingly. Nevertheless, we can flatten this list using the following code:

```
def flatten(sub_tree, flat_list):
    if type(sub_tree) is not list:
        flat_list.append(sub_tree)
    else:
        r, l = sub_tree
        flatten(r, flat_list)
        flatten(l, flat_list)
```

Now, we can get a member of `tree[0][0]`, as follows:

```
flat_list = []
flatten(tree[0][0], flat_list)
print(flat_list)
```

We can also mimic the output of `fit_predict` and build our own predicted labels using the following code snippet. It will assign the labels from zero to three to the members of the different branches of the tree we built. Let's call our predicted labels `y_pred_dash`:

```
n_samples = x.shape[0]
y_pred_dash = np.zeros(n_samples)
for i, j, label in [(0,0,0), (0,1,1), (1,0,2), (1,1,3)]:
    flat_list = []
    flatten(tree[i][j], flat_list)
    for sample_index in flat_list:
        y_pred_dash[sample_index] = label
```

To make sure our code works as expected, the values in `y_pred_dash` should match those in `y_pred` from the previous section. Nonetheless, nothing says whether the `tree[0][0]` part of the tree should be given the label 0, 1, 2, or 3. Our choice of labels is arbitrary. Therefore, we need a scoring function that compares the two predictions while taking into account that the label names may vary. That's the job of the adjusted Rand index, which is going to be the topic of the next section.

The adjusted Rand index

The **adjusted Rand index** is very similar to the accuracy score in terms of its classification. It calculates the level of agreement between two lists of labels, yet it accounts for the following issues that the accuracy score cannot deal with:

- The adjusted rand index doesn't care much about the actual labels, as long as the members of one cluster here are the same members of the cluster there.

- Unlike in classification, we may end up having too many clusters. In the extreme case of having each sample as its own cluster, any two lists of clusters will agree with each other if we ignore the names of the labels. Thus, the adjusted rand index discounts the possibility of the two clusters agreeing by chance.

The best-adjusted rand index is `1` when the two predictions match. Thus, we can use it to compare `y_pred` with our `y_pred_dash`. The score is symmetric, so the order of its parameters doesn't matter when calling the scoring function, as follows:

```
from sklearn.metrics import adjusted_rand_score
adjusted_rand_score(y_pred, y_pred_dash)
```

Since we get an adjusted rand index of `1`, we can rest assured that our code for inferring the cluster memberships from the children tree is correct.

I quickly mentioned that, in each iteration, the algorithm combines the two closest clusters. It is easy to imagine how distances are calculated between the two samples. They are basically two points and we have already used different distance measures, such as the Euclidean distance and Manhattan distance, before. However, a cluster is not a point. Where exactly should we measure the distances from? Shall we use the cluster's centroid? Shall we pick a specific data point within each cluster to calculate the distance from it? All these choices can be specified using the **linkage** hyperparameter. In the next section, we are going to see its different options.

Choosing the cluster linkage

By default, the **Euclidean** distance is used to decide which cluster pairs are closest to each other. This default metric can be changed using the **affinity** hyperparameter. Please refer to `Chapter 5`, *Image Processing with Nearest Neighbors*, if you want to know more about the different distance metrics, such as the **cosine** and **Manhattan** distance. When calculating the distance between two clusters, the **linkage** criterion decides how the distances can be measured, given the fact that a cluster usually contains more than one data point. In a *complete* linkage, the maximum distance between all the data points in the two clusters is used. Conversely, in a *single* linkage, the minimum distance is used. Clearly, the *average* linkage takes the average of all the distances between all sample pairs. In a *ward* linkage, two clusters are merged if the average Euclidean distances between each data point in the two clusters and the centroid of the merging cluster are at their minimum. Only Euclidean distances can be used with ward linkage.

To be able to compare the aforementioned linkage methods, we need to create a new dataset. The data points will be arranged in the form of two concentric circles. The smaller circle is enclaved into the bigger one, like Lesotho and South Africa. The `make_circles` function specifies the number of samples to generate (`n_samples`), how far apart the two circles are (`factor`), and how noisy the data is (`noise`):

```
from sklearn.datasets import make_circles
x, y = make_circles(n_samples=150, factor=0.5, noise=0.05, random_state=7)
df_circles = pd.DataFrame({'x1': x[:,0], 'x2': x[:,1], 'y': y})
```

I will display the resulting dataset in a bit, but first, let's use the agglomerative algorithm to cluster the new data samples. I will run the algorithm twice: first with a complete linkage and then with a single linkage. I will be using Manhattan distance this time:

```
from sklearn.cluster import AgglomerativeClustering

linkage_options = ['complete', 'single']

fig, axs = plt.subplots(1, len(linkage_options) + 1, figsize=(14, 6))

x, y = df_circles[['x1', 'x2']], df_circles['y']

plot_2d_clusters(x, y, axs[0])
axs[0].set_title(f'{axs[0].get_title()}\nActuals')

for i, linkage in enumerate(linkage_options, 1):
    y_pred = AgglomerativeClustering(
        n_clusters=2, affinity='manhattan', linkage=linkage
    ).fit_predict(x)

    plot_2d_clusters(x, y_pred, axs[i])

    axs[i].set_title(f'{axs[i].get_title()}\nAgglomerative\nLinkage=
{linkage}')
```

Here are the results of the two linkage methods side by side:

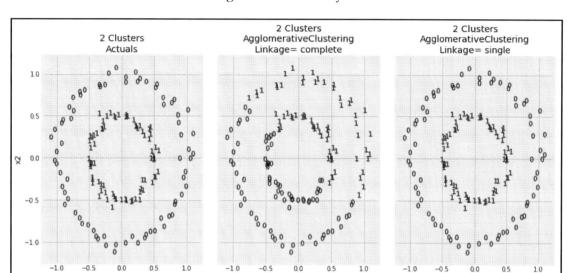

When a single linkage is used, the shortest distance between each cluster pair is considered. This allows it to identify the circular strip where the data points have been arranged. The compete linkage considers the longest distances between the clusters. This resulted in more biased results. Clearly, the single linkage had the best results here. Nevertheless, it is subject to noise due to its variance. To demonstrate this, we can regenerate the circular samples once more after increasing the noise from 0.05 to 0.08, as follows:

```
from sklearn.datasets import make_circles
x, y = make_circles(n_samples=150, factor=0.5, noise=0.08, random_state=7)
df_circles = pd.DataFrame({'x1': x[:,0], 'x2': x[:,1], 'y': y})
```

Running the same clustering algorithm on the new samples will give us the following results:

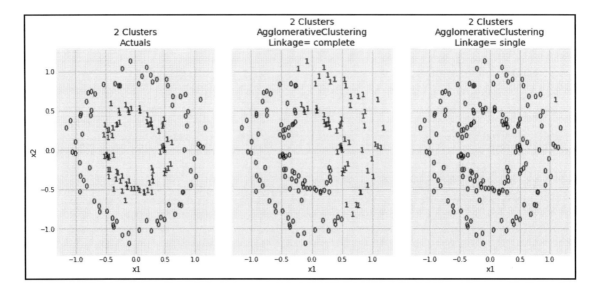

The noisy data confused our single linkage this time, while the outcome of the complete linkage did not vary much. In the single linkage, a noisy point that falls between two clusters may cause them to merge. The average linkage can be seen as a middle ground between the single and the complete linkage criteria. Due to the iterative nature of these algorithms, the three linkage methods cause the bigger clusters to grow even bigger. This may result in uneven cluster sizes. If having imbalanced clusters must be avoided, then the ward linkage should be favored over the other three linkage methods.

So far, the desired number of clusters had to be predefined for the K-means and agglomerative clustering algorithms. Agglomerative clustering is computationally expensive compared to the K-means algorithm, while the K-means algorithm cannot deal with non-convex data. In the next section, we are going to see a third algorithm that doesn't require the number of clusters to be predefined.

DBSCAN

"You never really understand a person until you consider things from his point of view."

- Harper Lee

The acronym **DBSCAN** stands for **density-based spatial clustering of applications with noise**. It sees clusters as areas of high density separated by areas of low density. This allows it to deal with clusters of any shape. This is in contrast to the K-means algorithm, which assumes clusters to be convex; that is, data blobs with centroids. The DBSCAN algorithm starts by identifying the core samples. These are points that have at least min_samples around them within a distance of eps (ε). Initially, a cluster is built out of its core samples. Once a core sample has been identified, its neighbors are also examined and added to the cluster if they meet the core sample criteria. Then, the cluster is expanded so that we can add non-core samples to it. These are samples that can be reached directly from the core samples within a distance of eps but are not core samples themselves. Once all the clusters have been identified, along with their core and non-core samples, the remaining samples are considered noise.

It is clear that the min_samples and eps hyperparameters play a big role in the final predictions. Here, we're setting min_samples to 3 and trying a different setting for eps:

```
from sklearn.cluster import DBSCAN

eps_options = [0.1, 1.0, 2.0, 5.0]

fig, axs = plt.subplots(1, len(eps_options) + 1, figsize=(14, 6))

x, y = df_blobs[['x1', 'x2']], df_blobs['y']

plot_2d_clusters(x, y, axs[0])
axs[0].set_title(f'{axs[0].get_title()}\nActuals')

for i, eps in enumerate(eps_options, 1):
    y_pred = DBSCAN(eps=eps, min_samples=3,
metric='euclidean').fit_predict(x)

    plot_2d_clusters(x, y_pred, axs[i])
    axs[i].set_title(f'{axs[i].get_title()}\nDBSCAN\neps = {eps}')
```

The resulting clusters for the blobs dataset help us identify the effect of the eps hyperparameter:

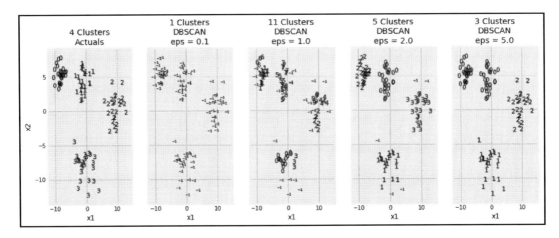

A very small eps does not allow any core samples to form. When eps was set to 0.1, almost all the points were treated as noise. The core points started to form as we increased the value of eps. However, at some point, when eps was set to 0.5, two clusters were mistakenly merged.

Similarly, the value of min_samples can make or break our clustering algorithm. Here, we're going to try different values of min_samples for our concentric data points:

```
from sklearn.cluster import DBSCAN

min_samples_options = [3, 5, 10]

fig, axs = plt.subplots(1, len(min_samples_options) + 1, figsize=(14, 6))

x, y = df_circles[['x1', 'x2']], df_circles['y']

plot_2d_clusters(x, y, axs[0])
axs[0].set_title(f'{axs[0].get_title()}\nActuals')

for i, min_samples in enumerate(min_samples_options, 1):
    y_pred = DBSCAN(
        eps=0.25, min_samples=min_samples, metric='euclidean', n_jobs=-1
    ).fit_predict(x)

    plot_2d_clusters(x, y_pred, axs[i])

    axs[i].set_title(f'{axs[i].get_title()}\nDBSCAN\nmin_samples = {min_samples}')
```

Here, we can see the effect of `min_samples` on our clustering results:

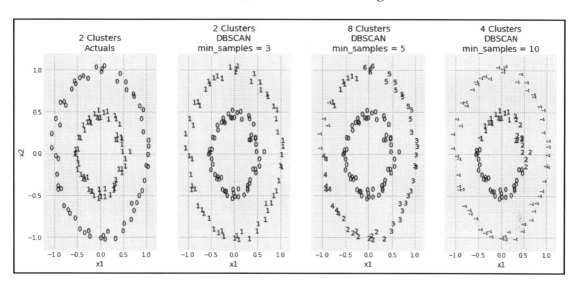

Once more, a careful choice of `min_samples` gave the best results. In contrast to `eps`, the bigger the value of `min_samples`, the harder it is for the core samples to form.

In addition to the aforementioned hyperparameters, we can also change the distance metric used by the algorithm. Usually, `min_samples` takes values above three.
Setting `min_samples` to one means that each sample will be its own cluster, while setting it to two will give similar results to the agglomerative clustering algorithm, but with a single linkage. You may start by setting the `min_samples` value to double the dimensionality of your data; that is, twice the number of features. Then, you may increase it if your data is known to be noisy and decrease it otherwise. As for `eps`, we can use the following **k-distance graph**.

In the concentric dataset, we set `min_samples` to three. Now, for each sample, we want to see how far its two neighbors are. The following code snippet calculates the distance between each point and its closest two neighbors:

```
from sklearn.neighbors import NearestNeighbors

x = df_circles[['x1', 'x2']]
distances, _ = NearestNeighbors(n_neighbors=2).fit(x).kneighbors()
```

If `min_samples` was set to any other number, we would have wanted to get as many neighbors as that number, minus one. Now, we can focus on the farthest neighbor of the two for each sample and plot all the resulting distances, as follows:

```
pd.Series(distances[:,-1]).sort_values().reset_index(drop=True).plot()
```

The resulting graph will look as follows:

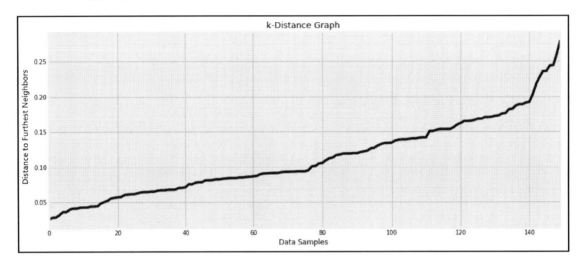

The point where the graph changes its slope dramatically gives us a rough estimate for our `eps` value. Here, when `min_samples` was set to three, an `eps` value of `0.2` sounded quite right. Furthermore, we can try different values for these two numbers and use the silhouette score or any other clustering metric to fine-tune our hyperparameters.

Summary

The British historian Arnold Toynbee once said, *"no tool is omnicompetent"*. In this chapter, we used three tools for clustering. Each of the three algorithms we discussed here approaches the problem from a different angle. The K-means clustering algorithm tries to find points that summarize the clusters and the centroids and builds its clusters around them. The agglomerative clustering approach is more of a bottom-up approach, while the DBSCAN clustering algorithm introduces new concepts such as core points and density. This chapter is the first of three chapters to deal with unsupervised learning problems. The lack of labels here forced us to learn about newer evaluation metrics, such as the adjusted rand index and the silhouette score.

In the next chapter, we are going to deal with our second unsupervised learning problem: **anomaly detection**. Luckily, the concepts discussed here, as well as the ones from Chapter 5, *Image Processing with Nearest Neighbors*, about nearest neighbors and nearest centroid algorithms will help us in the next chapter. Once more, we will be given unlabeled data samples, and we will be tasked with picking the odd samples out.

12

Anomaly Detection – Finding Outliers in Data

Detecting anomalies in data is a recurring theme in machine learning. In `Chapter 10`, *Imbalanced Learning – Not Even 1% Win the Lottery*, we learned how to spot these interesting minorities in our data. Back then, the data was labeled and the classification algorithms from the previous chapters were apt for the problem. Aside from **labeled anomaly detection** problems, there are cases where data is unlabeled.

In this chapter, we are going to learn how to identify outliers in our data, even when no labels are provided. We will use three different algorithms and we will learn about the two branches of **unlabeled anomaly detection**. Here are the topics that will be covered in this chapter:

- Unlabeled anomaly detection
- Detecting anomalies using basic statistics
- Detecting outliers using `EllipticEnvelope`
- Outlier and novelty detection using **Local Outlier Factor (LOF)**
- Detecting outliers using isolation forest

Unlabeled anomaly detection

In this chapter, we will start with some unlabeled data and we will need to spot the anomalous samples in it. We may be given inliers only, and we want to learn what normal data looks like from them. Then, after fitting a model on our inliers, we are given new data and need to spot any outliers that diverge from the data seen so far. These kinds of problems are referred to as **novelty detection**. On the other hand, if we fit our model on a dataset that consists of a combination of inliers and outliers, then this problem is referred to as an **outlier detection** problem.

Like any other unlabeled algorithm, the `fit` method ignores any labels given. This method's interface allows you to pass in both *x* and *y*, for the sake of consistency, but *y* is simply ignored. In cases of novelty detection, it is logical to first use the `fit` method on a dataset that includes no outliers, and then use the algorithm's `predict` method later on for data that includes both inliers and outliers. Conversely, for outlier detection problems, it is common to apply your `fit` method and predict all at once with the `fit_predict` method.

Before using any of our algorithms, we need to create a sample dataset to be used throughout this chapter. Our data will include 1,000 samples, with 98% of them coming from certain distributions and the remaining 2% coming from different distributions. In the next section, we are going to see how to create this sample data in detail.

Generating sample data

The `make_classification` function allows us to specify the number of samples, as well as the number of features. We can limit the number of informative features and make some features redundant—that is, dependent on the informative features. We can also make some features copies of any of the informative or redundant features. In our current use case, we will make sure that all our features are informative since we are going to limit ourselves to two features only. Since the `make_classification` function is meant to produce data for classification problems, it returns both *x* and *y*.

We will ignore *y* when building our models and only use it for evaluation later on. We will make sure each class comes from two different distributions by setting `n_clusters_per_class` to 2. We will keep the two features to the same scale by setting `scale` to a single value. We will also make sure the data is randomly shuffled (`shuffle=True`) and that no samples from one class are labeled as members of the other class (`flip_y=0`). Finally, we will set `random_state` to 0 to make sure we get the exact same random data when running the following code on our computer:

```
from sklearn.datasets import make_classification

x, y = make_classification(
    n_samples=1000, n_features=2, n_informative=2, n_redundant=0,
n_repeated=0,
    n_classes=2, n_clusters_per_class=2, weights=[0.98, ], class_sep=0.5,
    scale=1.0, shuffle=True, flip_y=0, random_state=0
)
```

Now that the sample data is ready, it is time to think of ways to detect the outliers in it.

Detecting anomalies using basic statistics

Rather than jumping straight into the available algorithms in scikit-learn, let's start by thinking about ways to detect the anomalous samples. Imagine measuring the traffic to your website every hour, which gives you the following numbers:

```
hourly_traffic = [
    120, 123, 124, 119, 196,
    121, 118, 117, 500, 132
]
```

Looking at these numbers, 500 sounds quite high compared to the others. Formally speaking, if the hourly traffic data is assumed to be normally distributed, then 500 is further away from its mean or expected value. We can measure this by calculating the mean of these numbers and then checking the numbers that are more than 2 or 3 standard deviations away from the mean. Similarly, we can calculate a high quantile and check which numbers are above it. Here, we find the values above the 95th percentile:

```
pd.Series(hourly_traffic) > pd.Series(hourly_traffic).quantile(0.95)
```

This code will give an array of the False values, except for the penultimate value, which is the one corresponding to 500. Before printing out the results, let's put the preceding code in the form of an estimator with its fit and predict methods. The fit method calculates the threshold and saves it, and the predict method compares the new data to the saved threshold. I also added a fit_predict method that carries out these two operations in sequence. Here is the code for the estimator:

```
class PercentileDetection:
    def __init__(self, percentile=0.9):
        self.percentile = percentile
    def fit(self, x, y=None):
        self.threshold = pd.Series(x).quantile(self.percentile)
    def predict(self, x, y=None):
        return (pd.Series(x) > self.threshold).values
    def fit_predict(self, x, y=None):
        self.fit(x)
        return self.predict(x)
```

We can now use our newly created estimator. In the following code snippet, we use the 95th percentile for our estimator. We then put the resulting predictions alongside the original data into a data frame. Finally, I added some styling logic to mark the rows with outliers in bold:

```
outlierd = PercentileDetection(percentile=0.95)
pd.DataFrame(
```

```
    {
        'hourly_traffic': hourly_traffic,
        'is_outlier': outlierd.fit_predict(hourly_traffic)
    }
).style.apply(
    lambda row: ['font-weight: bold'] * len(row)
        if row['is_outlier'] == True
        else ['font-weight: normal'] * len(row),
    axis=1
)
```

Here is the resulting data frame:

	user_height	is_outlier
0	120	False
1	123	False
2	124	False
3	119	False
4	196	False
5	121	False
6	118	False
7	117	False
8	**500**	**True**
9	132	False

Can we apply the same logic to the dataset from the previous section? Well, yes, but we need to figure out how to apply it to multi-dimensional data first.

Using percentiles for multi-dimensional data

Unlike the hourly_traffic data, the data we generated using the make_classification function is multi-dimensional. We have more than one feature to check this time. Obviously, we can check each feature separately. Here is the code for checking the outliers with respect to the first feature:

```
outlierd = PercentileDetection(percentile=0.98)
y_pred = outlierd.fit_predict(x[:,0])
```

We can do the same for the other feature as well:

```
outlierd = PercentileDetection(percentile=0.98)
y_pred = outlierd.fit_predict(x[:,1])
```

Now, we have ended up with two predictions. We can combine them in a way that each sample is marked as an outlier if it is an outlier with respect to any of the two features. In the following code snippet, we will tweak the PercentileDetection estimator to do that:

```
class PercentileDetection:
    def __init__(self, percentile=0.9):
        self.percentile = percentile
    def fit(self, x, y=None):
        self.thresholds = [
            pd.Series(x[:,i]).quantile(self.percentile)
            for i in range(x.shape[1])
        ]
    def predict(self, x, y=None):
        return (x > self.thresholds).max(axis=1)
    def fit_predict(self, x, y=None):
        self.fit(x)
        return self.predict(x)
```

Now, we can use the tweaked estimator as follows:

```
outlierd = PercentileDetection(percentile=0.98)
y_pred = outlierd.fit_predict(x)
```

We can also use the labels we ignored earlier to calculate the precision and recall of our new estimator. Since we care about the minority class, whose label is 1, we set pos_label to 1 in the following code snippet:

```
from sklearn.metrics import precision_score, recall_score

print(
    'Precision: {:.02%}, Recall: {:.02%} [Percentile Detection]'.format(
        precision_score(y, y_pred, pos_label=1),
        recall_score(y, y_pred, pos_label=1),
    )
)
```

This gives a precision of 4% and a recall of 5%. Did you expect better results? I did too. Maybe we need to plot our data to understand what might be the problem with our method. Here is the dataset, where each sample is marked according to its label:

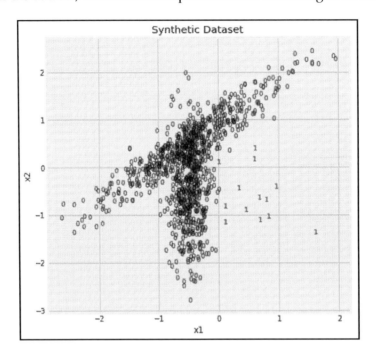

Our method checks each point and sees whether it is extreme on one of the two axes. Despite the fact that the outliers are further away from the inliers, there are still inliers that share the same horizontal or vertical position of each point of the outliers. In other words, if you project your points onto any of the two axes, you will not be able to separate the outliers from the inliers anymore. So, we need a way to consider the two axes at once. What if we find the mean point of the two axes—that is, the center of our data—and then draw a circle or an ellipse around it? Then, we can consider any point that falls outside this ellipse an outlier. Would this new strategy help? Luckily, that's what the EllipticEnvelope algorithm does.

Detecting outliers using EllipticEnvelope

"I'm intimidated by the fear of being average."

– Taylor Swift

The `EllipticEnvelope` algorithm finds the center of the data samples and then draws an ellipsoid around that center. The radii of the ellipsoid in each axis are measured in the **Mahalanobis** distance. You can think of the Mahalanobis distance as a Euclidean distance whose units are the number of standard deviations in each direction. After the ellipsoid is drawn, the points that fall outside it can be considered outliers.

The **multivariate Gaussian distribution** is a key concept of the `EllipticEnvelope` algorithm. It's a generalization of the one-dimensional Gaussian distribution. If the Gaussian distribution is defined by single-valued mean and variance, then the multivariate Gaussian distribution is defined by matrices for means and covariances. The multivariate Gaussian distribution is then used to draw an ellipsoid that defines what is normal and what is an outlier.

Here is how we use the `EllipticEnvelope` algorithm to detect the data outliers, using the algorithm's default settings. Keep in mind that the `predict` methods for all the outlier detection algorithms in this chapter return `-1` for outliers and `1` for inliers:

```
from sklearn.covariance import EllipticEnvelope

ee = EllipticEnvelope(random_state=0)
y_pred = ee.fit_predict(x) == -1
```

We can calculate the precision and the recall scores for the predictions using the exact same code from the previous section:

```
from sklearn.metrics import precision_score, recall_score

print(
    'Precision: {:.02%}, Recall: {:.02%} [EllipticEnvelope]'.format(
        precision_score(y, y_pred, pos_label=1),
    recall_score(y, y_pred, pos_label=1),
    )
)
```

This time, we get a precision of `9%` and a recall of `45%`. That's already better than the previous scores, but can we do better? Well, if you take another look at the data, you will notice that it is non-convex. We already know that the samples in each class come from more than one distribution, and so the shape of the points doesn't seem like it would perfectly fit into an ellipse. This means that we should instead use an algorithm that bases its decision on local distances and densities, rather than comparing everything to a fixed centroid. The **Local Outlier Factor** (**LOF**) gives us that feature. If the **k-means clustering algorithm** of the previous chapter falls into the same group as the elliptic envelope algorithm, then the LOF would be the counterpart of the **DBSCAN** algorithm.

Outlier and novelty detection using LOF

"Madness is rare in individuals – but in groups, parties, nations, and ages, it is the rule."

– Friedrich Nietzsche

LOF takes an opposite approach to Nietzsche's—it compares the density of a sample to the local densities of its neighbors. A sample existing in a low-density area compared to its neighbors is considered an outlier. Like any other neighbor-based algorithms, we have parameters to specify the number of neighbors to consider (n_neighbors) and the distance metric to use to find the neighbors (metric and p). By default, the Euclidean distance is used—that is, metric='minkowski' and p=2. You can refer to Chapter 5, *Image Processing with Nearest Neighbors*, for more information about the available distance metrics. Here is how we use LocalOutlierFactor for outlier detection, using 50 neighbors and its default distance metric:

```
from sklearn.neighbors import LocalOutlierFactor

lof = LocalOutlierFactor(n_neighbors=50)
y_pred = lof.fit_predict(x) == -1
```

The precision and recall scores have now further improved the event. We got a precision value of 26% and a recall value of 65%.

Just like the classifiers, which have the predict method as well as predict_proba, outlier detection algorithms not only give us binary predictions, but can also tell us how confident they are that a sample is an outlier. Once the LOF algorithm is fitted, it stores its outlier factor scores in negative_outlier_factor_. A sample is more likely to be an outlier if the score is closer to –1. So, we can use this score and set its bottom 1%, 2%, or 10% values as outliers, and consider the rest inliers. Here is a comparison for the different performance metrics at each of the aforementioned thresholds:

```
from sklearn.metrics import precision_score, recall_score

lof = LocalOutlierFactor(n_neighbors=50)
lof.fit(x)

for quantile in [0.01, 0.02, 0.1]:
    y_pred = lof.negative_outlier_factor_ < np.quantile(
        lof.negative_outlier_factor_, quantile
    )
    print(
        'LOF: Precision: {:.02%}, Recall: {:.02%}
```

```
[Quantile={:.0%}]'.format(
        precision_score(y, y_pred, pos_label=1),
        recall_score(y, y_pred, pos_label=1),
        quantile
    )
)
```

Here are the different precision and recall scores:

```
# LOF: Precision: 80.00%, Recall: 40.00% [Quantile=1%]
# LOF: Precision: 50.00%, Recall: 50.00% [Quantile=2%]
# LOF: Precision: 14.00%, Recall: 70.00% [Quantile=10%]
```

As in the case with the classifiers' probabilities, there is a trade-off here between the precision and recall scores for the different thresholds. This is how you can fine-tune your predictions to suit your needs. You can also use `negative_outlier_factor_` to plot the **Receiver Operating Characteristic (ROC)** or **Precision-Recall (PR)** curves if the true labels are known.

Aside from its use for outlier detection, the LOF algorithm can also be used for novelty detection.

Novelty detection using LOF

When used for outlier detection, the algorithm has to be fitted on the dataset with both its inliers and outliers. In the case of novelty detection, we are expected to fit the algorithm on the inliers only, and then predict on a contaminated dataset later on. Furthermore, to be used for novelty detection, you have `novelty=True` during the algorithm's initialization. Here, we remove the outliers from our data and use the resulting subsample, `x_inliers`, with the `fit` function. Then, we predict for the original dataset as normal:

```
from sklearn.neighbors import LocalOutlierFactor

x_inliers = x[y==0]

lof = LocalOutlierFactor(n_neighbors=50, novelty=True)
lof.fit(x_inliers)
y_pred = lof.predict(x) == -1
```

The resulting precision (`26.53%`) and recall (`65.00%`) values did not vary much compared to when we used the algorithm for outlier detection. In the end, the choice in terms of novelty detection versus the outlier detection approach is a tactical one. It depends on the available data when the model is built and whether it contains outliers.

You probably already know by now that I like using the ensemble methods, and so it is hard for me to end this chapter without presenting an ensemble algorithm for outlier detection. In the next section, we are going to look at the **isolation forest** algorithm.

Detecting outliers using isolation forest

In previous approaches, we started by defining what normal is, and then considered anything that doesn't conform to this as outliers. The isolation forest algorithm follows a different approach. Since the outliers are few and different, they are easier to isolate from the rest. So, when building a forest of random trees, a sample that ends in leaf nodes early in a tree—that is, it did not need a lot of branching effort to be isolated—is more likely to be an outlier.

As a tree-based ensemble, this algorithm shares many hyperparameters with its counterparts, such as the number of random trees to build (n_estimators), the ratio of samples to use when building each tree (max_samples), the ratio of features to consider when building each tree (max_features), and whether to sample with a replacement or not (bootstrap). You can also build the trees in parallel using all the available CPUs on your machine by setting n_jobs to –1. Here, we will build an isolation forest algorithm of 200 trees, then use it to predict the outliers in our dataset. Like all the other algorithms in this chapter, a prediction of –1 means that the sample is seen as an outlier:

```
from sklearn.ensemble import IsolationForest

iforest = IsolationForest(n_estimators=200, n_jobs=-1, random_state=10)
y_pred = iforest.fit_predict(x) == -1
```

The resulting precision (6.5%) and recall (60.0%) values are not as good as the previous approaches. Clearly, LOF is the most suitable algorithm for the data we have at hand here. We were able to compare the three algorithms since the original labels were available to us. In reality, labels are usually unavailable, and it is hard to decide which algorithm to use. The field of unlabeled anomaly detection evaluation is actively being researched, and I hope to see scikit-learn implement reliable evaluation metrics once they are available in the future.

In the case of supervised learning, you can use true labels to evaluate models using the PR curves. When it comes to unlabeled data, recent researchers are trying to tailor evaluation criteria, such as the **Excess-Mass (EM)** and **Mass-Volume (MV)** curves.

Summary

So far in this book, we have used supervised learning algorithms to spot anomalous samples. This chapter offered additional solutions when no labels are provided. The solutions explained here stem from different fields of machine learning, such as statistical learning, nearest-neighbor, and tree-based ensembles. Each one of the three tools explained here can excel, but also have disadvantages. We also learned that evaluating machine learning algorithms when no labels are provided is tricky.

This chapter will deal with unlabeled data. In the previous chapter, we learned how to cluster data, and then we learned how to detect the outliers in it here. We still have one more unsupervised learning topic to discuss in this book, though. In the next chapter, we will cover an important topic relating to e-commerce—recommendation engines. Since it is the last chapter of this book, I'd also like to go through the possible approaches to machine learning model deployment. We will learn how to save and load our models and how to deploy them on **Application Programming Interfaces (APIs)**.

13
Recommender System – Getting to Know Their Taste

A layperson might not know about the sophisticated machine learning algorithms controlling the high-frequency transactions taking place in the stock exchange. They may also not know about the algorithms detecting online crimes and controlling missions to outer space. Yet, they interact with recommendation engines every day. They are daily witnesses of the recommendation engines picking books for them to read on Amazon, selecting which movies they should watch next on Netflix, and influencing the news articles they read every day. The prevalence of recommendation engines in many businesses requires different flavors of recommendation algorithms.

In this chapter, we will learn about the different approaches used by recommender systems. We will mainly use a sister library to scikit-learn called Surprise. Surprise is a toolkit that implements different collaborative filtering algorithms. So, we will start by learning the differences between the *collaborative filtering* algorithms and the *content-based filtering* algorithms used in a recommendation engine. We will also learn how to package our trained models to be used by other software without the need for retraining. The following topics will be discussed here:

- The different recommendation paradigms
- Downloading Surprise and the dataset
- Using KNN-inspired algorithms
- Using baseline algorithms
- Using singular value decomposition
- Deploying machine learning models in production

The different recommendation paradigms

In a recommendation task, you have a set of users interacting with a set of items and your job is to figure out which items are suitable for which users. You may know a thing or two about each user: where they live, how much they earn, whether they are logged in via their phone or their tablet, and more. Similarly, for an item—say, a movie—you know its genre, its production year, and how many Academy Awards it has won. Clearly, this looks like a classification problem. You can combine the user features with the item features and build a classifier for each user-item pair, and then try to predict whether the user will like the item or not. This approach is known as **content-based filtering**. As its name suggests, it is as good as the content or the features extracted from each user and each item. In practice, you may only know basic information about each user. A user's location or gender may reveal enough about their tastes. This approach is also hard to generalize. Say we decided to expand our recommendation engine to recommend TV series as well. The number of Academy Awards may not be relevant, then, and we may need to replace this feature with the number of Golden Globe nominations instead. What if we expand it to music later? It makes sense to think of a different approach that is content-agnostic instead.

Collaborative filtering, on the other hand, doesn't care much about the user or the item features. Rather, it assumes that users who are already interested in some items will probably have the same interests in the future. To make a recommendation for you, it basically recruits other users who are similar to you and uses the decisions they make to suggest items to you in the future. One obvious problem here is the cold-start problem. When a new user joins, it is hard to know which users are similar to them right away. Also, for a new item, it will take a while for some users to discover it, and only then will the system be able to recommend it to other users.

Since each approach has its shortcomings, a hybrid approach of the two can be used. In its simplest form, we can just recommend to the new users the most popular items on the platform. Once these new users consume enough items for us to know their taste, we can start incorporating a more collaborative filtering approach to tailor their recommendations for them.

In this chapter, we are going to focus on the *collaborative filtering* paradigm. It is the more common approach, and we already learned in previous chapters how to build the classifiers needed for the *content-based filtering* approach. We will be using a library called Surprise to demonstrate the different collaborative filtering algorithms. In the next section, we are going to install Surprise and download the data needed for the rest of the chapter.

Downloading surprise and the dataset

Nicolas Hug created Surprise [`http://surpriselib.com`], which implements a number of the collaborative filtering algorithms we will use here. I am using version 1.1.0 of the library. To download the same version of the library via `pip`, you can run the following command in your terminal:

```
pip install -U scikit-surprise==1.1.0
```

Before using the library, we also need to download the dataset used in this chapter.

Downloading the KDD Cup 2012 dataset

We are going to use the same dataset that we used in Chapter 10, *Imbalanced Learning – Not Even 1% Win the Lottery*. The data is published on the **OpenML** platform. It contains a list of records. In each record, a user has seen an online advertisement, and there is an additional column stating whether the user clicked on the advertisement. In the aforementioned chapter, we built a classifier to predict whether the user clicked on the advertisement. We used the provided features for the advertisements and the visiting users in our classifier. In this chapter, we are going to frame the problem as a collaborative filtering problem. So, we will only use the IDs of the users and the advertisements. All the other features will be ignored, and this time, the target label will be the user rating. Here, we will download the data and put it into a data frame:

```
from sklearn.datasets import fetch_openml

data = fetch_openml(data_id=1220)

df = pd.DataFrame(
    data['data'],
    columns=data['feature_names']
)[['user_id', 'ad_id']].astype(int)


df['user_rating'] = pd.Series(data['target']).astype(int)
```

We converted all the columns into integers. The rating column takes binary values, where 1 indicates a click or a positive rating. We can see that only 16.8% of the records lead to a positive rating. We can check this by printing the mean of the user_rating column, as follows:

```
df['user_rating'].mean()
```

We can also display the first four rows of the dataset. Here, you can see the IDs of the users and the advertisements, as well as the given ratings:

	user_id	ad_id	user_rating
0	0	8343295	0
1	562934	20017077	1
2	11621116	21348354	0
3	8778348	20366086	0

The Surprise library expects the data columns to be in this exact order. So, no more data manipulations are required for now. In the next section, we are going to see how to load this data frame into the library and split it into training and test sets.

Processing and splitting the dataset

In its simplest form, two users are similar, from a collaborative filtering point of view, if they give the same ratings to the same items. It is hard to see this in the current data format. It would be better to put the data into a user-item rating matrix. Each row in this matrix represents a user, each column represents an item, and the values in each cell represent the rating given by each user to the corresponding item. We can use the pivot method in pandas to create this matrix. Here, I have created the matrix for the first 10 records of our dataset:

```
df.head(10).groupby(
    ['user_id', 'ad_id']
).max().reset_index().pivot(
    'user_id', 'ad_id', 'user_rating'
).fillna(0).astype(int)
```

Here is the resulting 10 users by 10 items matrix:

ad_id	6803526	8343295	9027213	20017077	20366086	20886690	21186478	21348354	21367376	21811752
user_id										
0	0	0	0	0	0	0	0	0	0	0
562934	0	0	0	1	0	0	0	0	0	0
579253	0	0	0	0	0	0	0	0	0	0
2886008	0	0	0	0	0	0	1	0	0	0
5277279	0	0	0	0	0	0	0	0	0	0
7589739	0	0	0	0	0	0	0	0	0	0
8778348	0	0	0	0	0	0	0	0	0	0
11621116	0	0	0	0	0	0	0	0	0	0
11808635	0	0	1	0	0	0	0	0	0	0
12118311	0	0	0	0	0	0	0	0	0	0

Doing this ourselves using data frames is not the most efficient approach. The Surprise library stores the data in a more efficient way. So, we will use the library's `Dataset` module instead. Before loading the data, we need to specify the scale of the ratings given. Here, we will use the `Reader` module to specify that our ratings take binary values. Then, we will load the data frame using the `load_from_df` method of the dataset. This method takes our data frame as well as an instance of the aforementioned reader:

```
from surprise.dataset import Dataset
from surprise import Reader

reader = Reader(rating_scale=(0, 1))
dataset = Dataset.load_from_df(df, reader)
```

The collaborative filtering algorithm is not considered a supervised learning algorithm due to the absence of concepts such as features and targets. Nevertheless, users give ratings to the item and we try to predict those ratings. This means that we can still evaluate our algorithm by comparing the actual ratings to the predicted ones. That's why it is common to split the data into training and test sets and use metrics to evaluate our predictions. Surprise has a similar function to scikit-learn's `train_test_split` function. We will use it here to split the data into 75% training versus 25% test sets:

```
from surprise.model_selection import train_test_split
trainset, testset = train_test_split(dataset, test_size=0.25)
```

In addition to the train-test split, we can also perform **K-Fold cross-validation**. We will use the **Mean Absolute Error (MAE)** and the **Root Mean Squared Error (RMSE)** to compare the predicted ratings to the actual ones. The following code uses 4-fold cross-validation and prints the average MAE and RMSE for the four folds. To make it easier to apply to different algorithms, I created a `predict_evaluate` function, which takes an instance of the algorithm we want to use. It also takes the entire dataset, and the name of the algorithm is used to print it alongside the results at the end. It then uses the `cross_validate` module od `surprise` to calculate the expected errors and print their averages:

```
from surprise.model_selection import cross_validate

def predict_evaluate(recsys, dataset, name='Algorithm'):
    scores = cross_validate(
        recsys, dataset, measures=['RMSE', 'MAE'], cv=4
    )
    print(
        'Testset Avg. MAE: {:.2f} & Avg. RMSE: {:.2f} [{}]'.format(
            scores['test_mae'].mean(),
            scores['test_rmse'].mean(),
            name
        )
    )
```

We will be using this function in the following sections. Before learning about the different algorithms, we need to create a reference algorithm—a line in the sand with which to compare the remaining algorithms. In the next section, we are going to create a recommendation system that gives random results. This will be our reference algorithm further down the road.

Creating a random recommender

We know that 16.8% of the records lead to positive ratings. Thus, a recommender that randomly gives positive ratings to 16.8% of the cases seems like a good reference to compare the other algorithms. By the way, I am deliberately avoiding the term *baseline* here and using terms such as *reference* instead, since one of the algorithms used here is called *baseline*. Anyway, we can create our reference algorithm by creating a `RandomRating` class that inherits from the Surprise library's `AlgoBase` class. All the algorithms in the library are driven from the `AlgoBase` base class and they are expected to implement an estimate method.

This method is called with each user-item pair and it is expected to return the predicted rating for this particular user-item pair. Since we are returning random ratings here, we will use NumPy's `random` module. Here, we set n=1 in the binomial method, which turns it into a Bernoulli distribution. The value given to p during the class initialization specifies the probability of returning ones. By default, 50% of the user-item pairs will get a rating of 1 and 50% of them will get a rating of 0. We will override this default and set it to 16.8% when using the class later on. Here is the code for the newly created method:

```
from surprise import AlgoBase

class RandomRating(AlgoBase):

    def __init__(self, p=0.5):
        self.p = p
        AlgoBase.__init__(self)

    def estimate(self, u, i):
        return np.random.binomial(n=1, p=self.p, size=1)[0]
```

We need to change the default value of p to `16.8%`. We can then pass the `RandomRating` instance to `predict_evaluate` to get the estimated errors:

```
recsys = RandomRating(p=0.168)
predict_evaluate(recsys, dataset, 'RandomRating')
```

The previous code gives us an average MAE of `0.28` and an average RMSE of `0.53`. Remember, we are using K-fold cross-validation. So, we calculate the average of the average errors returned for each fold. Keep these error numbers in mind as we expect more advanced algorithms to give lower errors. In the next section, we will meet the most basic family of the collaborative filtering algorithms, inspired by the **K-Nearest Neighbors (KNN)** algorithms.

Using KNN-inspired algorithms

We have encountered enough variants of the KNN algorithm for it be our first choice for solving the recommendation problem. In the user-item rating matrix from the previous section, each row represents a user and each column represents an item. Thus, similar rows represent users who have similar tastes and identical columns represent items liked by the same users. Therefore, if we want to estimate the rating ($r_{u,i}$), given by the user (u) to the item (i), we can get the KNNs to the user (u), find their ratings for the item (i), and calculate the average of their rating as an estimate for ($r_{u,i}$). Nevertheless, since some of these neighbors are more similar to the user (u) than others, we may need to use a weighted average instead. Ratings given by more similar users should be given more weight than the others. Here is a formula where a similarity score is used to weigh the ratings given by the user's neighbors:

$$Expected(r_{u,i}) = \frac{\sum_v Similarity(u, v) \times r_{v,i}}{\sum_v Similarity(u, v)}$$

We refer to the neighbors of *u* with the term *v*. Therefore, $r_{v,i}$ is the rating given by each of them to the item (i). Conversely, we can base our estimation on *item similarities* rather than *user similarities*. Then, the expected rating ($r_{u,i}$) would be the weighted average of the ratings given by the user (u) to their most similar items (i).

You may be wondering whether we can now set the number of neighbors and whether there are multiple similarity metrics to choose from. The answer to both questions is yes. We will dig deeper into the algorithm's hyperparameters in a bit, but for now, let's use it with its default values. Once `KNNBasic` is initialized, we can pass it to the `predict_evaluate` function, the same way we passed the `RandomRating` estimator to it in the previous section. Make sure you have enough memory on your computer before running the following code:

```
from surprise.prediction_algorithms.knns import KNNBasic
recsys = KNNBasic()
predict_evaluate(recsys, dataset, 'KNNBasic')
```

We get an average MAE of 0.28 and an average RMSE of 0.38 this time. The improvement in the squared error is expected, given that the `RandomRating` estimator was blindly making random predictions, while `KNNBasic` bases its decision on users' similarities.

The ratings in the dataset used here are binary values. In some other scenarios, users may be allowed to give 5-star ratings, or even give scores from 0 to 100. In those scenarios, one user may be more generous with their numbers than another. We both may have the same taste, but for me, a 5-star rating signals the movie is great, while you never give a 5-star rating yourself, and your favorite movies get 4-star rating tops. The `KNNWithMeans` algorithm deals with this problem. It is an almost identical algorithm to `KNNBasic`, except for the fact that it initially normalizes the ratings given by each user to make them comparable.

As stated earlier, we can choose the number for K, as well as the similarity score used. Additionally, we can decide whether we want to base our estimation on user similarities or on item similarities. Here, we set the number of neighbors to 20, use cosine similarity, and base our estimation on item similarities:

```
from surprise.prediction_algorithms.knns import KNNBasic

sim_options = {
    'name': 'cosine', 'user_based': False
}
recsys = KNNBasic(k=20, sim_options=sim_options, verbose=False)
predict_evaluate(recsys, dataset, 'KNNBasic')
```

The resulting errors are worse than before. We get an average MAE of 0.29 and an average RMSE of 0.39. Clearly, we need to try different hyperparameters until we get the best results. Luckily, Surprise provides a `GridSearchCV` helper for tuning the algorithm's hyperparameters. We basically provide a list of the hyperparameter values and specify the measures we need to use to evaluate the algorithms. In the following code snippet, we set the measures to `rmse` and `mae`. We use 4-fold cross-validation and use all the available processors in our machines when running the grid search. You probably know by now that KNN algorithms are slow with their prediction time. So, to speed up this process, I only ran the search on a subset of our dataset, as follows:

```
from surprise.model_selection import GridSearchCV
from surprise.prediction_algorithms.knns import KNNBasic

param_grid = {
    'sim_options': {
        'name':['cosine', 'pearson'],
    },
    'k': [5, 10, 20, 40],
    'verbose': [True],
}

dataset_subset = Dataset.load_from_df(
```

```
    df.sample(frac=0.25, random_state=0), reader
)
gscv = GridSearchCV(
    KNNBasic, param_grid, measures=['rmse', 'mae'],
    cv=4, n_jobs=-1
)
gscv.fit(dataset_subset)

print('Best MAE:', gscv.best_score['mae'].round(2))
print('Best RMSE:', gscv.best_score['rmse'].round(2))
print('Best Params', gscv.best_params['rmse'])
```

We get an average MAE of 0.28 and an average RMSE of 0.38. These are the same results as with the default hyperparameters. However, `GridSearchCV` chose a K value of 20 versus the default of 40. It also chose the **Pearson correlation coefficient** as its similarity measure.

The KNN algorithm is slow and did not give the best performance for our dataset. Therefore, in the next section, we are going to try a non-instance-based learner instead.

Using baseline algorithms

The simplicity of the nearest neighbors algorithm is a double-edged sword. On the one hand, it is easier to grasp, but on the other hand, it lacks an objective function that we can optimize during training. This also means that the majority of its computation is performed during prediction time. To overcome these problems, Yehuda Koren formulated the recommendation problem in terms of an optimization task. Still, for each user-item pair, we need to estimate a rating ($r_{u,i}$). The expected rating this time is the summation of the following triplet:

- μ: The overall average rating given by all users to all items
- b_u: A term for how the user (u) deviates from the overall average rating
- b_i: A term for how the item (i) deviates from the average rating

Here is the formula for the expected ratings:

$$Expected(r_{u,i}) = \mu + b_u + b_i$$

For each user-item pair in our training set, we know its actual rating ($r_{u,i}$), and all we need to do now is to figure out the optimal values of b_u and b_i. We are after values that minimize the difference between the actual rating ($r_{u,i}$) and the *expected rating* ($r_{u,i}$) from the aforementioned formula. In other words, we need a solver to learn the values of the terms when given the training data. In practice, the baseline algorithm tries to minimize the average squared difference between the actual and the expected ratings. It also adds a regularization term that penalizes (b_u) and (b_i) to avoid overfitting. Please refer to `Chapter 3, Making Decisions with Linear Equations`, for a better understanding of the concept of regularization.

The learned coefficients (b_u and b_i) are vectors describing each user and each item. At prediction time, if a new user is encountered, b_u is set to 0. Similarly, if a new item that wasn't seen in the training set is encountered, b_i is set to 0.

Two solvers are available for solving this optimization problem: **Stochastic Gradient Descent (SGD)** and **Alternating Least Squares (ALS)**. ALS is used by default. Each of the two solvers has its own settings, such as the maximum number of epochs and the learning rate. Moreover, you can also tune the regularization parameters.

Here is how the model is used with its default hyperparameters:

```
from surprise.prediction_algorithms.baseline_only import BaselineOnly
recsys = BaselineOnly(verbose=False)
predict_evaluate(recsys, dataset, 'BaselineOnly')
```

This time, we get an average MAE of 0.27 and an average RMSE of 0.37. Once more, `GridSearchCV` can be used to tune the model's hyperparameters. I will leave the parameter tuning for you to try. Now, it is time to move on to our third algorithm: **Singular Value Decomposition (SVD)**.

Using singular value decomposition

The user-item rating matrix is usually a huge matrix. The one we got from our dataset here comprises 30,114 rows and 19,228 columns, and most of the values in this matrix (99.999%) are zeros. This is expected. Say you own a streaming service with thousands of movies in your library. It is very unlikely that a user will watch more than a few dozen of them. This sparsity creates another problem. If one user watched the movie *The Hangover: Part 1* and another user watched *The Hangover: Part 2*, from the matrix's point of view, they watched two different movies. We already know that collaborative filtering algorithms don't use users or item features. Thus, it is not aware of the fact that the two parts of *The Hangover* movie belong to the same franchise, let alone knowing that they both are comedies. To deal with this shortcoming, we need to transform our user-item rating matrix. We want the new matrix, or matrices, to be smaller and to capture the similarities between the users and the items better.

The **SVD** is a matrix factorization algorithm that is used for dimensionality reduction. It is very similar to **Principal Component Analysis (PCA)**, which we looked at in Chapter 5, *Image Processing with Nearest Neighbors*. The resulting singular values, as opposed to the principal components in PCA, capture latent information about the users and the item in the user-item rating matrix. Don't worry if the previous sentence is not clear yet. In the next section, we will understand the algorithm better via an example.

Extracting latent information via SVD

Nothing spells taste like music. Let's take the following dataset. Here, we have six users, each voting for the musicians they like:

```
music_ratings = [('U1', 'Metallica'), ('U1', 'Rammstein'), ('U2',
'Rammstein'), ('U3', 'Tiesto'), ('U3', 'Paul van Dyk'), ('U2',
'Metallica'), ('U4', 'Tiesto'), ('U4', 'Paul van Dyk'), ('U5',
'Metallica'), ('U5', 'Slipknot'), ('U6', 'Tiesto'), ('U6', 'Aly & Fila'),
('U3', 'Aly & Fila')]
```

We can put these ratings into a data frame and convert it into a user-item rating matrix, using the data frame's `pivot` method, as follows:

```
df_music_ratings = pd.DataFrame(music_ratings, columns=['User', 'Artist'])
df_music_ratings['Rating'] = 1

df_music_ratings_pivoted = df_music_ratings.pivot(
    'User', 'Artist', 'Rating'
).fillna(0)
```

Here is the resulting matrix. I used `pandas` styling to give the different ratings different colors for clarity:

Artist User	Aly & Fila	Metallica	Paul van Dyk	Rammstein	Slipknot	Tiesto
U1	0	1	0	1	0	0
U2	0	1	0	1	0	0
U3	1	0	1	0	0	1
U4	0	0	1	0	0	1
U5	0	1	0	0	1	0
U6	1	0	0	0	0	1

Clearly, users 1, 2, and 5 like metal music, while users 3, 4, and 6 like trance music. We can see this despite the fact that user 5 only shares one band with users 1 and 2. We could perhaps also see this because we are aware of these musicians and because we have a holistic view of the matrix instead of focusing on individual pairs. We can use scikit-learn's `TruncatedSVD` function to reduce the dimensionality of the matrix and represent each user and musician via N components (single vectors). The following snippet calculates `TruncatedSVD` with two *single vectors*. Then, the `transform` function returns a new matrix, where each row represents one of the six users, and each of its two columns corresponds to one of the two single vectors:

```
from sklearn.decomposition import TruncatedSVD
svd = TruncatedSVD(n_components=2)
svd.fit_transform(df_music_ratings_pivoted).round(2)
```

Once more, I put the resulting matrix into a data frame and used its styling to color the cells according to their values. Here is the code for that:

```
pd.DataFrame(
    svd.fit_transform(df_music_ratings_pivoted),
    index=df_music_ratings_pivoted.index,
    columns=['SV1', 'SV2'],
).round(2).style.bar(
    subset=['SV1', 'SV2'], align='mid', color='#AAA'
)
```

This is the resulting data frame:

User	SV1	SV2
U1	0	1.37
U2	0	1.37
U3	1.71	-0
U4	1.21	-0
U5	0	1
U6	1.21	-0

You can treat each of the two components as a music genre. It is clear that the smaller matrix was able to capture the user's taste in terms of genres. Users 1, 2, and 5 are brought closer to each other now, as are users 3, 4, and 6, who are closer to each other than they were in the original matrix. We will use the cosine similarity score to show this more clearly in the next section.

The concept used here is also used with textual data. Words such as `search`, `find`, and `forage` carry similar meanings. Thus, the `TruncatedSVD` transformer can be used to compress a **Vector Space Model (VSM)** into a lower space before using it in a supervised or an unsupervised learning algorithm. When used in that context, it is known as **Latent Semantic Analysis (LSA)**.

This compression not only captures the latent information that is not clear in the bigger matrix, but also helps with distance calculations. We already know that algorithms such as KNN work best with lower dimensions. Don't take my word for it. In the next section, we will compare the cosine distances when calculated based on the original user-item rating matrix versus the two-dimensional one.

Comparing the similarity measures for the two matrices

We can calculate the cosine similarities between all users. We will start with the original user-item rating matrix. After calculating pairwise cosine similarities for users 1, 2, 3, and 5, we put the results into a data frame and apply some styling for clarity:

```
from sklearn.metrics.pairwise import cosine_similarity

user_ids = ['U1', 'U2', 'U3', 'U5']
```

```
pd.DataFrame(
    cosine_similarity(
        df_music_ratings_pivoted.loc[user_ids, :].values
    ),
    index=user_ids,
    columns=user_ids
).round(2).style.bar(
    subset=user_ids, align='mid', color='#AAA'
)
```

Here are the resulting pairwise similarities between the four users:

	U1	U2	U3	U5
U1	1	1	0	1
U2	1	1	-0	1
U3	0	-0	1	-0
U5	1	1	-0	1

Indeed, user 5 is more similar to users 1 and 2, compared to user 3. However, they are not as similar as we expected them to be. Let's now calculate the same similarities by using TruncatedSVD this time:

```
from sklearn.metrics.pairwise import cosine_similarity
from sklearn.decomposition import TruncatedSVD

user_ids = ['U1', 'U2', 'U3', 'U5']

svd = TruncatedSVD(n_components=2)
df_user_svd = pd.DataFrame(
    svd.fit_transform(df_music_ratings_pivoted),
    index=df_music_ratings_pivoted.index,
    columns=['SV1', 'SV2'],
)

pd.DataFrame(
    cosine_similarity(
        df_user_svd.loc[user_ids, :].values
    ),
    index=user_ids,
    columns=user_ids
).round(2).style.bar(
    subset=user_ids, align='mid', color='#AAA'
)
```

The new calculations capture the latent similarities between the musicians this time and incorporate this when comparing the users. Here is the new similarity matrix:

	U1	U2	U3	U5
U1	1	1	0	1
U2	1	1	-0	1
U3	0	-0	1	-0
U5	1	1	-0	1

Clearly, user 5 is more similar to users 1 and 2 than before. Ignore the negative signs before some of the zeros here. This is because of Python's implementation of the **IEEE (Institute of Electrical and Electronics Engineers)** standard for floating-point arithmetic.

Naturally, we can also represent the musicians in terms of their genres (single vectors). This other matrix can be retrieved via `svd.components_`. Then, we can calculate the similarities between the different musicians. This transformation is also advised as a preliminary step before clusters sparse data.

Now that this version of SVD is clear, in practice, when dealing with large datasets, more scalable factorization algorithms are usually used. **Probabilistic Matrix Factorization (PMF)** scales linearly with the number of observations and performs well on sparse and imbalanced datasets. We are going to use Surprise's implementation of PMF in the next section.

Click prediction using SVD

We can now use Surprise's SVD algorithm to predict the clicks in our dataset. Let's start with the algorithm's default parameters, and then explain it later on:

```
from surprise.prediction_algorithms.matrix_factorization import SVD
recsys = SVD()
predict_evaluate(recsys, dataset, 'SVD')
```

This time, we get an average MAE of 0.27 and an average RMSE of 0.37. These are similar results to the baseline algorithm used earlier. In fact, Surprise's implementation of SVD is a combination of the baseline algorithm and SVD. It expresses the user-item ratings using the following formula:

$$Expected(r_{u,i}) = \mu + b_u + b_i + q_i^T p_u$$

The first three terms of the equation (μ, b_u, and b_i) are the same as in the baseline algorithm. The fourth term represents the product of two similar matrices to the ones we got from TruncatedSVD. The q_i matrix expresses each item as a number of single vectors. Similarly, the p_u matrix expresses each user as a number of single vectors. The item matrix is transposed, hence the letter T on top of it. The algorithm then uses **SGD** to minimize the squared difference between the expected ratings and the actual ones. Similar to the baseline model, it also regularizes the coefficients of the expected rating (b_u, b_i, q_i, and p_u) to avoid overfitting.

We can ignore the baseline part of the equation—that is, remove the first three coefficients of it (μ, b_u, and b_i) by setting biased=False. The number of single vectors to use is set using the n_factors hyperparameter. We can also control the number of epochs for SGD via n_epochs. Furthermore, there are additional hyperparameters for setting the algorithm's learning rate, regularization, and the initial values of its coefficients. You can find the best mix for these parameters using the parameter-tuning helpers provided by surprise—that is, GridSearchCV or RandomizedSearchCV.

Our discussion of the recommender systems, along with their various algorithms, marks an end to the machine learning topics discussed in this book. Like all the other algorithms discussed here, they are only useful when putting in production for others to use them. In the next section, we are going to see how we can deploy a trained algorithm and make it accessible to others.

Deploying machine learning models in production

There are two main modes of using machine learning models:

- **Batch predictions**: In this mode, you load a bunch of data records after a certain period—for example, every night or every month. You then make predictions for this data. Usually, latency is not an issue here, and you can afford to put your training and prediction code into single batch jobs. One exception to this is if you need to run your job too frequently that you do not have enough time to retrain the model every time the job runs. Then, it makes sense to train the model once, store it somewhere, and load it each time new batch predictions are to be made.

- **Online predictions**: In this model, your model is usually deployed behind an **Application Programming Interface (API)**. Your API is usually called with a single data record each time, and it is supposed to make predictions for this single record and return it. Having low latency is paramount here and it is typically advised to train the model once, store it somewhere, and use the pre-trained model whenever a new API call is made.

As you can see, in both cases, we may need to separate the code used during the model's training from the one used at prediction time. Whether it is a supervised learning algorithm or an unsupervised learning one, besides the lines of code it is written in, a fitted model also depends on the coefficients and parameters learned from the data. Thus, we need a way to store the code and the learned parameters as one unit. This single unit can be saved after training and then used later on at prediction time. To be able to store functions or objects in files or share them over the internet, we need to convert them into a standard format or protocol. This process is known as serialization. `pickle` is one of the most commonly used serialization protocols in Python. The Python standard library provides tools for pickling objects; however, `joblib` is a more efficient option when dealing with NumPy arrays. To be able to use the library, you need to install it via `pip` by running the following in your terminal:

```
pip install joblib
```

Once installed, you can use `joblib` to save anything onto a file on disk. For example, after fitting a baseline algorithm, we can store the fitted object using the `joblib` function's `dump` method. The method expects, along with the model's object, the name of the file to save the object in. We usually use a `.pkl` extension to refer to `pickle` files:

```
import joblib
from surprise.prediction_algorithms.baseline_only import BaselineOnly

recsys = BaselineOnly()
recsys.fit(trainset)
joblib.dump(recsys, 'recsys.pkl')
```

Once saved to a disk, any other Python code can load the same model again and use it right away without the need for refitting. Here, we load the pickled algorithm and use it to make predictions for the test set:

```
from surprise import accuracy
recsys = joblib.load('recsys.pkl')
predictions = recsys.test(testset)
```

A `surprise` estimator was used here since this is the library we used throughout this chapter. Nevertheless, any Python object can be pickled and loaded in the same way. Any of the estimators used in the previous chapters can be used the same way. Furthermore, you can also write your own classes, instantiate them, and pickle the resulting objects.

To deploy your model as an API, you may need to use a web framework, such as **Flask** or **CherryPy**. Developing web applications is beyond the scope of this book, but once you know how to build them, loading pickled models should be straightforward. It's advised to load the pickled object when the web application is starting. This way, you do not introduce any additional latency if you reload the objects each time you receive a new request.

Summary

This chapter marks the end of this book. I hope all the concepts discussed here are clear by now. I also hope the mixture of the theoretical background of each algorithm and its practical use paved the way for you to adapt the solutions offered here for the different problems you meet in practice in real life. Obviously, no book can be conclusive, and new algorithms and tools will be available to you in the future. Nevertheless, Pedro Domingos groups the machine learning algorithms into five tribes. Except for the evolutionary algorithms, we have met algorithms that belong to four out of Domingos' five tribes. Thus, I hope the various algorithms discussed here, each with their own approach, will serve as a good foundation when dealing with any new machine learning solutions in the future.

All books are a work in progress. Their value is not only in their content but goes beyond that to include the value that comes from the future discussions they spark. Be assured that you will make the author of any book happy each time you share something you built based on the knowledge you gained from that book. You will make them equally happy each time you quote them, share new and better ways to explain things in their books, or even correct mistakes they made. I, too, am looking forward to such invaluable contributions from you.

Other Books You May Enjoy

If you enjoyed this book, you may be interested in these other books by Packt:

Python Machine Learning - Third Edition
Sebastian Raschka, Vahid Mirjalili

ISBN: 978-1-78995-575-0

- Master the frameworks, models, and techniques that enable machines to 'learn' from data
- Use scikit-learn for machine learning and TensorFlow for deep learning
- Apply machine learning to image classification, sentiment analysis, intelligent web applications, and more
- Build and train neural networks, GANs, and other models
- Discover best practices for evaluating and tuning models
- Predict continuous target outcomes using regression analysis
- Dig deeper into textual and social media data using sentiment analysis

Mastering Machine Learning Algorithms - Second Edition

Giuseppe Bonaccorso

ISBN: 978-1-83882-029-9

- Understand the characteristics of a machine learning algorithm
- Implement algorithms from supervised, semi-supervised, unsupervised, and RL domains
- Learn how regression works in time-series analysis and risk prediction
- Create, model, and train complex probabilistic models
- Cluster high-dimensional data and evaluate model accuracy
- Discover how artificial neural networks work – train, optimize, and validate them
- Work with autoencoders, Hebbian networks, and GANs

Leave a review - let other readers know what you think

Please share your thoughts on this book with others by leaving a review on the site that you bought it from. If you purchased the book from Amazon, please leave us an honest review on this book's Amazon page. This is vital so that other potential readers can see and use your unbiased opinion to make purchasing decisions, we can understand what our customers think about our products, and our authors can see your feedback on the title that they have worked with Packt to create. It will only take a few minutes of your time, but is valuable to other potential customers, our authors, and Packt. Thank you!

Index